Economic Growth and Social Equity
in Developing Countries

Economic Growth and Social Equity in Developing Countries

IRMA ADELMAN & CYNTHIA TAFT MORRIS

Stanford University Press, Stanford, California 1973

Much of the material used in Chapters 1 and 2 of
this book originally appeared in the authors'
*Society, Politics, and Economic Development: A
Quantitative Approach* (Baltimore: Johns Hopkins
Press, 1967; rev. ed. 1971), and is reproduced
here with the kind permission of the publishers.

Stanford University Press, Stanford, California
© 1973 by the Board of Trustees of the
Leland Stanford Junior University
Printed in the United States of America
ISBN 0-8047-0837-1   LC 73-80616

*To our children who, like us, have more
questions than answers*

Preface

This book is a quantitative investigation of the interactions among economic growth, political participation, and the distribution of income in noncommunist developing nations. We apply statistical techniques to qualitative measures of institutional characteristics of nations in order to generate hypotheses about the impact of economic growth and institutional change upon social equity in underdeveloped countries.

Our methodological approach, which does not rely on a narrowly specified theoretical model, provides a way to break out of conventional circles of thought about the consequences of economic growth for equity and participation. In our view such a break with past thinking is essential in order to overcome the strong tendency for the prevailing views of the discipline to become institutionalized—a tendency that occurs less by intention than as a consequence of the limitations of men's minds.

The results of our analyses came as a shock to us. Although we had believed economic growth to have unfavorable social, cultural, and ecological consequences, we had shared the prevailing view among economists that economic growth was economically beneficial to most nations. We had also not greatly questioned the relevance today of the historical association of successful economic growth with the spread of parliamentary democracy. Our results proved to be at variance with our preconceptions. In view of their unexpectedness, we undertook a variety of cross-checks during the two years before we sought their present publication. Case studies and other historical and contemporary evidence coming to our attention have been so overwhelmingly consistent with our findings that, despite major data deficiencies, we present them here with considerable confidence in their validity.

The limitations of our work are considerable. We provide no answers to the pressing problems involved in promoting greater social equity in underdeveloped nations. At best, our results suggest the general directions in which to look for solutions. Our data are neither sufficiently discriminating nor concrete enough for us to investigate the detailed microprocesses whereby institutional changes affect the distribution of income and power in villages, regions, and even countries. We have also not shown the way for development planning to incorporate the goal of social equity. This critical task will require greatly increased knowledge of the social and institutional setting as well as of the details of the complex interactions among the society, the bureaucracy, and the economy. Irma Adelman is currently working on the construction of planning models capable of including some of these influences.

We are grateful to the Agency for International Development for contributing to the financing of the research upon which Chapters 3 and 4 are based and to The American University for varied services. We are indebted to the National Science Foundation for the eight years of support provided to Cynthia Taft Morris for her work on joint research that includes the present project. We appreciate greatly the research fellowship given by the Center for Advanced Study in the Behavioral Sciences at Stanford University to Irma Adelman during 1971–72 that permitted her to devote time to the first revision of the present studies. We are also obligated to the World Bank for contributing to her work on the final revision.

We wish to acknowledge the kind permission of The Johns Hopkins Press to include in Chapters 1 and 2 material previously published in our earlier book, *Society, Politics, and Economic Development*.

We are obligated to many individuals for their contributions to the development of our research and thinking. We are particularly indebted to Princeton Lyman for his encouragement of our original undertaking and to Joan Nelson for her continued interest in and comments on various stages of our research. We have also benefited from the helpful comments of Marian Redetski, Christian Morrisson, and George Dalton. We wish to thank Charles Pepper and Frank Adelman for their skillful editing of various chapters of the book. Our gratitude is also due to Jane Ross for her invaluable work on our indicator of political participation and to Donald Masters for his great success in the collection of available income distribution data. We owe special thanks to over 100 country and regional experts for contributing to the validation of our classifications of 74 countries with respect to the extent of political participation. For her excellent typing of the final manuscript we are obligated to Mary Ann Khojandi. Finally, we are deeply indebted to our respective husbands for their steady encouragement of our work and their continuing interest in its outcome.

IRMA ADELMAN

CYNTHIA TAFT MORRIS

September 20, 1973

Contents

*Economic Growth and Social Equity
in Developing Countries*

Introduction

In the 1950's the community of development economists and other specialists addressed the question of whether economic growth in underdeveloped countries could be increased. The 1960's showed that indeed it could. Many development specialists were satisfied with that answer. They thought that if policy actions were taken to speed up a country's economic growth, increased popular participation in the political process and a more equitable distribution of income would eventually follow. They assumed, in other words, that increases in the rate of growth of such components of economic development as industrialization, agricultural productivity, physical overhead capital, investment, and per capita GNP were closely associated with increases in the extent of political and economic participation.

Since about 1965, however, development specialists have begun to realize that development does not work in the expected way. During the 1960's, for example, Brazil's GNP per capita grew, in real terms, by 2.5 percent annually. Yet the relative share of the national income received by the poorest 40 percent of the population declined from 10 percent in 1960 to 8 percent in 1970, while the relative share of the richest 5 percent increased from 29 percent to 38 percent.[1] Nor is there any evidence of an increase in political participation; on the contrary, there was a marked decrease in participation between the early 1960's, when the left liberals under Quadros and Goulart triumphed, and the early 1970's, when a military dictatorship was in full control. Unfortunately, this experience is not unique. Indeed, it has become clear that economic growth itself not only tends to be accompanied by actual declines in political participation but is one of the prime causes of income inequality. These conclusions emerge from our study of a large sample of developing countries in Chapters 3 and 4. From the viewpoint of those deeply concerned with improving the distribution of the benefits from growth, it follows that the development strategies of the 1960's must be rethought. But how?

This study is a preliminary effort to answer that question. By a quantitative examination of the various social, political, and economic factors that account for differences in political participation and the distribution of income in developing countries, we have tried to assess the relative importance of these factors in the formulation of possible development policies to be adopted by these countries. In the process, our study sheds light on the complex relationship between political participation, economic participation, and economic growth. Our results are intended primarily to clarify the policy choices of the countries themselves, though they are also relevant to the policies of external aid-giving agencies.

Chapters 1 and 2 present the data. They consist of 48 qualitative measures of the social, economic, and political characteristics of the 74 countries in our sample. We discuss the reasons for our choice of variables and the criteria we use for scoring countries on each variable. These data, which are from our earlier study of economic performance in underdeveloped countries, *Society, Politics, and Economic Development*,[2] cover an unusually wide range of the various facets of underdevelopment.

In Chapter 3 we show the results of applying the technique of discriminant analysis to a study of forces tending to increase political participation in the 74 developing countries, and in Chapter 4 the results of applying a similar analysis to the achievement of a more equitable distribution of income. In each of these chapters, after analyzing influences contributing to the failure of the old development policies to achieve results, we suggest the major components of alternative development strategies for countries at different levels of development. The final chapter summarizes our findings.

Before we proceed with the detailed account of our analysis, we must warn the reader that this study is necessarily exploratory in nature and that our analytical approach has inherent limitations. The conclusions are based on the authors' interpretations of the analysis, bearing in mind the limitations of the data and methodology. It should be noted particularly that the sample of 74 countries, though unusually large, is still a limited one; that the study covers only a limited period of time; and that the analysis is based on a single set of cross-sectional rather than multi-country time-series data. In addition, it should be stressed that our qualitative indices are only crude measures of the various national traits they represent and that the income distribution data in particular are of varying and uncertain quality. It should also be pointed out that the validity of the political results for the least developed group of countries is particularly unclear because so many of the countries of sub-Saharan Africa are newly independent.

The inclusion of a broad spectrum of qualitative phenomena in our analyses permits us to explore much more fully than do conventional studies the forces contributing to increased political and economic participation in low-income countries. Our conclusions, while necessarily tentative, point strongly to the importance of social, institutional, and political transformations for the achievement of greater political and economic equality; and they underline the urgent need to discard as outmoded the view that economic growth in low-income countries typically benefits the masses.

CHAPTER ONE

Methodology: Sociocultural Indicators

Both the nature of the data and the methodology of the study deviate from the "classical" methodology of economics. These aspects of the current analysis therefore require some discussion.

STATISTICAL METHODOLOGY

Contrary to common preconceived notions, no optimal scientific research strategy exists for all problems at all points of time. The most appropriate research design varies with the state of theoretical and empirical knowledge about the subject under study, the research resources available, and the comparative advantage of the investigator. The standard methodology propounded in econometrics courses has four steps: (1) formulate the problem; (2) specify a simplified theoretical model capable of empirical implementation to represent the relevant interactions; (3) fit the model statistically; and (4) accept or reject the hypothesis underlying the specification of the model. Even in standard econometric work, these procedures are seldom honored except in the breach. Rather, there is an iterative process in which the model is successively refined as the statistical results become available, so that the final model presented as the "original" hypothesis is a hybrid reflecting an interaction between a priori conceptions and empirical information.*

Our contention is that, in exploratory studies of subjects for which theoretical knowledge is crude and fuzzy, the classical procedure

---

* Witness the preponderance of studies in which the author's hypothesis is accepted.

is inefficient and may also be extremely misleading, since prior hunches and biases are used to rule out phenomena that may be important.

In formulating a research design, it is useful to distinguish between subjects about which much is known and those on which there is very little validated knowledge.[1] For subjects characterized by much prior information, the formulation and empirical testing of theoretically based models are desirable. For subjects characterized by little prior information, the use of statistical tools to describe more simply the structure of the actual world in order to formulate empirically well-grounded hypotheses for future testing appears more appropriate. This is because the early stages of knowledge in a discipline do not meet the requirements for hypothesis testing. Appropriate models are either lacking or, equally serious, there is a multiplicity of poorly articulated models that are not clearly distinct and for which the empirical referends are not at all obvious. The hypothesis-testing approach is extremely inefficient under these circumstances, since it requires that, in each test, there be only one hypothesis tested against a well-specified alternative.

The subject of national development and its effects on distributive justice clearly is characterized by little prior information. Development economics and social philosophy provide some assistance in selecting variables representing particular aspects of the development process. However, none of the subdisciplines of economics, sociology, and political science provide even partially validated models for studying the interrelations among economic, social, and political change and their impact on distributive justice. This gap in development theory places the subject matter of the present analysis squarely in the class of problems for which the hypothesis-testing approach is inefficient. Hence, a sound first step appears to be the use of powerful deductive statistical techniques whose purpose is to provide empirical foundations for subsequent theory construction.

As in all statistical analyses, the techniques used in this book provide information that is useful only to the extent that the data are valid and represent the relevant aspects of the problems under study. In addition, they give direct information only on statistical associations or lack of them and not on causality. Their role in the acquisition of scientific knowledge is rather like the role of Newton's apple in the construction of Newton's postulates: by calling attention to certain complicated multidimensional regularities, these analyses point out those systematic characteristics that require explanation in a theoretical model of the phenomenon being studied.

The Role of Theory

Our stress on empirical regularities might appear antitheoretical. Such is not our intention. Theoretical considerations have played a major role in virtually all aspects of the present study. They have guided our choice of variables; they have shaped our measurement procedure; and finally, they have helped us interpret the results. Theoretical reasoning is particularly important in helping to disentangle causation from association and from indirect interaction, since statistical analysis alone can achieve neither. This deductive use of theory is as valid as the use of theory to formulate a model. In both cases, theory is used to impose a causal structure on empirical phenomena. When theory is used to interpret statistical results, the empirical regularities evident in the results may be used to impose a theoretical structure on the hypothesis formulated. By contrast, when theory is used a priori, it is often not clear to what empirical referends the model system corresponds, or, indeed, whether the model corresponds to any real economy at all.

Choice of Techniques

Our choice of statistical techniques for the present study was guided by our wish to determine those national characteristics that best discriminate statistically between different extents of economic and political participation.* The wide range of development levels included in our sample required provision for non-

---

* The techniques are described in greater detail in Chapters 3 and 4.

linearity in the relationships among the variables. In our study of political participation, adequate data for 74 countries permitted stratification of the sample. To allow for variations in patterns of association at different levels of development, we applied linear discriminant analysis to the data for each of three subsamples. Discriminant theory is sufficiently developed so that tests for statistical significance could also be applied to overall relationships. In our study of economic participation the paucity of data on income distributions limited the sample to only 44 countries and precluded sufficient sample stratification to take account of the obvious nonlinearities in the relationships between income distribution and other socioeconomic and political characteristics. Hence, we chose an extremely flexible alternative technique, the analysis of hierarchical interactions that places no constraints on the form of relationships (with respect to their linearity or nonlinearity) but has the disadvantage that the tests of statistical significance that have been developed provide only crude approximations.

Caveats

The present study applies statistical tools to explore the associations among leading socioeconomic and political characteristics of nations likely to affect their levels of political and economic participation. The choice of variables is intentionally broad in keeping with the rudimentary state of a priori knowledge about the interrelationships involved in the spread of participation in the distribution of power and in the sharing of the benefits of economic growth. In our choice of statistical techniques, we have studiously avoided the conventional assumption that linear relationships characterize socioeconomic and political processes in underdeveloped countries and have sought to discover leading empirical regularities in the broad phenomena studied in order to constrain our formulation of hypotheses for future testing by salient characteristics of the actual world. "Conclusions" drawn from our quantitative results thus play a different role than in standard econometric work. They are rather themselves hypotheses formulated through the interaction of our empirical findings and a priori knowledge, and may appropriately be used for subsequent hypothesis testing by ourselves and others. Our present efforts thus represent an earlier stage of research than does the usual hypothesis-testing type of study, and should be viewed as an essential preliminary to the formulation of empirically sound models for future econometric work on the subjects of economic and political participation.

MEASUREMENT OF INSTITUTIONAL CHARACTERISTICS

A major barrier to the quantitative investigation of interactions between economic and noneconomic influences in economic development is the lack of adequate indicators of institutional traits of nations. To include measures of these traits in our statistical analyses of economic development, we were therefore obliged to devise experimental indicators of a wide range of qualitative national characteristics. The preparation of these data involved the establishment of rules for ranking 74 underdeveloped countries with respect to each of 50 characteristics; it thus required "measurement" (in the broad sense of the word) of qualitative institutional phenomena.

Several characteristics of our data should be pointed out. First, they are, without exception, ordinal. Even the conventional "quantitative" variables such as investment rates and literacy rates are ordinal, since we view them as representing underlying concepts to which they are, at best, monotonically related. Insofar as we have used empirical and theoretical information to determine the spacing of intervals and the distribution of observations between adjacent intervals, our data are of the ordered metric variety.

Second, by far the greatest difficulties we faced in developing indicators were those of conceptualization and definition, lacking theories as precise and acceptable as those on which production and cost-of-living indices, for example, are based.* Concepts such as social tension, political participation, mass communication,

---

* Even where relatively explicit and acceptable theories exist, as in the case of measurement of social mobility, we were obliged by data deficiencies to select indexes other than those that would be most desirable theoretically.

modernization of outlook, national integration, and political stability are all extremely important in theorizing about political and social change in underdeveloped countries, and yet they do not have widely agreed-upon operational definitions appropriate to classifying primary observable facts. Thus, a major challenge of the present investigation was to develop empirical equivalents for complex theoretical concepts in the face of major constraints upon data availability.

Third, the scarcity and irregularity of primary data greatly constrained the number of feasible alternatives for the measurement of each influence. Furthermore, since we chose to include countries for which all data were poor (usually those at the lowest level of development), and thereby to avoid a major bias present in most cross-section studies of developing countries, we were restricted to measurement by intervals sufficiently wide so that, when point estimates were unavailable, we could use descriptive and judgmental information to make reasonably reliable interval estimates.

Method of Successive Definition

In preparing our qualitative multidimensional indicators, we began with theoretically motivated definitions. Next, we studied the descriptive data in order to see how well actual country situations fit our formulation of the concept. The inadequacies of the initial fit were then used to reformulate the concept to fit better the characteristics of the real world. We then consulted expert opinion and again reformulated the definitions. We continued this process of confronting successive reformulations with information on actual country situations until we were able to classify the countries in our sample with reasonable confidence.

This procedure of successive definition is well illustrated by the indicator of political participation, which is discussed in detail in Chapter 4. Our indicator of the extent of socioeconomic dualism provides a further example of the interaction of conceptualization and testing against the actual world that took place in the preparation of our data.

Example of the Dualism Indicator

In the literature on economic development, "dualism" is not defined with sufficient concreteness to classify actual country situations. For example, J. H. Boeke uses the term to describe "societies showing a distinct cleavage of two synchronic and full grown social styles," while Benjamin Higgins and others point to dualistic cleavages between sectors having sharply different production functions.[2] Fei and Ranis stress the coexistence of a traditional subsistence agricultural sector and an advanced "dynamic and vigorous" industrial sector.[3] In attempting to define dualism with sufficient concreteness to classify actual economies, our major conceptual difficulty was the ranking of two intermediate categories, for we characterized both ends of the continuum by the absence of marked dualism. Dualism is absent at the lower end by reason of the overwhelming predominance of nonmarket subsistence agriculture combined with the extremely limited growth of a market-oriented sector; the upper end is not markedly dualistic because the intermingling of modern and traditional elements throughout the economy resulted in the absence of a clearcut geographic cleavage between a market-oriented sector and a distinct, predominantly nonmonetized traditional sector. In our initial definition, we conceived of a single intermediate category characterized by sharp social, economic, and technological contrasts between a geographically distinct and important plantation or extractive or industrial sector using advanced technology and a major subsistence nonmarket agricultural sector.

When we confronted our original definition with descriptive data from country studies, we immediately discovered that it made no provision for countries with a geographically quite distinct, important, and rapidly growing market sector characterized by the predominance of indigenous cash-cropping with conventional techniques. The countries in which peasant cash-cropping dominates the market sector differ significantly from those in which extractive or plantation enterprises using advanced technologies dominate the market sector. In particular, resource flows in the latter countries are limited primarily to intermittent labor flows, while in the former countries, resource flows include movements of land, labor, and capital.

In reformulating the dualism indicator we therefore gave weight to the extent of intersectoral resource flows as well as to socio-economic and technological contrasts and to the presence or absence of a relatively clearcut cleavage between market and non-market sectors. We defined two intermediate categories for countries with both a geographically distinct and important market sector and a relatively large, predominantly nonmonetized traditional sector. We gave higher scores to countries in which (a) the market sector was characterized by the predominance of indigenous cash-cropping; (b) less marked contrast existed between technologies and styles of life; and (c) more extensive economic interaction occurred between traditional and modern sectors. We did so because of our judgment that these countries were further along the path to the pervasive intermingling of modern and traditional elements throughout the economy characteristic of the upper end of the spectrum.

The reformulated four-way classification scheme enabled us to rank the great majority of countries in our sample. An examination of additional sources of country information led to only minor reformulations of the category descriptions so as to take better account of the diversity of individual country situations.

The procedure of successive definition we are describing is that which was followed historically in the development of measures of national income. The theoretically derived empirical construct was confronted with actual data on income and output; the inconsistencies between construct and primary data then stimulated reformulations of the construct, which was again tested for consistency with primary facts. This is not, of course, to say that our indicators are either as reliable or as precise as measures of GNP in advanced countries; it is only to emphasize that at the exploratory stage in development of new measures of institutional phenomena the method of successive definition must be applied in order to obtain operational definitions consistent with observable phenomena and therefore suitable for classifying them.

Validation of Measurement

The process of conceptualization and definition that we followed in constructing our composite indicators is a procedure well tried in the history of scientific inquiry—in the physical as well as the social sciences. In *The Conduct of Inquiry*, Abraham Kaplan says:[4]

In short, the process of specifying meaning is a part of the process of inquiry itself. In every context of inquiry we begin with terms that are undefined—not indefinables, but terms for which *that* context does not provide a specification. As we proceed, empirical findings are taken up into our conceptual structure by way of new specifications of meaning, and former indications and references in turn become matters of empirical fact. . . . What I have tried to sketch here is how such a process of "successive definition" can be understood so as to take account of the openness of meaning of scientific terms. *For the closure that strict definition consists in is not a precondition of scientific inquiry but its culmination.* To start with we do not know just what we mean by our terms, much as we do not know just what to think about our subject-matter. We can, indeed, begin with precise meanings, as we choose; but so long as we are in ignorance, we cannot choose wisely. It is this ignorance that makes the closure premature.

The validity of the measures constructed by the procedure depends not only on keeping the degree of error (in its various senses) within tolerable limits but also on their substantive validity.[5]

Although our socioeconomic and political indicators are necessarily crude, several considerations point to the validity of using them in our exploratory quantitative studies.

First, limited experimentation with selected variables indicates that our statistical results are not very sensitive to reasonable alternative specifications for the concepts measured. This finding is consistent with exploratory research by other investigators showing considerable substitutability between alternative crude indices based on subsets from a larger group of closely correlated indicants of the concept measured.

Second, the statistical interconnections among the 48 measures in our study are both interpretable and broadly consistent with knowledge based on historical and comparative studies. Furthermore, variations in results between subsets of observations as well as between subsets of variables reinforce the overall results. The sensibleness of the findings thus, in and of itself, offers partial validation of the measurement procedures.

Third, as for the "qualitative" nature of our variables, rejection by economists of institutional measures as only ordinal is unwarranted unless they simultaneously reject all economic composites including price, production, and productivity indexes. These latter measures are also ordinal if taken to represent concepts of any theoretical interest. All indices are subject to the difficulty that they cannot, without arbitrariness, be subjected to standard methods of statistical analysis. The validity of treating them as cardinal must be established case by case on the basis of actual sensitivity studies.

That such tests are only partial is evident. The present investigation does not attempt, nor could it attempt with our limited resources, direct validation of the various indexes by comparison with the results of fundamental measurement procedures. Nor does it attempt the type of direct collection of primary data in underdeveloped countries that would be necessary to establish fully the reliability of the measures. It is rather an exploratory study to provide the kind of experimentation with conceptualization, and the kind of information about empirical interconnections, without which more detailed on-the-spot collection of primary qualitative data is a waste of resources.

Ultimately, the usefulness of the measures we have constructed will depend upon their success in serving the purposes for which they were designed. These are, first, to give insights into the nature and relative weight of the various interactions involved in economic development and, second, to provide a good starting point for a process of experimentation, by ourselves and other investigators, in which further empirical testing and theoretical reasoning must interact.

Principles Guiding the Choice of Indicators

Before turning to a detailed consideration of the indicators, we shall explain briefly the general principles influencing our choice of variables. In making the choice, we were guided by two possibly conflicting principles: those of inclusiveness and parsimony.

For the first, we strove to represent in our measures those aspects of economic, social, and political institutions and performance that might affect the distribution of economic benefits and political power. We wished to include a broad selection of indicators that would describe the many facets of low-income countries relevant not only to economic, social, and political development but also to distributive justice. More specifically, the social variables were chosen to portray the principal social aspects of urbanization and industrialization; the political indicators were selected to represent various aspects of political structure, performance, and the distribution of power in modern states; and the economic indexes were designed to summarize the changes in economic structure and institutions typical of industrialization and economic growth. We found it necessary at an early stage of classifying countries to reject several indicators that appeared theoretically desirable, but that could not be formulated with sufficient concreteness to permit unambiguous classifications.

With respect to the second principle influencing our choice of variables, parsimony, we strove not to multiply our indices of any particular feature of society but rather to combine within each single classification scheme interrelated aspects of the relevant feature. In the definition of composite indicators, we sought to include closely intercorrelated traits conceptually relevant to the fundamental country characteristic we wished to describe. It should be noted, of course, that in order to avoid ambiguous statistical results, we tried to include in any single indicator only elements that were closely interrelated. The indicator of the level of effectiveness of tax systems illustrates the application of the principle of parsimony. Three main aspects of tax systems were included in a single index: the ratio of total government revenues to GNP, the ratio of direct tax revenue to total government revenues, and the presence or absence of widespread difficulties in collecting taxes. In general, attempts to introduce into previous analyses a large number of narrow indexes, no one of which was adequate in itself to characterize any given feature of institutions or performance, tended to yield results that were considerably less amenable to interpretation than results obtained with broad indicators. Thus, the final choice of variables for our investigation covers a broad range of the salient sociopolitical and economic features of developing countries without, however, including a multiplicity of narrow indicators of any particular feature. These variables are listed below in the order in which they will be discussed.

Sociocultural Indicators
Size of the traditional agricultural sector
Extent of dualism
Extent of urbanization
Importance of the indigenous middle class
Extent of social mobility
Extent of literacy
Extent of mass communication
Degree of cultural and ethnic homogeneity
Degree of social tension
Crude fertility rate
Degree of modernization of outlook
Predominant type of religion
Level of socioeconomic development

Political Indicators
Degree of national integration and sense of national unity
Degree of centralization of political power
Extent of political participation*
Degree of freedom of political opposition and the press
Degree of competitiveness of political parties
Predominant basis of the political party system
Strength of the labor movement
Political strength of the traditional elite
Political strength of the military
Political and social influence of religious organization
Degree of administrative efficiency

* This indicator is defined in Chapter 3.

Extent of leadership commitment to economic development
Extent of direct government economic activity
Length of colonial experience
Type of colonial experience
Recency of self-government
Extent of political stability

Economic Indicators
Per capita GNP in 1961
Growth rate of real per capita GNP, 1950/51–1963/64
Abundance of natural resources
Gross investment rate
Modernization of industry
Industrialization, 1950–63
Character of agricultural organization
Modernization of techniques in agriculture
Improvement in agricultural productivity, 1950–63
Adequacy of physical overhead capital
Effectiveness of the tax system
Improvement in the tax system, 1950–63
Effectiveness of financial institutions
Improvement in financial institutions, 1950–63
Improvement in human resources
Structure of foreign trade
Rate of population growth
Country size and orientation of development strategy

SOCIOCULTURAL INDICATORS

The interdependence of changes in social organization and values and economic growth has long been recognized by social scientists, although it has undergone relatively little formal investigation. Karl Marx was one of the first to point to changes in social relations as a keystone in the theory of economic development. Since his time, economic historians have frequently underlined the importance of social structure in influencing the pattern of economic change. Familiar examples of their concern with social factors in the growth process are Sombart's analysis of the "spirit of capitalism" as a moving force in the rise of Western industry, Tawney's study of the impact upon economic growth of the Protestant ethic, and recent investigations into the role of social structure in explaining differences in rates of economic growth in the nineteenth century.[6] In addition, development economists almost invariably underline the importance of social transformations in initiating economic growth, although they rarely attempt to incorporate noneconomic influences into their formal theories.

In view of the acknowledged importance of the social and cultural aspects of the process of economic development, our study includes a wide range of sociocultural indicators.

Size of the Traditional Agricultural Sector

The problem of poverty in developing countries is in large measure a problem of rural poverty, and the problem of increasing inequality in the distribution of income is in large measure a problem of stagnant subsistence agriculture.

Inherent in the processes of industrialization and economic growth is a major shift of population from the agricultural to the urban industrial sector of the economy. It is typical of low-income countries that large proportions of their populations live in relatively self-contained low-income agricultural communities in which production is primarily for local consumption.

A program of income equalization requires a policy focus upon rural development; economic growth requires an expansion of agricultural output and productivity. The importance to economic growth of expanding agricultural output lies partly in the need to provide increased food supplies to growing urban areas and in the additional market for domestic output created by increases in agricultural cash incomes. In addition, increases in agricultural productivity are required to release to industry the labor required for its expansion.* Although both goals imply a certain policy emphasis upon the agrarian sector, the policies pursued under each are not necessarily consistent with the other. Increases in agricultural output, if not accompanied by income expansion among consumers, may imply falling rural incomes and much increasing inequality between the countryside and the city. Increases in agricultural

---

* There are, of course, other reasons as well for the emphasis made by development economists upon the importance of increased agricultural production. See B. F. Johnston and J. W. Mellor, "The Role of Agriculture in Economic Development," *American Economic Review*, 51 (1961): 566–93.

productivity tend to benefit the larger, more progressive farmers disproportionately in both absolute and relative terms because of unequal access to subsidized inputs, and hence tend to increase inequalities within the rural sector.

The indicator we have chosen to summarize variations in the relative weight of the traditional agricultural sector measures the proportion of the population engaged in self-sufficient subsistence agriculture. It is well known, of course, that employment data, like most data for low-income countries, are poor or nonexistent. In most less developed countries, until very recently censuses were taken at irregular intervals or not at all. Even where censuses have been taken, their coverage has usually been limited or their results otherwise unreliable. Furthermore, censuses usually do not include the information on different types of agricultural establishments necessary to estimate either employment or residence on farms in the nonmarket sector.

In view of the overwhelming deficiencies of the basic data on the relative size of the nonmonetized agricultural sector, we established four rather broad categories with respect to this indicator. The grouping of countries into relatively few categories enabled us, where data were lacking or inadequate, to use expert opinion in assigning countries to their appropriate category. The use of judgmental information to obtain point estimates would have been considerably less appropriate.

The classification of individual countries with respect to the relative importance of their traditional agricultural sectors was accomplished in two stages. The first step was to obtain estimates of the proportion of the total population involved in agriculture as of about 1960. The relevant United Nations data covered less than one-third of the countries included in our investigation.[7] Estimates for about 25 additional countries were secured by adjusting Yale Data Program statistics on the proportion of the labor force in agriculture[8] and cross-checking the results with recent country studies. For the remaining third of the countries in the sample, principally African ones, we relied primarily upon rough estimates contained in recent country studies, both published and unpublished. The second step in the classification of countries was then to exclude the population engaged primarily in modern commercial agriculture or in indigenous cash-crop agriculture. For this purpose, qualitative information on the relative weight of different types of agriculture was relied upon to a great extent.[9] Statistical information was used, however, for the minority of countries for which it was available; in this connection, several studies made by the International Labour Organization were particularly useful.[10] Our final country classifications are, of course, only broadly indicative of the relative quantitative weight of traditional subsistence agriculture.

Four principal categories of less developed countries were distinguished with respect to the size of their traditional subsistence sectors as of about 1960.

A. Countries with 80 percent or more of their population in traditional subsistence agriculture in which the marketing of crops was of relatively minor importance.

B. Countries with from 55 to 79 percent of their population in traditional subsistence agriculture in which the marketing of crops was of relatively minor importance.

C. Countries with from 25 to 54 percent of their population in traditional subsistence agriculture in which the marketing of crops was of relatively minor importance.

D. Countries with less than 25 percent of their population in traditional subsistence agriculture in which the marketing of crops was of relatively minor importance.

Extent of Dualism

One of the most striking characteristics of the socioeconomic structure of many developing nations is that, side by side with a dominant traditional sector in which conventional techniques and communal self-sufficiency prevail, there exists a rapidly growing exchange sector. Technology in the exchange sector tends to be modern where expansion has been largely the result of foreign investment in extractive, plantation, or estate activities; it tends to be traditional where expansion has taken place through shifts of indigenous producers into the small-scale cultivation of cash crops. Partly as a consequence of the limited interaction between the two sectors, these differences in technology are accompanied by intersectoral differences in factor productivities and hence in per capita incomes. In addition, dualistic productive patterns are typically associated with differences in institutional arrangements that contribute to contrasting divisions of the national product among labor, domestic capital, and foreign capital. Finally, intersectoral differences in the ownership of wealth tend to produce related differences in the distribution of political power and the extent of political participation.

The precise criteria used in classifying countries with respect to the extent of dualism as of about 1960 are presented below.

A. Countries characterized by some significant modernization of methods of production in almost all sectors of the economy and in which there was no clear-cut sectoral or geographic cleavage between the modern and nonmodern segments of the economy; that is, traditional and modern production methods existed side by side in almost all sectors of the economy.

B. Countries characterized by a moderately definite sectoral or geographic cleavage between (1) an important industrial and/or mining and/or agricultural exchange sector where modern technology may or may not have prevailed and (2) a predominantly nonmonetized sector where traditional hand and animal production methods prevailed. Countries in this category differ from those in category C in two respects: (1) a single, geographically distinct, traditional nonmonetized sector was not overwhelmingly predominant; if such a sector existed, it tended to be less important than the exchange sector; (2) these countries had only moderately contrasting socioeconomic organization and styles of life between the exchange sector and the traditional nonmonetized sector. Included in this category and classified B— are a number of countries in which the exchange sector consisted of important, large, modern, expatriate or government activities and significant indigenous small-scale commercial enterprises, in which there was also a fairly large and distinct nonmonetized traditional sector.

C. Countries in which there was a sharp and pervasive sectoral or geographic cleavage between an important exchange sector and an important traditional nonmonetized sector. These countries were characterized (1) by a sharp contrast between levels of technology, types of economic organization, and social styles of life in the exchange sector and the traditional sector and (2) by the predominance of a traditional nonmonetized sector in which strong traditional patterns of social organization remained relatively untouched by the activities of the exchange sector in spite of significant intermittent labor flows into the exchange sector.

D. Countries not characterized by significant dualism by reason of the extremely limited development of their exchange sector combined with the overwhelming predominance of the nonmonetized traditional sector.

Extent of Urbanization

The positive association of urbanization with industrialization, participation, and economic growth is well known. Cities provide concentrations of population from which industrial labor may be drawn; they also contain a greater variety of skills and resources than do rural areas. Even more important perhaps, urbanization promotes values favorable to participation, entrepreneurship, and industrial growth; in particular, cities typically tend to favor a propensity to analyze traditional institutions and to innovate and accept change, since in the relatively impersonal and fragmented setting of urban life the all-embracing bonds of traditional community systems are difficult to maintain.[11] Income distribution within cities tends to be quite unequal, since the majority of both well-off elites and badly-off squatters live in urban areas. Whether urban inequality exceeds that of the countryside depends, however, on the nature of the city, the country's stage of development, and the extent of dualism. The tendency for the majority of the middle class to reside in cities and the growth in importance of middle-class incomes may more than counterbalance the tendency for cities to incorporate the extremes of the income distribution.

The role of urbanization in increasing political participation in developing countries is far-reaching.[12] The dislocations accompanying rapid urban growth have led to the politization of those groups whom they most affect, including both new urban migrants and long-term residents discontented by destabilizing impacts of urbanization.[13]

In general, it seems likely that, once some minimum extent of urbanization is reached, the importance of cities in the process of economic development lies less in their more concentrated provision of human resources than in their role as an agent in fostering those changes in social structure and political and economic values that are essential to enhancing political participation, entrepreneurial activity, occupational mobility, and thus, indirectly, to economic growth and political change.

Our indicator of the extent of urbanization is a straightforward statistical one in which all the data were obtained from a prepublication copy of *Urbanization: Expanding Population and Shrinking World,* made available to us through the courtesy of the Urban Land Institute.[14] In fact, it is notable that this indicator is the only one included in our study for which a complete series of recent and comparable data was available. The following are categories into which we grouped the countries in our sample with respect to the proportion of the population living in urban areas containing over 20,000 people in the early 1960's.

A. Countries with 30 percent or more of their total population in urban areas of 20,000 or more inhabitants.

B. Countries with at least 20 but less than 30 percent of their total population in urban areas of 20,000 or more inhabitants.

C. Countries with at least 10 but less than 20 percent of their total population in urban areas of 20,000 or more inhabitants.

D. Countries with at least 5 but less than 10 percent of their total population in urban areas of 20,000 or more inhabitants.

E. Countries with less than 5 percent of their total population in urban areas of 20,000 or more inhabitants.

Importance of the Indigenous Middle Class

The widening of political participation to include the indigenous middle class is an important first step in broadening the distribution of political power. Economic benefits also tend to accrue to the middle class during industrialization, since both the expansion of industry and the development of bureaucracies greatly expand the demand for commercial, entrepreneurial, professional, and technical talents typically provided by "middle-class" occupational groups. It is clear from many country studies that the growth of a robust middle class remains of crucial importance in contemporary low-income nations. However, the specific groups that contribute most to economic development may differ greatly, and, indeed, the very term "middle class" with its Western "bourgeois" connotation is not very appropriate. In developing countries today, for example, it often happens that salaried government officials, rather than private businessmen, provide the leadership for economic change and innovation. Furthermore, to an even greater extent than in nineteenth-century Europe, a large part of the available talent important for economic growth is often found among expatriate groups in the population. At the same time, current experience with the problems of developing nations suggests that the presence of active indigenous groups in the middle class is considerably more conducive to the initiation of a widespread growth process than is the existence of expatriate groups that characteristically tend to concentrate their efforts within the existing modern sectors. Therefore, in deriving our indicator of the size of the middle class, we have ranked the presence of indigenous groups considerably higher than the presence of expatriate elements.

Our indicator of the importance of the indigenous middle class as of about 1960 assigns less developed countries to five principal categories on the basis of (1) statistical estimates of the importance of selected middle-class occupations, together with (2) qualitative information concerning the comparative weight of indigenous and expatriate elements in the middle class. As mentioned above, statistical estimates of employment for most low-income countries are extremely poor. United Nations data on the distribution of the active male population by broad occupational groups provided us with information for less than half the countries in our sample.[15] For a few additional countries appropriate estimates were available from recent country studies. These data on the distribution of employment were used to determine whether, as of about 1960, less than 10 percent, from 10 to 19 percent, or over 19 percent of the male labor force was in commerce, banking, insurance, or in technical, professional, managerial, administrative, or clerical employments. For the large number of countries for which no precise employment estimates could be obtained, one of two approaches was taken. First, all countries for which qualitative information indicated an overwhelming predominance of expatriate elements in the middle class were assigned to a special category.[16] Where qualitative information indicated the simultaneous presence of a small, growing indigenous class, the country was given a higher score. The majority of countries for which employment data were lacking was classified by these characteristics. Second, it was assumed that all countries that had less than 20 percent of their total population outside the agricultural sector also had less than 10 percent of their active male population employed in the middle-class occupations listed above;[17] this assumption enabled us to complete the classification of almost all of the remaining countries for which employment data were unavailable. A few doubtful cases were resolved by interview.

The precise classification scheme follows for the indicator of the importance of the indigenous middle class, as of about 1960.

A. Countries with a relatively important indigenous middle class in which at least 20 percent of the active male population was in commerce, banking, insurance, or in technical, professional, managerial, administrative, or clerical employments. Excluded from this category, however, are countries meeting this statistical criterion in which the middle class was dominated by expatriate elements.

B. Countries with a significant but fairly small indigenous middle class in which at least 10 percent but not more than 19 percent of the active male population was in commerce, banking, insurance, or in technical, professional, managerial, administrative, or clerical employments. Excluded from this category, however, are countries meeting this criterion in which the middle class was dominated by expatriate elements.

C. Countries in which expatriate entrepreneurial, commercial, administrative, and technical groups dominated the middle class but in which a growing, though still small, indigenous middle class also existed.

D. Countries in which expatriate entrepreneurial, commercial, administrative, and technical groups dominated the middle class almost completely; indigenous middle-class groups were negligible. Countries in which an important settled expatriate group consisting of over 1 percent of the population operated in several sectors of the economy are classified *D+*.

E. Countries in which the indigenous middle class was extremely small or negligible and in which there was no important expatriate middle class. All countries for which it is estimated that less than 10 percent of the active male population was in the middle-class occupations listed above and in which there was not an important expatriate middle class are included in this category.

Extent of Social Mobility

The extent of vertical social mobility has direct equity implications as well as important social and political consequences. In countries where the growth process entrains movements from rags to riches to rags in three generations, for example, a given amount of inequality may create less injustice than in countries with a rigid stratification system where the current poor have a negligible chance of upward mobility.

The positive association between social mobility and industrialization has often been emphasized. The multiple facets of social mobility, however, and their varying importance to economic growth and social equity are not always made clear. There are attitudinal aspects of mobility: the degree to which individual attainments are met with social recognition and advance, and in particular, the extent to which economic achievements receive positive social approval. Closely related to the attitudes affecting social mobility is the extent of opportunity for an individual to advance by means of ability rather than social status. Of course, it is to be expected that the possibilities for vertical mobility will be greater, the larger the number of jobs requiring special proficiency. Furthermore, the expansion of industry normally entails an increase in employment opportunities and thus upward mobility. Finally, a significant aspect of social mobility is the extent of opportunity in a society to obtain skills and education; inevitably a narrow educational base limits the scope for individual improvements in status. Thus, the process of industrialization and the increase in opportunities for social mobility interact as countries proceed toward sustained economic development.[18]

In choosing a variable to represent the extent of social mobility, we looked for reasonably specific characteristics that would summarize the important aspects of social mobility. One element included in the definition of an index of social mobility was the extent of access to education. The measure of educational opportunity that we used was the ratio of the population five to 19 years of age enrolled in primary and secondary schools.[19] A second element incorporated in the classification scheme was the extent of opportunity to advance into middle-class occupations (clerical, administrative, technical, managerial, commercial). We measured this aspect of social mobility by the importance of the indigenous middle class.* The final element in the definition was the presence or absence of prohibitive cultural or ethnic barriers to upward social mobility. No special category was provided for the few countries having such barriers; rather, for each country with such barriers, the score received on the basis of the other two elements in the scheme was reduced by one letter grade. In our original formulation of the indicator of social mobility, we included an index of the openness of access to political leadership presented in *A Cross-Polity Survey*.[20] However, it proved not to be closely related to the other aspects of mobility and resulted in ambiguity in our statistical results.[21]

In the final definitional scheme, three broad categories of social mobility were distinguished as of about 1960.

A. Countries that were characterized by considerable social mobility, measured by the standards of less developed countries, as

---

* See the discussion of our indicator of the importance of the indigenous middle class for the sources of these data, p. 23.

indicated by relatively broad access to educational attainments (i.e. a school enrollment ratio of over 40 percent) and fairly good opportunities to enter middle-class occupations. (Clerical, administrative, technical, commercial, and professional occupations represent at least 10 percent of the active male population.) In addition, countries in this category are characterized by the absence of prohibitive cultural or ethnic barriers affecting important segments of the population. Countries in which either the above middle-class occupations form more than 20 percent of the active male population or the school enrollment ratio is more than 50 percent are classified A+. Countries in which there is nevertheless a marked degree of social stratification are classified A−.

B. Countries that were characterized by fairly limited social mobility, as indicated by school enrollment ratios of less than 40 percent but more than 25 percent and by the fact that middle-class occupations formed only 5–10 percent of the active male population. Also included in this category are a few countries that meet the first two criteria for category A but in which the presence of prohibitive ethnic or cultural barriers affects significant segments of the population.

C. Countries that were characterized by a low degree of social mobility, as indicated by very limited access to education (school enrollment ratios of less than 25 percent) and the existence of little opportunity to enter middle-class occupations. Countries that also had rigid, traditionally determined social castes are classified C−. Countries that, generally speaking, had extremely low social mobility but in which either (1) registered school enrollment ratios were nevertheless above 25 percent or (2) the middle class, while very small, was rapidly growing are classified C+. Also included in this category are a few countries that meet the criteria for category B except for the presence of prohibitive cultural or ethnic barriers affecting significant segments of the population.

Extent of Literacy

It is certainly generally accepted that literacy is an essential economic asset in industrial urban occupations, facilitating the training of unskilled as well as skilled workers. In addition, it is an important modern mechanism for integrating both the social and political structures of a nation. Indeed, it has been maintained that literacy is the basic personal skill underlying the whole process of modernization.[22]

While most students of the subject would agree that literacy is important economically and politically, it is often stressed that the productivity of investment in literacy varies at different stages of development. In particular, the economic gains from increased literacy at very low stages of socioeconomic evolution may level off quickly and may not become very marked again until the society reaches a point at which widespread transformations of social structure facilitate the full use of literacy. The political effects of increased literacy may also be destabilizing at early stages of development. Increases in literacy often generate demands for participation that threaten rudimentary and fragile political systems. They also increase the political stresses arising from increased competition between traditional and modern loyalties.

Of course, it would have been desirable to devise a broader and more accurate indicator of the stock of education embodied in the working population than the rate of literacy. However, appropriate data on years of schooling of various segments of the population, for example, are available for only a handful of developing countries. Data on school enrollment ratios are not suitable, since they refer only to additions to the stock of education.

Our indicator of the extent of literacy is a purely quantitative one, for which the basic source was Russett et al., *World Handbook of Political and Social Indicators.*[23] For a few countries having poor data, however, the judgment of country experts was used to adjust published figures that were clearly overestimates. While the dates of available estimates of literacy vary from country to country, most of them related to 1958. In view of the large margin of error in many of these estimates, we have checked them where possible with estimates from other sources.

The following is the classification scheme for the indicator of the extent of literacy.

A. Countries in which at least 65 percent of the adult population was literate. Those in which over 85 percent was literate are classified *A*+; those in which 75–85 percent was literate are classified *A*; and those in which 65–74 percent was literate are classified *A*−.

B. Countries in which 35–64 percent of the adult population was literate. Those in which rates of literacy were 55–64 percent are classified *B*+; those in which rates of literacy were 45–54 percent are classified *B*; and those in which rates of literacy were 35–44 percent are classified *B*−.

C. Countries in which 16–34 percent of the adult population was literate. Those in which rates of literacy were 30–34 percent are classified *C*+; those in which rates of literacy were 23–29 percent are classified *C*; and those in which rates of literacy were 16–22 percent are classified *C*−.

D. Countries in which less than 16 percent of the adult population was literate. Those in which rates of literacy were 11–15 percent are classified *D*+; those in which rates of literacy were 6–10 percent are classified *D*; and those in which rates of literacy were under 6 percent are classified *D*−.

Extent of Mass Communication

The importance of mass communication to social and political change has been emphasized in recent years by the rapid expansion of communications research oriented toward the problems of less developed countries.[24] As is often pointed out, modern media systems are an important mechanism both for diffusing thought patterns and demands for industrial products and for inducing greater participation in national political systems.[25] It is indeed a fact in advanced societies that both newspapers and radios are important means for the articulation of group political interests and thus for the effective working of participant political systems.

The role of mass communication media in the modernizing process appears to vary systematically with different stages of development. In a study of the Middle East, it is suggested that the modernization of social systems characteristically shows three phases: the first marked by rapid urbanization, the second by a sharp increase in literacy, and the third by greatly expanded media participation.* This suggestion is to some extent supported by statistical analyses indicating that literacy rates and urbanization show greater elasticity than does the use of radios with respect to variations in per capita income in the lowest ranges of per capita GNP, while the reverse is true in the higher ranges of per capita GNP that include less developed countries.[26]

In selecting an indicator of mass communication, we have chosen a composite index based on daily newspaper circulation and number of radio receivers. The former has been given somewhat greater weight since it appears to be the more reliable series.† The principal sources for the information used are the United Nations data reported in the *World Handbook of Political and Social Indicators*. The classification of each country depends upon the deciles within which it falls when all countries for which data are available are ranked.[27] The detailed basis for the classification is shown in the following tabulation:

Classification	Case deciles of news-paper circulation	Case deciles of radios licensed or in use
A+	2	2 or 3
A	2	4
A	3	3 or 4
A—	4	3 or 4 or 5
B+	5	3 or 4 or 5
B	5	6
B—	6	5 or 6 or 7
B—	7	5
C+	6	8
C+	7	5 or 6 or 7
C+	8	5
C	7	8
C—	7	9
C—	8	7 or 8 or 9
C—	9	6
C—	10	5
D+	8	10
D+	9	8 or 9 or 10
D	9	10
D—	10	9 or 10

* Lerner, *The Passing of Traditional Society*, pp. 61–63. His index of media participation is a composite indicator of daily newspaper circulation, number of radio receivers, and cinema seating capacity.

† There is a slight tendency toward understatement in countries reporting radios licensed rather than radios in use. See Russett, p. 118.

Degree of Cultural and Ethnic Homogeneity

A familiar characteristic of many less developed countries is the presence of diversity in language, culture, religion, and race. Among countries at the earliest stage of social and economic development, the "primordial attachments" of kinship, race, language, religion, and custom tend to be very strong.[28] The resulting lack of social and economic integration contributes to their difficulties in initiating a process of economic growth. In addition, these primordial attachments characteristically come into severe conflict with the requirements for effective political integration and, in particular, with the need for more generalized commitments to a relatively impersonal nationwide civil order. Not only does cultural and ethnic heterogeneity tend to hamper the early stages of nation building and economic growth, but in addition, the initial effects of urbanization and industrialization may be to intensify awareness of religious, racial, and cultural differences and thus to produce social tensions that, in the short run at least, create additional impediments to socioeconomic and political development. The presence of social, ethnic, or religious minorities may also exacerbate the political consequences of inequalities in the distribution of income and power, since in a heterogeneous nation the dominant ethnic group often tends to be favored disproportionately in both economic and political arenas. In general, therefore, it seems reasonable to conclude that, other things being equal, less developed countries that are relatively homogeneous with respect to cultural, religious, and ethnic characteristics are less hampered in the achievement of social and political integration and in the initiation of continuous economic growth than more heterogeneous societies.*

In defining an indicator of cultural and ethnic homogeneity, we combined three country characteristics into a single index: the extent of linguistic, religious, and racial homogeneity. The element

---

* However, for a contrasting view—that the more integrated society is less likely to adapt to change than the poorly integrated one—see Ralph Linton, "Cultural and Personality Factors Affecting Economic Growth," in B. F. Hoselitz, ed., *The Progress of Underdeveloped Areas* (Chicago, 1952), pp. 87–88.

receiving the greatest weight, the proportion of the population speaking the dominant language, was chosen to summarize the overall degree of homogeneity of the culture. The *World Handbook of Political and Social Indicators*[29] provided the basic information on linguistic homogeneity for about two-thirds of the countries in our sample. The remaining countries were classified with the help of Banks and Textor's *A Cross-Polity Survey*,[30] the *Encyclopaedia Britannica*, and a small number of interviews. The principal sources of data on religious and racial homogeneity were *A Cross-Polity Survey*[31] and the *Encyclopaedia Britannica*. Country studies and interviews were also helpful in completing a number of classifications.

A. Countries in which, generally speaking, over 85 percent of the population spoke the dominant language and in which over 70 percent of the population was of the same race. The countries meeting these criteria are divided into two groups: (1) countries in which over 90 percent of the population was of the same race and in which the religion was relatively homogeneous are classified A+;* (2) countries in which over 90 percent of the population was of the same race but in which the religion was heterogeneous are classified A. Countries in which the religion was homogeneous but in which the predominant race constituted only 71–90 percent of the population are also classified A.

B. Countries in which over 70 percent of the population spoke the dominant language but in which (1) less than 71 percent of the population was of the same race, or (2) the religion was heterogeneous, or (3) both characteristics (1) and (2) apply. The following tabulation specifies the gradations within this category:

Score	Language (pct)	Race (pct)	Religion
B+	Over 85%	71–90%	Homogeneous
B+	Over 85	51–70	Heterogeneous
B	Over 85	51–70	Homogeneous
B	Over 85	Under 51	Either
B	71–85	Over 90	Either
B−	71–85	Under 91	Either

* The definitions of religious homogeneity and religious heterogeneity used in this classification system are those given in *A Cross-Polity Survey*; that is, a country is homogeneous with respect to religion if 80–85 percent

C. Countries in which 51–70 percent of the population spoke the dominant language. The countries meeting this criterion are divided into three groups: (1) those in which over 90 percent of the population was of the same race and in which the religion was homogeneous are classified *C*+; (2) those in which either (*a*) over 90 percent of the population was of the same race but the religion was heterogeneous or (*b*) 71–90 percent of the population was of the same race with no specification about religion are classified *C*; (3) all countries in which 51–70 percent of the population spoke the dominant language and in which less than 71 percent was of the same race are classified *C*−.

D. Countries in which less than 51 percent of the population spoke the dominant language. The countries in this category were divided into two groups: (1) those in which over 90 percent of the population was of the same race and in which the religion was homogeneous are classified *D*+; (2) all the remaining countries in which less than 51 percent of the population spoke the dominant language are classified *D*.

Degree of Social Tension

The frequent occurrence of serious social tensions and social conflict often accompanies the early stages of industrialization, urbanization, and modernization. In the first place, the breakup of the traditional kinship and tribal groups that are characteristic of low-income countries produces tensions, both personal and social, between primary loyalties to the small community and the new, broader loyalties demanded by the modern nation-state; tensions of this type have varied manifestations such as caste conflicts or struggles between central and tribal political authorities. As mentioned in discussing cultural homogeneity, another source of tension arises because the process of nation building acts to intensify conflicts within the nation between groups that have different and opposing bonds of culture, race, custom, or religion.[32] Finally, the process of broadening political participation to include

---

of the population was of the predominant religion, and it is heterogeneous if less than 80–85 percent was of the predominant religion.

previously excluded ethnic or socioeconomic groups is often accompanied by a heightening of social tensions. Thus, it is not surprising to find evidence that at the early stages of industrialization and urbanization there is an interaction between socioeconomic changes that produce tensions, which in turn may slow down further economic development.

The indicator of the degree of social tension we have chosen for our study is a purely qualitative one, several attributes of which should be specially noted. In the first place, in order to obtain reasonably unambiguous category descriptions, evidence of overt social tensions was of necessity weighted more heavily than evidence of potential underlying tensions. Second, for final country classifications we relied greatly upon consultation with about 30 regional experts to whom a statement of category descriptions and preliminary country scores was circulated. Preliminary classifications were based upon recent country studies; a useful cross-check on these was also provided by Banks and Textor's *A Cross-Polity Survey*.[33] Finally, it should be emphasized that the judgments with respect to the degree of social tension refer only to the period 1957–62, for which we had reasonably adequate interview information; a number of countries would have been scored differently had the time period been extended to the present.

The classification scheme for this indicator distinguishes between three principal categories.

A. Countries that during the period 1957–62 were suffering from marked social tensions accompanied by considerable violence and social instability arising from racial, tribal, religious, or cultural tensions.

B. Countries characterized by important social tensions during the period 1957–62, accompanied by some violence or other overt manifestations of tension, which were not, however, widespread. These tensions may have arisen from any of the sources mentioned in the definition of category *A.* Countries experiencing occasional or frequent but very small-scale violence connected with social unrest are classified *B+*.

C. Countries characterized by insignificant social tensions or by moderate social tensions of which there were very few or no overt signs during the period 1957–62.

Crude Fertility Rate

It is generally accepted that patterns of population growth intimately condition a country's success in raising its standard of living. Furthermore, there is considerable evidence that suggests the existence of a systematic tendency for mortality rates and fertility rates to decline as countries progress to higher levels of development. Historically, in Western Europe, for example, economic development was accompanied by dramatic decreases in mortality rates, later succeeded by declines in birth rates caused largely by decreases in average family size. Most recent authors agree that this historical decline in rates of fertility resulted from a complex of interrelated social changes that accompanied the process of industrialization and urbanization.[34]

While there are thus good reasons to expect lower fertility to accompany economic development in the long run, the exact nature of the relationship and its impact on income distribution are by no means clear. High fertility rates in rural areas tend to reduce the marketable surplus of agricultural products, shifting the terms of trade against industry. At the same time, however, a larger agricultural population generates a larger "reserve army" of urban unemployed. The net impact of high fertility on income distribution depends on the relative strength of these influences, and thus on the level and geographical spread of economic development as well as social policy with respect to wage minima.

Our indicator of fertility is a purely statistical one based upon estimates of crude fertility rates for the period 1955–59 in the majority of cases. The principal source for these estimates was information collected by the United Nations.[35] As is well known, data on fertility are often unreliable. Wherever possible, therefore, estimates based on sample surveys or demographic analyses of census data were used, even if they were for an earlier or more recent period than 1955–59. Since fertility rates tend to change rather slowly, we felt that differences of a few years in time period were not important. In contrast, differences between informal estimates originating within countries and subsequently published census-based estimates were in some instances very large. For countries for which reliable estimates were not available for any period, several cross-checks were made of data obtained from United Nations sources and country studies. First, the data were checked for consistency with estimates contained in recent country studies of overall population growth rates, mortality rates, and average life expectancy.* Second, they were cross-checked with qualitative information on practices of family limitation. Finally, where possible, they were cross-checked with more reliable estimates for similar neighboring countries.

The less developed countries in our sample were grouped into the following broad categories according to their crude fertility rates. Unless otherwise noted, plus and minus scores are assigned to countries having fertility rates close to the limits of the category.

A. Countries with crude fertility rates of 50 per 1,000 population or more.

B. Countries with crude fertility rates of from 40 to 49 per 1,000 population.

C. Countries with crude fertility rates of from 30 to 39 per 1,000 population.

D. Countries with crude fertility rates of under 30 per 1,000 population. Those in which the fertility rate was from 26 to 29 per 1,000 population are classified D+.

Degree of Modernization of Outlook

In discussing indicators of social and cultural change, we have on several occasions mentioned the importance to economic growth of the creation of attitudes favorable to change and innovation. Indeed, many social scientists would agree with W. E. Moore that an essential aspect of the transformation of a less developed soci-

---

* For example, if a country had an estimated average life expectancy of 35 years, we assumed that its mortality rate could not be less than 25 per 1,000. Given an estimate for population growth of 3 percent per annum, it appeared that any estimate of the crude fertility rate of less than 50 per 1,000 could be taken as unreasonable.

ety into a developed one is the "transformation of the contents of the minds of the elite who direct and of the men who man" the society and polity.[36] Various authors have attempted to define the essence of that "modernization" of men's outlook that they stress is necessary to social, economic, and political change. Daniel Lerner, a student of transitional societies, emphasizes the individual's sense of participation as the essence of the "modern" outlook. In probing the sources of the participant society, he maintains that the essential element in the makeup of the modern man is a "psychic mobility" that enables him to identify with new aspects of his environment and to adapt readily to them.[37]

In developing an index of the degree of modernization of outlook, we were obliged to depend on a broad characterization of less developed countries that was based largely upon judgmental information. Two qualitative elements were combined in the index. First, we divided countries into two broad classes: those in which the outlook of educated urban groups was "significantly" modernized and those in which it was not. Countries were judged to have significant modernization of outlook only if the adoption of Western or modern styles of living had gone considerably farther than external forms and dress, and had entailed the evolution of at least some important modern forms of social and political participation such as voluntary associations. The second element in the index was a judgment of whether programs of political, social, and economic modernization (health programs, economic institution building) have or have not gained significant support among the urban population and among some of the rural population. The principal sources of information for these judgments were recently published country studies, in addition to a small number of interviews with regional experts who were personally familiar with a large number of countries in their region. Valuable cross-checks for our classifications of some of the countries in the sample were provided by Banks and Textor's *A Cross-Polity Survey*.[38] In our final definition of the indicator of the degree of modernization of outlook as of about 1960, three principal categories of less developed countries were distinguished.

A. Countries in which the outlook of the urban educated population was significantly modernized, judging by the standards of less developed countries, and in which programs of political, social, and economic modernization had gained significant support among both the urban and rural populations.

B. Countries in which the outlook of the urban educated population was significantly modernized but in which programs of political, social, and economic modernization had gained significant support only among the urban population.

C. Countries in which the outlook of the educated urban sector was partially but not significantly modernized and in which programs of modernization, if they existed, had gained relatively little support among either the urban or the rural population.

Predominant Type of Religion

Economic historians have written at length on the subject of the interrelationship between religion and economic growth. Max Weber suggested that the Puritan religious values developed in the sixteenth century were particularly favorable to capitalist economic growth.[39] His ideas have stimulated studies as diverse as Tawney's inquiry into religion's impact on attitudes toward business activity in sixteenth-century England,[40] varied investigations of Puritanism in early America,[41] and studies of the impact of religious values on the growth of selected Asian countries.[42]

In general, religions that stress belief in the individual's control over his personal activities and fate might be expected to produce attitudes more favorable to striving toward economic success and participation. Religious values stressing individual control over the environment might also be expected to favor participation in the political process. The present indicator defines four categories of countries that are distinguished and ranked according to the degree to which the predominant religion stresses belief in the individual's control over his personal fate. Both the characterizations of the individual types of religion and the classification of countries with respect to them are drawn from Banks and Textor, *A Cross-Polity Survey*.[43]

The general lines of the classification scheme are as follows:

A. Countries in which the predominant religion emphasizes the individual's responsibility for his actions and his ability to influence his environment.

B and *C*. Countries in which the predominant religion promotes moderately fatalistic attitudes toward man's capacity to alter his destiny.

D. Countries in which the predominant religion teaches that man is subject to the power of his physical and social environment.

The detailed classification scheme provides gradations for countries of mixed religion:

Classification	Type of religion
A+	Mixed Christian; Jewish
A	Catholic; East Orthodox
A−	Mixed: Christian; literate non-Christian
B+	Mixed: Christian; nonliterate
B	Muslim
C+	Mixed: literate non-Christian
C	Buddhist; Hindu
C−	Mixed: literate non-Christian; nonliterate
D	Mixed: nonliterate; literate non-Christian; Christian

Level of Socioeconomic Development

The inadequacies of per capita GNP as a measure of national development have led to various attempts to devise broader indexes of development status and performance.[44] Some merely supplement per capita GNP with indicators of levels of living and structural change.[45] Others attempt to devise broader aggregates that incorporate other components of modernization. The present variable is in the latter spirit.

Our aggregate measure of socioeconomic development is composed of the indicators of social and socioeconomic modernization discussed above, (except for social tension and type of religion), as well as per capita GNP and a measure of degree of national integration and sense of national unity discussed in the next chapter. The selection of variables to be included in our measure of socioeconomic development and their relative weighting were derived by factor analysis from a set of 25 socioeconomic and political variables. The variables selected were those that grouped in the first factor, and together they accounted for over 50 percent of the overall variance of all the variables included.

For this variable, each country is given its factor score on the first factor that we interpret to summarize the level of social and economic development. The individual factor scores and a description of the factor analysis from which the scores are taken may be found in Adelman and Morris, *Society, Politics, and Economic Development*, Chap. 4.[46]

CHAPTER TWO

Methodology: Political and Economic Indicators

POLITICAL INDICATORS

The relationship between the political characteristics of developing nations and economic growth has received considerable attention in recent years.[1] Both the contemporary scene and historical experience provide instances of successful economic development under quite diverse political systems. In Western Europe, for example, successful economic performance has been associated with political democracy and a moderately important government economic role; in contrast, the rapid economic development of the Soviet Union has been achieved with an authoritarian form of government and massive government economic activity. Although similar contrasts may be drawn from among less developed countries, recent investigations of the political systems of developing nations suggest that there may nevertheless be systematic patterns of political change associated with economic development.

While there is general agreement on the importance of the interaction of political influences and economic growth, the literature on the subject is complicated by lack of agreement on the nature of political development. Each approach to political development tends to produce its own distinct view of the political transformations typically accompanying urbanization and industrialization.[2]

In our choice of political variables, therefore, we have attempted to represent several important spheres of the political life of a developing society. One broad sphere depicted by several variables reflects the evolution of "stable but sensitive political mechanisms for relating the interests and the demands of the society to political power."[3] The variables chosen for this purpose were the degree of competitiveness of political parties, the predominant basis of the political party system, the extent of political participation, the strength of the labor movement, the extent of freedom of political opposition and of the press, and the degree of centralization of political power. A second important group of political variables incorporated in our studies describes the character and orientation of political administration and leadership. This group is composed of the indicators of the degree of administrative efficiency, the political strength of the traditional elite, the political strength of the military, the extent of direct government economic activity, and the extent of leadership commitment to economic development. Finally, we incorporated in our analysis a measure of the extent of political stability.

Degree of National Integration and Sense of National Unity

An important aspect of the growth of modern nation-states is the process of integrating the political system and of creating a sense of national unity among the population. As mentioned above, the greater the initial cultural and ethnic heterogeneity of a society, the less likely it is that modern integrative mechanisms such as education and mass communication media will be effective in promoting a unified polity and society. In addition, there is a purely political aspect of the lack of integration. In countries where the ties of most of the population are still "primordial," such as those of kin, tribe, and race, the creation of a national government is likely, for a time at least, to result in parallel and non-integrated structures of authority: on the one hand, a multiplicity of purely local traditional (often tribal) authorities, and on the other hand, a national political structure that lacks grass roots mechanisms for the articulation of local interests. As countries develop and become more integrated economically and socially, it becomes more likely that their formal political institutions will reflect the spread of the more generalized commitments to a nation-state that are characteristic of the advanced countries of the world.[4] Thus, in the long run, economic and social development tends to be accompanied by a process of gradual transference of social and political loyalties from traditional communally based sociopolitical organizations to the more aggregated political structures typical of higher levels of development.

In defining a variable to represent the process of national integration, we chose a purely qualitative one. Our first attempt involved the combination of two qualitative elements into a single index: the intensity of the political and economic nationalism of a country's leaders and the pervasiveness among the population of a sense of national unity. A statement of category descriptions, together with our preliminary country classifications, was circulated to some 30 regional experts with a request for corrections and suggestions. It appeared from their comments that the two elements included in the index were not necessarily associated with each other.* As a result, we decided after further study that an indicator measuring both cultural and political aspects of the degree of national integration would be better conceptually than one that included extent of nationalistic feeling or chauvinism of the leadership. In our redefinition we combined statistical information on the proportion of the population speaking a common language[5] with two qualitative aspects of integration: the degree of integration of local political structures with national political institutions and the prevalence among the population of a sense of national identity. The principal sources of qualitative information for this indicator were recent country studies and the interviews referred to above.

In the final classification scheme, less developed countries were grouped into four broad categories.

A. Countries characterized by a marked degree of national integration, as indicated by the overwhelming predominance of a common language and culture and by the reasonably effective

---

* For a definition of this index and for results in which it was incorporated, see the study by the present authors, "A Factor Analysis of the Interrelationship between Social and Political Variables and Per Capita Gross National Product," *Quarterly Journal of Economics*, 79 (1965): 559ff. We are also grateful to Everett E. Hagen for his suggestion that we treat the two elements separately.

integration of central and local political systems. In addition, well-developed senses of national unity prevailed in these countries.

B. Countries characterized by a moderate degree of national integration. In all these countries political systems were fairly well integrated, over 60 percent of the population spoke the predominant language, and a majority of the population had a well-developed sense of national unity. However, important minorities existed in these countries that did not speak the predominant language and/or did not share in the sense of national identity of the majority.

C. Countries characterized by a small degree of national integration in which, however, the majority of the population spoke a common language. In these countries local and central political systems were poorly integrated and the sense of overall national unity was weak among most of the population.

D. Countries characterized by a marked absence of national integration, as indicated by the absence of a common language and culture, ineffective integration of local and central political systems, and little or no sense of overall national unity. In all these countries less than half the population spoke a common language.

Degree of Centralization of Political Power

The relationship between the degree of centralization of political power and economic performance appears to vary at different levels of socioeconomic evolution. Contemporary developing countries in the lowest income bracket generally have not yet achieved effective national unification on either the economic or the political plane. Indeed, they often suffer from marked discontinuity between central government structures and local traditional tribal authorities.[6] Among countries at this low stage of socioeconomic growth, a movement from very low to somewhat higher levels of development is typically accompanied by greater centralization of political power in the sense of the firmer establishment of an effective nationwide network of government authority.[7] There is also historical evidence that politically more unified countries tended to perform better economically. Growth rates in nineteenth-century Germany and Italy, for example, were higher following unification than before.*

The relations between political centralization and economic and political participation are not clear a priori. In underdeveloped countries, increases in centralization may be, but by no means always are, accompanied by more participant political mechanisms and more equal distributions of income. Indeed, a common justification of centralization of power is that it is necessary in order to implement egalitarian reforms opposed by influential nongovernment elites.

Our indicator of the degree of centralization of political power defines four categories of countries, the lowest of which is characterized by marked discontinuity between independent, local, traditional authorities and the central government, and the highest of which is characterized by a highly centralized, relatively unified, authoritarian central governmental structure. Intermediate between these are centralized nonauthoritarian governments and moderately centralized governments tending toward democratic decentralization. In our preliminary definition of this indicator, we were doubtful about the rank order of the two categories of relative decentralization: that defined by democratic decentralization and that defined by a cleavage between traditional local political authorities and central, often authoritarian, governments. We finally decided that the latter represented a lesser degree of effective centralization than the former.† Thus, the final indicator represents a continuum with respect to degree of centralization. Strictly interpreted, this variable is not intended to represent a movement from more democratic systems to less democratic sys-

---

* Change in the extent of political unification was, of course, only one of a number of influences that accounted for changes in economic performance. For a general discussion of, and data on, growth rates in various countries in the latter half of the nineteenth century, see S. J. Patel, "Rates of Industrial Growth in the Last Century, 1860–1958," *Economic Development and Cultural Change*, 9 (1961): 316–50.

† We are grateful to E. E. Hagen for underlining this difficulty and for suggesting the order of rank that we finally accepted. For results based upon the alternative ordering, see our study "A Factor Analysis of the Interrelationship between Social and Political Variables and Per Capita Gross National Product."

tems, although it is evident that it may be related to such a movement.

The primary sources of information for this classification were recent country studies and a series of more than 30 consultations with regional and country experts. These were found to be necessary because of the tendency of written published and unpublished reports to characterize almost all governments of less developed countries as centralized without sufficiently differentiating among them. In our cross-check of country classifications, several raw characteristics from Banks and Textor's *A Cross-Polity Survey* were also consulted.[8]

Below is the precise classification scheme for our indicator of the degree of centralization of political power during the period 1957–62.

A. Countries with highly centralized authoritarian governments in which most major decisions were referred to the central executive, in which central government control was at least reasonably effective throughout most of the country, and in which regional and local government authorities had relatively little political power. In addition, countries in this category were characterized by considerable repression of opposition by the central government.

B. Countries with highly centralized, reasonably effective government control throughout most of the country and weakness of local and regional government institutions. Countries in this category are distinguished from those in category *A* by the absence of significant measures of repression by the central government.

C. Countries characterized by a movement toward administrative decentralization of political power. Central governments may have continued to be strong, but decentralized national, regional, or local government authorities had, or were gaining, significant political power.

D. Countries characterized by centralization of government authority without marked repression of opposition, in which, however, central governments did not maintain effective administrative control throughout important parts of the country. Local village or tribal authorities continued to be the key administrative units in many areas.

Degree of Freedom of Political Opposition and the Press

An important aspect of the strength of democratic institutions is the degree of freedom of political opposition and of the press. Of course, these freedoms may exist before the evolution of effective mechanisms for individual participation in a democratic political system; however, once specialized institutions have been created to articulate and aggregate specific group interests in national politics, the presence in the society of reasonable freedom of expression and of political opposition becomes a sine qua non of effective democracy.

Since relatively few less developed countries have extensive freedom of opposition or of the press, it is useful when defining an indicator to represent them to distinguish among the many countries having some form of restrictions. Therefore we have assigned relatively high scores to countries in which restrictions on the press and on political opposition are only occasional or fairly limited. Successively lower scores were given to countries having increasingly restrictive government controls. Two further points should be noted about the definition of this indicator. First, the degree of freedom of political opposition was weighted more heavily than the degree of freedom of the press, since the former was felt to be a better indicator of genuine institutional freedom. Second, the presence or absence of controls over foreign newspapers was excluded from consideration.

The primary sources for the preliminary classification of countries were recent country studies. Once again, the indexes of freedom of the press and freedom of group opposition presented in *A Cross-Polity Survey*[9] gave us a valuable independent cross-check on the judgmental information gathered from other sources. As a result, only a handful of interviews was required to resolve doubtful cases.

The final classification scheme summarizing the degree of freedom of political opposition and the press during the period 1957–62 is presented below.

A. Countries in which political parties (other than extremist parties opposing constitutional forms of government) were free to organize, operate, and oppose the government throughout all or most of the period 1957–62. Countries in which domestic freedom of the press was nevertheless somewhat restricted or intermittent are classified A−.

B. Countries in which political parties, while generally free to organize, were limited in their political activities and in their freedom to oppose the government during part or all of the 1957–62 period. Countries in which domestic freedom of the press was restricted or intermittent during the period are classified B−.

C. Countries in which political parties were limited to nonpolitical activities or in which political opposition to the government was banned during the period 1957–62. Those in which political opposition was banned and in which domestic freedom of the press was absent are classified C−. The remaining countries are classified C.

Degree of Competitiveness of Political Parties

The presence of competitiveness among political parties is one dimension of an effective democratic system. At the lower end of the scale of political competitiveness, a movement from a pure dictatorship to a system with a national unity party, and subsequently to a system with two competing parties, clearly represents a movement toward greater democracy. However, while at least two competing parties are necessary for a political system to assure representation of the diverse groups in a society, further multiplication of parties does not necessarily produce a more participant democratic system, even though, strictly speaking, it may lead to an increase in the degree of political competitiveness. With respect to the relationship between competition among parties and economic change, there is evidence (cited above in our discussion of the strength of democratic institutions) of a tendency for countries with no political parties or with only a single party to rank low on indexes of the level of economic development as well as on most spectra of political development. There are, however, no a priori grounds for expecting a relationship between competitiveness of the political party system and distribution of income. A multiplicity of parties may be representative of only a narrow segment of the population or, alternatively, may have very little influence on national decision making; in either case, their impact in increasing equity would be negligible.

In deriving an index of the competitiveness of parties during the period 1957–62, we differentiated only slightly between countries having two parties and countries having more than two parties operating at a national level.* We did differentiate significantly between countries with two or more parties in which there was reasonable expectation of rotation or sharing of government control among parties and those in which there was not. Finally, it should be noted, of course, that classification of a country with respect to the number of political parties sharing or rotating control of the political system is not tantamount to classification according to strength of the democratic system. A country may have two nationally operative political parties, for example, and yet be characterized by extremely low voter participation, significant restrictions on freedom of the press, or marked instability of the party system.

The primary source of information on degree of competitiveness used in classifying individual countries was Banks and Textor's *A Cross-Polity Survey*, raw characteristic number 41 (party system: quantitative). Recent country studies were consulted as a cross-check on the particular time period used in our definition of the indicator. Where a country had an operative party system during only part of the period 1957–62, classification was made on the basis of the longest consistent subperiod.

A. Countries in which there were two or more reasonably effective political parties, between at least two of which rotation or

---

* In this connection we are grateful to E. E. Hagen for his suggestion that we redefine this indicator.

sharing of government control could reasonably be expected. Countries in which there were more than two national parties are classified *A* and those in which there were only two are classified *A*—.

B. Countries in which there were two or more effective political parties without a reasonable expectation that rotation or sharing of government control would occur. Countries in which at least two parties had significant power at the national level but in which one of these was unable to win a majority are classified *B.* Those in which only one party was effective at the national level but in which one or more other parties retained their identity in national elections are classified *B*—.

C. Countries in which there was only one political party effective at the national level and in which all others had been banned or were adjuncts to the dominant party.

D. Countries in which there were no political parties effective at the national level.

Predominant Basis of the Political Party System

The broad contrast between the nature of political parties in advanced democracies and in most underdeveloped countries is well known. Generally speaking, in most economically developed democracies each of several competitive parties tends to represent a fairly wide range of interests having a given class or ideological orientation and to formulate pragmatic programs that combine and articulate these interests. In contrast, most low-income nations have either noncompetitive political systems or competitive systems in which particularistic (ethnic, religious, regional) or highly personalistic parties predominate. Within the range of income represented by most contemporary developing nations, it is not quite so clear how the character of political parties is related to differences in economic performance.

We have defined an indicator of the predominant basis of political party systems in terms of a spectrum, the lower end of which is marked by the absence of parties or by the dominance of a single party with nationalistic appeal, and the upper end characterized by articulate aggregative parties having a class or ideological orientation. Thus, progression along the scale involves (1) a movement toward greater articulation of, first, primordial particularist interests, then personalistic interests, and finally associational interests (such as those of labor unions and industrialists); and (2) a movement toward greater combination or aggregation of small group interests into larger associations with more rationally formulated pragmatic national programs.

The primary data for the country classifications were taken from *A Cross-Polity Survey.*[10] Two difficulties experienced in classifying countries should be noted. The first was the problem of scaling an essentially typological characteristic; we resolved this difficulty along the lines discussed above. A second related difficulty arose with respect to countries having mixed party systems: for example, those having both ideological and personalistic parties or those having both personalistic and particularist parties.* The solution to the first problem helped resolve the second problem. Where a country had an approximately equal weight of parties defined by two adjacent categories, a score lying between the two was taken to represent its mixed system. As it happened, almost every ambiguous case could be resolved in this manner. In the remaining cases we were able with the help of expert opinion to make a definite judgment regarding the type of party that predominated. As with the indicator of competitiveness, where a country had an operative political party system during only part of the period 1957–62, classification was made on the basis of the longest subperiod.

The definition of our indicator of the predominant basis of the political party system during the period 1957–62 follows.

A. Countries with political systems characterized by the predominance of a party or parties having, among other things, significant class or ideological orientation. Countries in which political parties had a mixture of important ideological and personalistic elements are classified A−. Excluded from this category are countries in which there is an important exclusively mass-directed or national unity party.

* Other combinations were rare.

B. Countries in which political parties in general were highly personalistic rather than doctrinal or nationalistic. Party systems in some of these countries were characterized by extensive political opportunism. Countries in which political parties had a mixture of significant personalistic and religious, cultural, ethnic, or regional elements are classified *B−*.

C. Countries in which the predominant basis of political parties was the regional, ethnic, cultural, or religious groupings of the population.

D. Countries in which the dominant national unity party did not have a significant class or ideological orientation.

E. Countries in which there were no effective political parties or in which all parties had been banned for more than three years of the period 1957–62.

Strength of the Labor Movement

A familiar sociopolitical concomitant of the process of industrialization is the growth of trade union organization. While there have been historical instances of unions of agricultural workers, the creation of durable, stable labor organizations has typically accompanied the growth of industrial enterprise. A number of reasons have been put forth for the association of trade union growth with industrialization. One contemporary explanation suggests that only fully urbanized industrial workers who have no expectation of returning to their rural homes are likely to become so committed to the urban industrial way of life that their protests and demands will take the form of permanently organized economic and political action.[11] The political consequences of the growth of unions derive from their key role as a channel for increased participation by workers in the political process.[12] Typically in underdeveloped countries the spread of political participation through labor unions comes at a later stage of national development than does the broadening of political participation to include the middle classes, while participation by rural groups comes last of all.

There is considerable controversy with respect to the short-run relationship between unions, economic growth, and income distribution. One view, held by John Dunlop and Karl De Schweinitz, for example, is that because trade unions favor consumption they tend to reduce (or prevent an increase in) the proportion of resources going into investment and thus to retard the rate of economic growth. Other points of view emphasize the positive effects of unions as modernizing influences and agents of social welfare.[13] The net impact of unionization on income distribution is unclear. The creation of a unionized working elite may stimulate the use of more capital-intensive techniques and thus slow the rate of growth of employment, while also increasing inequality among wage earners. On the other hand, unions typically support programs designed to improve income distribution.

The derivation of an index of the strength of the labor movement was complicated by the absence of data on trade union memberships for most of the countries in our sample. The indicator chosen was a primarily qualitative composite of several aspects of labor union strength: extent of political power, freedom from political restrictions, independence of government influence, and extent of popular support. Finally, within each category a lower score was given to countries having a very small industrial labor force from which unions could potentially draw their membership.

In classifying individual countries with respect to the strength of their labor movements during the period 1957–62, recent studies of labor movements in less developed countries were the principal source of information.[14] Preliminary judgments based on these data were cross-checked by several interviews with regional experts, directed at assigning doubtful cases to specific categories.

A. Countries in which labor movements were relatively well established and active and had considerable popular support (judging by the standards of less developed countries), considerable independent political power, and significant freedom to oppose the government. The labor organizations in these countries, though substantially independent, were usually allied with one or more political parties. Countries in which, as of about 1960, the industrial labor force was 30 percent of or less than the total nonagricultural labor force are classified A—.

B. Countries with fairly well-established independent labor movements that had moderate political power but that in most instances were limited in their freedom to oppose the government. In a number of these countries political parties dominated the labor movement; however, excluded from this category are countries in which the labor movement was controlled by a single political party that dominated the nation. Countries that had a very small industrial labor force are classified *B−*.

C. Countries in which a fairly well-established labor movement was either government-sponsored or seriously restricted in its activities by the government. This category includes countries in which a single political party dominated the labor movement. Countries that had a very small industrial labor force are classified *C−*.

D. Countries in which the labor movement was negligible or in effect proscribed. Countries with a very small independent labor movement that had negligible political influence are classified *D+*. Countries in which labor organization was banned completely are classified *D−*. The remaining countries are classified *D*.

Political Strength of the Traditional Elite

The emergence of a political leadership committed to economic modernization is generally agreed to be essential to the socioeconomic transformation that a traditional society must undergo for an effective take-off into self-sustained growth. At very low levels of development the breakup of the social and political control exercised by traditional land-owning elites or other tradition-oriented bureaucratic, military, or religious elites is important for the initiation of economic growth, for at least two interrelated reasons. First, control of the wealth of a country by a traditional elite tends to result in spending by wealth-owners for services, luxury goods, land, and other real estate rather than for the expansion of business enterprise. Second, tradition-oriented actions and ideologies tend to be dominated by ascriptive particularistic norms that often conflict with the requirements for economic modernization and technological change,[15] as well as with the dictates of social equity.

Thus, the extent of the social and political influence of the traditional elite is an aspect of the social structure of low-income countries that is very relevant to a study of economic development and social equity.

In classifying less developed countries with respect to the role of the traditional elite, we grouped them into three broad categories according to the political strength of their tradition-oriented elites during the period 1957–62. We interpreted the traditional elites to include both traditional landholding elites and bureaucratic, religious, or military elites who favored the preservation of traditional political, social, and economic organization, institutions, and values. Qualitative information from recent country studies was the principal source used in the preliminary classification of individual countries.[16]

Once preliminary country scores were assigned, we consulted twelve regional experts for clarification of doubtful classifications. These consultations made it evident that our preliminary category descriptions did not provide for countries under colonial rule during part of the 1957–62 period or for countries in which the role of traditional national elites changed significantly during that period. To deal with the former group, we introduced a distinction between tradition-oriented and modernizing colonial elites; to deal with the latter, we assigned a special score to countries in which the power of the traditional elite showed a marked decline during the period.

The classification scheme for the indicator of political strength of the traditional elite during the period 1957–62 groups countries into three principal categories.

A. Countries in which traditional landowning and/or other tradition-oriented national elites were politically dominant during the greater part of the period 1957–62. Any country in which a feudal-type landed aristocracy was in complete control is classified A+. Countries in which no important landed aristocracies existed but in which the controlling elites nevertheless exhibited clearly traditional attitudes are classified A−. The remaining countries are classified A.

B. Countries in which tradition-oriented national or colonial elites had moderate political influence during an important part of the period 1957–62. In many of these countries, commercial and industrial groups, modernizing military leaders, or modernizing bureaucrats exercised growing political power during the period. Countries in which the latter groups were or became more influential than the traditional elites during the period are classified *B*−.

C. Countries in which tradition-oriented elites had little or no political power during most of the period 1957–62. This category includes countries in which modernizing colonial regimes were succeeded by modernizing national governments during the period. Countries in which traditional elites were excluded from political activity either by legislation or by force during most of the period are classified *C*−.

Political Strength of the Military

Although the incidence of military intervention in civilian politics is quite high in developing countries, relatively few studies have been made of the relationship between military institutions and economic or political participation. Until recently a view commonly held was that militarism is inherently antipathetic both to the evolution of democracy and to broadly based economic growth. In the past few years, however, a number of political scientists have undertaken the study of armies in underdeveloped countries as potentially modern political structures capable of acting as effective modernizing agents. As Lucian Pye pointed out at a 1959 conference on the role of the military in underdeveloped countries, the members of the army of a low-income nation may be more receptive to Western technology and organization and more divorced from traditional patterns of action than are civil bureaucracies.[17] In addition, armies often provide training in specialized modern skills and offer a vehicle for the creation of a generalized sense of national identity. Finally, they can provide a channel for upward social mobility.

While opinions of the relationship between the military and economic development vary, it is clear that the political strength of the military is relevant to a study of the process of economic growth and of the distribution of the benefits from growth. In defining an indicator to represent variations in the role of the military, we grouped less developed countries into three broad categories determined respectively by a marked, moderate, or negligible military influence in the political arena. For our preliminary classification of the individual countries, the primary sources were recent country studies together with, for Latin American countries, Edwin Lieuwen's *Arms and Politics in Latin America*.[18] When Banks and Textor's *A Cross-Polity Survey* became available to us, it also proved extremely useful, since its definition of the military's political participation was very similar to ours.[19] Finally, various essays in *The Role of the Military in Underdeveloped Countries* offered us a cross-check on a number of our classifications.[20]

The classification scheme for our indicator of the political strength of the military during the period 1957–62 is presented below.

A. Countries in which the military was in direct political control during some part of the period 1957–62. Those in which the military was in direct control during the entire period are classified A+. Those in which the military controlled the civilian government for only one or two years of the period are classified A−. The remaining countries are classified A.

B. Countries in which the military was an important *political* influence but was not in direct political control during most of the period 1957–62. Those in which the tie between the military and the civilian government was very close are classified B+. Those in which military influence was significant during less than the entire period 1957–62 are classified B−. The remaining countries are classified B.

C. Countries in which the military had little or no political influence during the period 1957–62.

Political and Social Influence of Religious Organization

The relationship between organized religion and the national state changed greatly in Western Europe during the fifteenth, sixteenth, and seventeenth centuries. With the development of centralized "modern" states, the growth of more explicitly capitalist forms of economic activity, and the spread of modern science, an increasingly sharp division evolved between sacred and secular activities of both individuals and institutions. This complex of changes favored more widespread pursuit of economic goals and a gradual separation of the sphere of organized religion from that of the nation-state.[21] Outside Western Europe and its overseas settlements, however, the relationships between organized religion and the national state remained much stronger, and religious influences remained closely intertwined with political and social life. In countries where traditional long-established religious organizations tend toward the authoritarian, it might be expected that the greater political strength of religious organizations would favor less participant forms of political activity. Insofar as the influence of organized religion contributes to higher birthrates among the poor, it might also be expected to favor a more skewed income distribution. On the other hand, where powerful religious organizations dampen the operation of economic incentives and thereby retard economic growth rates, they would slow the trend toward inequality.

The following classification of countries by the political and social influence of religious organization stresses the extent of legal and de facto secularization of the state, the importance of religious law, the extent of national political influence of national religious organizations, and the extent of local social and political influence of regional religious organizations as of about 1960.

A. Countries in which there was a close identity of religion and the state and in which religious law was paramount. The political and social influence of religious organization was pervasive.

B. Countries in which there was no official separation of religion and the state, but in which there was considerable practical secularization of the state. National religious organization had considerable social and political influence, and religious law may have predominated in matters of personal status.

C. Countries in which there was official separation of religion and the state, but in which religious organizations nevertheless had considerable national political influence. Religion may have been taught in state schools, and/or religious schools may have been of considerable importance.

Countries in which there was de facto secularization of the state, with only a moderately important role of organized religion in national political life, are classified $C-$.

D. Countries in which religious organizations had relatively little national political influence. However, local religious organizations (including traditional tribal religious authorities) had considerable local and regional influence. Religion may have been taught in the state schools, and/or religious schools may have been of considerable importance.

E. Countries in which there was official separation of religion and the state and in which religious teaching in state schools was excluded. Religious organization may have been formally excluded from political activity. Religion may, nevertheless, have had considerable local influence.

Degree of Administrative Efficiency

The contributions that an effective bureaucracy can make to economic development have frequently been noted by social scientists. Rationally organized administrative services can help establish and strengthen the legal and public service facilities necessary for steady growth; they can help create financial institutions and tax instruments favorable to the expansion of private economic activity, or they can take direct responsibility for initiating development projects and plans.[22] They can also help to implement (or hinder) measures for the redistribution of income and wealth. Finally, bureaucracies operate as special interest groups that can inject either a socialist or a highly individualistic ethos into the process of development planning, depending on the character of the ruling bureaucratic elite.

In line with Max Weber's classical formulation of bureaucracy, modernization of bureaucratic administration may be said to involve the creation of such attributes within the bureaucracy as "hierarchy, responsibility, rationality, achievement orientation, specialization and differentiation, discipline, professionalization."[23] The indicator of administrative efficiency chosen for our study was a qualitative one in which interviews with regional and country experts were an important source of information in classifying individual countries. Another main source of information was recent country studies. The classifications were cross-checked with Banks and Textor's *A Cross-Polity Survey*, raw characteristic number 53 (character of bureaucracy).

Several criteria were used in grouping countries into three broad categories of degree of efficiency of the public administration: in particular, the degree of permanence and training of administrators (an indirect measure of whether recruitment is based upon qualifications for the job); the extent to which corruption, inefficiency, and incompetence seriously hamper government functioning; and the extent to which instability of policy at higher levels of administration promotes inefficiency. Classification of individual countries was based upon judgments regarding the period 1957–62. In the event of marked changes during the period, greater weight was given to the more recent years.

The classification scheme for the indicator of the extent of administrative efficiency follows.

A. Countries in which public administration was reasonably efficient. These countries had relatively well-trained civil services and did not suffer from instability of policy at higher administrative levels. Corruption was not widespread. Finally, bureaucratic inefficiency was not as marked as in most less developed countries.

B. Countries in which public administration was marked by considerable bureaucratic inefficiency but in which there was, nevertheless, a permanent body of administrators. Corruption may have been common, and there may have been moderate instability of policy at higher levels of administration, but the phenomena did not operate to the point where they seriously interfered with government functioning.

C. Countries in which public administration was characterized by extreme bureaucratic inefficiency and/or widespread corruption and/or serious instability of policy at higher administrative levels. Countries in which all three of these phenomena prevailed are classified C−.

Extent of Leadership Commitment to Economic Development

It is almost a truism to point out that the extent of commitment of the political leadership of a country to economic development is a significant determinant of its success in raising the country's standard of living. This is particularly true of contemporary low-income countries in which sociostructural, cultural, and attitudinal barriers to development are sufficiently strong to render unlikely a pattern of economic growth based primarily on individual enterprise. More specifically, many developing nations today suffer from marked imbalances in their economies and a variety of bottlenecks that seriously impede production and distribution. Given the weakness of their private sectors, they are unlikely to move forward economically without effective action on the part of their governmental leadership.[24]

The orientation of leadership toward social equity also affects the distribution of income through its impact on development programs. Depending on the goals and attitudes of the leadership, development plans may stress raising growth rates at the expense of equity or may emphasize redistributive measures and social justice. Of course, the power of development-oriented leadership groups relative to traditional bureaucracies, wealthy elites, or the military greatly affects the capacity of leaderships to achieve their goals.

The appropriate concept for judging leadership commitment to growth appears to be the extent and nature of activities that promote development by what has been called the "central guidance cluster." This guidance cluster would normally include a variety of government or even semiprivate agencies such as the head of the central bank, the financial minister, the head of the budget office, or government cabinet members and others who participate in the central decisions that guide the economy.[25] It is the attitudes of these leadership groups and the extent of their willingness to make purposive attempts to achieve institutional change that are relevant to an evaluation of leadership commitment to economic development.

In defining an indicator of leadership commitment to development during the period 1957–62, we have differentiated three broad categories on the basis of the following judgments:* (1) whether the heads of government and semiofficial national agencies (such as ministries of finance, planning agencies, and privately owned central banks) involved in direct or indirect central guidance of the economy typically make concerted efforts to promote the economic growth of the country; (2) whether or not this planning effort includes purposive attempts to alter institutional arrangements that clearly block the achievement of development goals; and (3) whether or not there are a national plan and a planning group functioning within the government that are charged full time with executing the plan. The details of the classification scheme and the individual country classifications follow.

A. Countries in which government leadership exhibited sustained and reasonably effective commitment to economic development (during the period 1957–62). This was indicated by the concerted efforts of leaders in government and other semiofficial agencies involved in central guidance of the economy to promote economic growth, and by purposive attempts by the government leadership to alter institutional arrangements unfavorable to growth. In addition, most countries in this category practiced some form of reasonably effective development planning.

B. Countries in which some government leaders evidenced a definite commitment to economic development (during the period 1957–62), as indicated by the practice of some form of national development planning. However, it was typical of the countries in this category that the activities of agencies involved in central guidance of the economy were poorly coordinated and that government attempts to alter institutional arrangements unfavorable to economic growth were infrequent or poorly sustained.

---

* These criteria would no longer suffice to differentiate among countries, since in the 1960's (1) and (3) have become ubiquitous.

C. Countries in which there was little or no evidence of leadership commitment to economic development (during the period 1957–62), as indicated by the absence of development plans and government planning groups. In addition, concerted efforts by agencies not formally engaged in planning to promote economic growth were lacking.

Extent of Direct Government Economic Activity

It is not surprising that most governments of contemporary developing countries play a major, direct role in promoting economic growth. In contrast to the historical experience of Western Europe, in which robust middle classes responsive to opportunities for industrial expansion were key carriers of economic progress, the exigencies of underdevelopment in today's low income nations turn many of them in the direction of government-stimulated and -managed development efforts. It is true that, even in the predominantly private enterprise economies in the West, the economic role of governments in the provision of transportation and other services was almost universally significant.[26] For a variety of reasons, however, contemporary developing nations often turn in the direction of greatly enlarged areas of government economic activity. Their indigenous middle classes tend to be very small or mo tivated toward purely commercial ventures; the extent of their social and physical overhead capital tends to be extremely limited; and in addition, the relative weight of the non-market sector with its traditional social organization and customs is often so great that, even with an active, urban, indigenous, entrepreneurial group, the expansion of indigenous economic activity tends to be very slow.[27] Alexander Eckstein, in investigating the role of government in economic growth, hypothesizes specifically that the role of the state in promoting development tends to be larger the greater the range of goals and the higher the level of attainment sought, the more rapid the rate of economic growth desired, the more unfavorable the factor and resource endowments, the greater the institutional barriers to economic change, and the greater the relative backwardness of the economy.[28] It is of course among lower-income nations that relative backwardness, poor factor endowments, and high aspirations for economic betterment are associated together, with the result that there are some grounds for expecting a larger economic role by the government than among more advanced nations.

On the other hand, if government economic activity is interpreted broadly to include expenditures on human resources, one might expect the economic role of the government to be not larger, but smaller, among lower-income nations. Quantitative investigations based on samples of countries in all income ranges show a mild tendency for the size of the public sector to be larger at higher levels of per capita GNP. One explanation for this tendency is that the advanced economies tend to spend relatively larger amounts upon social welfare, education, and other public services than does the typical lower-income economy.[29]

One might expect government ownership of productive enterprise to reduce the share of the uppermost income receivers in the total product. It is not clear, however, whether the gains in income from nationalization accrue to the poorest members of society or to the middle and upper (though not uppermost) income groups.

In our research on the role of the government in economic activity, we collected data on two aspects of governmental economic behavior. One type of data was qualitative information on the extent to which governments intervene in the economic life of the country through regulations, licensing, and the like. Second, we collected both judgmental and statistical data on the relative importance in the economy of direct government economic activities such as the building of infrastructure or direct engagement in industrial enterprise. Data on total government expenditures as a percentage of gross national product[30] turned out to be a rather poor measure for differentiating among countries with respect to direct government economic activity, although a useful cross-check on the classification of some countries. The difficulty with these data for our purpose was that they included greatly varying proportions of government consumption expenditures. In contrast, data on the proportion of net national investment undertaken by governments that we were able to obtain for a small number of countries were very useful. In the end, we relied upon qualitative indications of the relative significance of direct government economic activity to supplement the scant data available from U.N. sources and recent country studies.[31]

Our final indicator of the economic role of the government was based exclusively on estimates of the relative weight in the economy of direct government economic activity. We decided to eliminate the element of government interventionism as not conceptually close enough to the extent of direct government management of economic activities.* The final classification scheme follows.

A. Countries in which the direct economic role of the government was of major importance in the economy, as indicated by substantial government investment in infrastructure, health, and education. In all these countries the share of net investment undertaken by the government was large and, in many instances, greater than the share of private industry.

B. Countries in which direct government economic activity was moderately important. This category includes those countries in which there was a large public sector but in which the government nevertheless did not invest heavily in social and physical infrastructure. In these countries the share of net investment undertaken by the government was smaller than the share of the private sector.

C. Countries in which the direct economic role of the government was relatively small, as indicated by a relatively small government contribution to net investment and a relatively small public sector.

Length of Colonial Experience

The overwhelming majority of contemporary underdeveloped countries have been colonial dependencies during some important

---

* We are grateful to E. E. Hagen for his comments in this regard. We did not find our qualitative information on government interventionism sufficiently complete to introduce this aspect of the government's role as a separate indicator; it would only have permitted a two-way classification of countries.

part of their history. Controversies over the political and economic impact of colonialism have been rife.[32] Defenders of colonial rule have stressed benefits of training in Western forms of government and political participation and improvements in educational and health systems, as well as positive economic benefits from trade likely to have raised colonial standards of living. Attackers have viewed both political and economic consequences of colonial rule as detrimental on a wide variety of grounds, including its frequent tendency to prevent the development of indigenous forms of national government, the accrual of the major benefits of trade to colonial rulers, and the tendency for dualistic development to worsen strikingly the relative distribution of income.

The present classification groups countries into four categories according to the length of time a country was a colony prior to 1960.

A. Countries that were colonies for over 200 years.

B. Countries that were colonies for 101 to 200 years.

C. Countries that were colonies for 60 to 100 years.

D. Countries that were colonies for less than 60 years.

E. Countries that were never colonies.

Type of Colonial Experience

Colonial political and economic policies in contemporary underdeveloped countries varied considerably from one colonial ruler to another as well as from country to country.[33] Economic exploitation for the material benefit of the ruling country was a major goal of all colonial rulers. However, political policies varied greatly. British policy in its later phases treated colonies as semiautonomous political units, typically granting a share in political administration to indigenous officials, often with the explicit goal of providing qualified administrators for eventual independence. The stress laid upon indigenous control over local affairs might be expected to favor the growth of indigenous representative institutions. French policy in the same period attempted rather to integrate leading colonies with France and made little provision for training indigenous officials for independence or political participation. The policies of other rulers typically gave no constructive attention to national political institutions and often were destructive toward tribal institutions. Their economic policies might, therefore, be expected to contribute to even greater inequality of income distribution than in British and French colonies because of the lesser possibilities for indigenous elites to benefit from colonial development.

The following classification groups countries into four categories according to their colonial status between 1913 and 1960. The ranking of the categories is according to the extent to which the growth of indigenous political institutions might be expected to take place: with independent countries first, British colonies next, French colonies next, and other colonies last. The individual country classifications are based primarily on Banks and Textor, *A Cross-Polity Survey*, raw characteristics number 19 (date of independence) and number 21 (former colonial ruler).

A. Countries that were independent in 1913.

B. Countries not independent in 1913, that were British colonies.

C. Countries not independent in 1913, that were French colonies.

D. Countries not independent in 1913, that were colonies of rulers other than Britain or France.

Recency of Self-Government

The achievement of national independence has frequently provided a crucial stimulus to the growth of indigenous political institutions. One might therefore expect to find more advanced participant political mechanisms in countries which have been independent for longer periods of time. On the other hand, for very underdeveloped countries, it can be argued that independence and the rising expectations for economic betterment typically accompanying it produce political and social unrest which in turn leads to threat of revolution and authoritarianism rather than to more political participation. Since colonialism has typically contributed to a highly skewed income distribution, the expulsion of colonial rulers might be expected to produce a more equal distribution of income.

The present classification groups countries into six categories according to the recency of their independence. It is based in large part upon Banks and Textor, *A Cross-Polity Survey*, raw characteristic number 19 (date of independence).

A. Countries that were not independent in 1960.

B. Countries that gained independence between 1956 and 1960.

C. Countries that gained independence between 1946 and 1955.

D. Countries that gained independence between 1914 and 1945.

E. Countries that gained independence between 1800 and 1913.

F. Countries that gained independence before the nineteenth century.

Extent of Political Stability

The importance of political stability to sustained economic growth is almost self-evident. Since the expansion of both industrial enterprise and physical infrastructure rely heavily upon fixed capital formation, returns on which may involve considerable time lags, reasonable assurance regarding the stability of the general political framework is necessary to induce investment and innovation in these areas. This is not to say that transfers of political power may not occur without disrupting economic processes; it means rather that the impact of changes in legislation, administration, and political procedures should be sufficiently foreseeable to permit long-term commitment of resources.[34]

The contribution of political stability to widening political and economic participation is uncertain. On the one hand, improvements in the distribution of wealth and power may invite grass-roots pressures for radical change or revolution. Empirical studies suggest that civil disorders and internal violence typically increase in intensity after distribution and participation start improving. It is also argued that large disparities in economic and political participation will inevitably lead to a revolt of the downtrodden masses. On the other hand, it is sometimes suggested that political instability is a necessary stimulant to greater economic and political participation, even though it may lead to strong measures by traditional elites to reestablish law and order.

Several aspects of political stability were combined in deriving our overall stability index: (1) the extent of internal security throughout the country; (2) the extent of continuity in form of government; and (3) the extent of consensus about the prevailing form of government. In estimating the extent of internal security throughout the country, we used evidence on actual rather than potential violence. We combined data on deaths from domestic group violence per one million population (1950–62), available for 44 of the countries of our sample in the *World Handbook of Political and Social Indicators*,[35] with qualitative information from recent country studies on the extent and frequency of group violence. In our evaluation of countries with respect to continuity in form of government, we did not interpret a single reasonably peaceful change in form of government at the time of, or within a few years of, independence as evidence of political instability. Nor were frequent changes in the political leaders of a parliamentary system considered indicative of political instability unless they were accompanied by marked alterations in, or uncertainty about, legislation or administrative procedures. The primary evidence of significant lack of continuity in form of government used in classifying individual countries was the frequency and importance of military and other radical coups. Recent country and regional studies were the principal sources of information used on the incidence and violence of coups. The final element in our index, extent of consensus about the form of government, information on which also came from country studies, was used mainly to differentiate between reasonably stable polities and those characterized by moderate political instability. Of necessity, overt manifestations of lack of consensus, such as intense political antagonisms or significant communist subversion, were used rather than judgments regarding unexpressed lack of consensus.

Once our preliminary country classifications were prepared, interviews with country experts were very helpful in resolving doubtful cases. In addition, we cross-checked our classifications with two of the indicators in Banks and Textor's *A Cross-Polity Survey*: governmental stability and stability of party system.[36]

The classification scheme for our indicator of the extent of political stability during the period 1950–63 follows. It should be
noted that this is the only one of our sociocultural or political indicators for which the time period is longer than five years.*

A. Countries characterized by reasonable political stability (during the period 1950–63), judging by the standards of less developed countries, as indicated by relatively effective internal security,
considerable continuity in form of government, and the absence
of overt indications of lack of consensus about the prevailing political system. Included in this category are countries in which a
single change in form of government was achieved quite peacefully
at the time of, or within a few years of, the country's independence.

B. Countries characterized by moderate political instability
without much domestic violence. Included in this category are
countries in which there had been important nonviolent changes
in form of government (other than peaceful ones associated with
independence), marked internal political antagonisms, and/or significant communist subversion without much violence. Also included here are countries in which there had been sporadic and
relatively insignificant violence that did not threaten the internal
security of the country.

C. Countries characterized by moderate political instability and
significant domestic violence. Included in this category are (1)
countries with considerable continuity in form of government combined with sporadic but important domestic violence that did not,
however, threaten the internal security of the country for more
than a brief period; and (2) countries in which one or two coups
accompanied by limited violence were followed and/or preceded
by considerable periods of moderate political stability. Countries
in which there was extensive short-lived violence, followed and/or
preceded by considerable periods of moderate stability, are classified *C*–.

D. Countries characterized by considerable political instability

* The indicator of political stability used in our article "A Factor Analysis
of the Interrelationship between Social and Political Variables and Per Capita
Gross National Product," pp. 555–78, was a three-way classification based on
the period 1957–62 only.

during an important part of the period 1950–63, as indicated by violent coups, violent domestic outbreaks, and/or insurrections. Most of these countries had relatively high rates of death from domestic violence. Countries in which insurrections were widespread or of long duration, resulting in the continued absence of effective government control over the country, are classified $D-$.

ECONOMIC INDICATORS

Since the economic characteristics of developing countries are traditionally the primary domain that economists explore in investigating the phenomenon of economic development, little justification for the inclusion of economic indicators in our study is required. Indeed, one may view all the noneconomic attributes of nations discussed above as influential in economic development and distribution primarily through their impact upon the supplies and uses of the conventional factors or "agents" of production: resources, capital, and labor.

In choosing economic indicators for our investigation, we have attempted to include a variety of variables representing major characteristics of economic structure and institutions as of about 1961.

Per Capita GNP in 1961 / Growth Rate of Real
per Capita GNP, 1950/51–1963/64

Current estimates of national income per capita are deficient in several respects as measures of intercountry differences in levels of economic welfare[37] or of variations among countries in success in raising economic welfare. In the first place, what matters for economic welfare are levels of consumption rather than of overall production; investment expenditures, capital consumption allowances, and intermediate goods (e.g. private transport expenses) should be excluded from welfare-oriented measures of national performance.[38] Second, national income estimates generally fail to include nonmarketed output and services, which vary greatly in importance from country to country. Third, comparisons based on national income per capita are distorted by differences among countries in the distribution of income and in patterns of consumer preferences. These distortions may be particularly large for predominantly subsistence economies in which a large proportion of the value of marketed output originates in a rapidly expanding foreign extractive sector.[39] A further difficulty arises when estimates made in local currencies are translated into common units of measurement. The use of foreign exchange rates for this purpose is often unsatisfactory because exchange rates fail to reflect the prices of domestically consumed goods that do not enter into foreign trade. This source of distortion is likely to become particularly important when countries at widely varied levels of development are compared.*

If we define economic performance as the extent of success in increasing not economic welfare but rather the ability to produce goods and services, then the national income or product may be viewed as a measure of the differences in productive capacity. While this interpretation of economic performance avoids the problems associated with differences among countries in income distributions and tastes, it introduces the equally difficult problem of comparing aggregate products associated with different compositions of output and produced by different techniques.[40]

The maximization of the growth of real per capita gross national product is widely used as the criterion of development policy, even though the deficiencies of this criterion as a measure of economic welfare are widely recognized. To the extent that differences in per capita GNP are *not* monotonically related to differences in per capita welfare, the use of rate of growth of per capita GNP as a planning goal is dangerously misleading. It is therefore important to investigate the relationship between this indicator of performance and the distribution of income and welfare.

Per capita GNP in 1961. For our study we obtained almost all

---

* It has been suggested that there is a systematic tendency for the use of foreign exchange rates to undervalue a low-income country's output by a greater degree, the greater the disparity in per capita income between the two countries being compared. See E. E. Hagen, "Some Facts About Income Levels and Economic Growth," *Review of Economics and Statistics,* 42 (1960): 67.

the estimates of per capita GNP in 1961 from a single source.[41] For countries that lacked national income accounts, these estimates represent expert guesses based on knowledge of both the particular country and countries having similar levels and structures of production. It should be noted that no adjustments have been made to correct distortions arising from the use of official exchange rates, since the price data necessary for this purpose were inadequate or entirely lacking.

The rate of growth of real per capita GNP in constant prices between 1950/51 and 1963/64 suffers from many of the same deficiencies as point estimates for a single year. In making comparisons among countries, the comparison of rates of change obviates the problem of conversion into common units through the use of foreign exchange rates. At the same time, however, the problems arising from differences in the distribution of income and in the structure of production are complicated by changes within as well as among countries. The most serious problem arises for countries in which an extremely small modern sector expanded rapidly after 1950 while the subsistence agricultural sector of the country remained largely stagnant. Although we made no adjustment for many countries where this was true, we did make an adjustment for a few extreme cases. Four African countries in which, as of 1960, 90 percent of the population had been negligibly affected by the growth process were classified in a special category just above the category defined by very small growth rates of per capita GNP, even though monetary growth rates alone would have put them in a higher category.

Growth rate of real per capita GNP, 1950/51–1963/64. The classification scheme is shown as follows.

A. Countries with average annual growth rates in real per capita GNP of 3 percent or more during the period 1950/51–1963/64. Countries with average annual growth rates of 5 percent or more are classified A+. Excluded from this category are countries in which, as of about 1960, over 90 percent of the population was in the traditional subsistence sector where per capita income had not changed significantly since 1950.

B. Countries with average annual growth rates in real per capita GNP of from 2.0 to 2.9 percent during the period 1950/51–1963/64. Excluded from this category are countries in which, as of about 1960, over 90 percent of the population was in the traditional subsistence sector where per capita GNP had not changed significantly since 1950.

C. Countries with average annual growth rates in real per capita GNP of from 1.0 to 1.9 percent during the period 1950/51–1963/64. Excluded from this category are countries in which, as of about 1960, over 90 percent of the population was in the traditional subsistence sector where per capita GNP had not changed significantly since 1950.

D. Countries in which average annual growth rates in real per capita GNP of 1 percent or more were reported but in which, as of about 1960, over 90 percent of the population was in the traditional subsistence sector where per capita income had not changed significantly since 1950. Of these countries, those reporting average annual growth rates of 3 percent or more are classified D+, those reporting growth rates of from 2.0 to 2.9 percent are classified D, and those reporting growth rates of from 1.0 to 1.9 percent are classified D−.

E. Countries with average annual growth rates in real per capita GNP of from 0.0 to 0.9 percent during the period 1950/51–1963/64.

F. Countries in which negative average annual rates of change in per capita GNP occurred during the period 1950/51–1963/64.

Abundance of Natural Resources

The relationship between the abundance of natural resources and economic growth has long been of interest to economists. Indeed, classical economics was called the "dismal science" because of its basic premise that within countries the increasing scarcity of natural resources relative to population would eventually lead to decreasing returns to economic activity.[42]

There is little discussion in the literature concerning the relationship between natural resource abundance and the distribution of income and political power. We nevertheless include it in our study because, a priori, one expects natural resource abundance to be related to economic growth patterns, which in turn affect levels of participation.

The selection of a composite indicator to represent natural resource abundance is difficult, because any choice requires judgment regarding the nature and extent of substitutability among different classes of resources. The alternative solution of using a narrow indicator is conceptually unsatisfactory, since there is no a priori reason to expect the abundance of any single type of resource, taken alone, to be systematically associated with economic performance. In deriving a composite index of resource abundance, therefore, we defined abundance primarily in terms of three broad classes of resources: agricultural land, fuel, and mineral resources other than fuel.

Our final definition of natural resource abundance was based on general judgments regarding the abundance and variety of fuel and nonfuel mineral resources, together with data on the amount of agricultural land available per capita. The latter statistic was obtained for most countries either from the production yearbooks of the Food and Agricultural Organization or from individual country studies. "Agricultural land" in this connection includes arable land and land under tree crops, together with permanent meadows and pastures. Our principal sources for information on fuel and mineral resources were country studies, together with other sources.[48]

The classification scheme for this indicator follows.

A. Countries with an overall abundance and wide variety of known natural resources, as indicated in most instances by more than three acres of agricultural land per capita and the presence of important fuel, nonfuel mineral, and forest resources. Also included in this category and classified A— are a few countries with generally abundant resources but with only from one to three acres of agricultural land per capita and/or with significant deficiencies in either known nonfuel mineral or forest resources (but not in both). Excluded from this category are all countries without important known fuel resources or with less than one acre of agricultural land per capita.

B. Countries with either (1) relatively abundant agricultural resources (one acre or more of agricultural land per capita), together with a marked deficiency in all fuel resources or significant deficiencies in both known nonfuel mineral and forest resources, or (2) limited agricultural resources (less than one acre of agricultural land per capita), together with an overall abundance of known forest, fuel, and nonfuel mineral resources. In order to meet criterion (1), a country must have some important nonagricultural resources in addition to relatively abundant agricultural resources.

C. Countries with either (1) limited agricultural resources (less than one acre of agricultural land per capita), together with some important known fuel, nonfuel mineral, or forest resources (but not an overall abundance of these resources), or (2) relatively abundant agricultural resources (one acre or more of agricultural land per capita), together with the absence of any significant known nonagricultural resources. Excluded from this category, however, are countries meeting criterion (2) in which agricultural resources consist overwhelmingly of meadows and pastureland.

D. Countries with either (1) limited agricultural resources (less than one acre per capita), together with no significant known fuel and nonfuel mineral resources and no accessible exploitable forests, or (2) one acre or more of agricultural land per capita consisting overwhelmingly of meadows and pastureland, together with no significant known nonagricultural resources.

Gross Investment Rate

If one were to choose a single influence upon the pace of economic growth that over the years has received the most attention from economists, it would probably be the supply of capital. The classical economists gave it close attention, and when problems of economic growth again took the stage in the twentieth century, capital scarcity was for a time considered the crucial bottleneck in the development process.[44]

The importance of capital formation has also led economists to emphasize the role of savings in fostering development. Some have stressed that, since the bulk of savings comes from profits and high incomes, income inequality is necessary to accelerate growth. The empirical evidence, however, is unclear, with some recent studies casting doubt on the strength of the association between greater inequality and higher savings rates.[45]

In addition, although capital formation continues to be stressed as an important element in economic development, there has been a marked shift in emphasis in recent years toward other influences on development, such as improvements in technology, the supply of entrepreneurship, and the wide variety of noneconomic influences that underlie the supplies of production factors.[46] Furthermore, economists are once again stressing the long-familiar proposition that efficiency in the allocation and use of capital is at least as important as the size of the total investment fund.[47]

In defining an indicator of capital formation, we established six categories for grouping countries with respect to the average ratio of gross investment to gross national product for the period 1957–62. Data for classifying individual countries were obtained from the United Nations and the Agency for International Development.[48] For a number of countries that do not have national income accounts, the estimates obtained refer to a single year rather than to the entire period; for these estimates, we sought some confirmation from expert opinion and cross-checked them with Rosenstein-Rodan's estimates for 1961.[49]

The classification scheme for the indicator of gross investment rates during the period 1957–62 follows.

A. Countries in which gross investment rates were 23 percent or more. Countries in which the overwhelming proportion of investment originated in a single foreign-financed extractive sector are excluded, however.

B. Countries in which gross investment rates were from 18.0 to 22.9 percent. Countries in which the overwhelming proportion of investment originated in a single foreign-financed extractive sector are excluded.

C. Countries in which gross investment rates were from 16.0 to 17.9 percent. Also included in this category and classified *C*— are countries that had gross investment rates of 16 percent or more in which the overwhelming proportion of investment originated in a single foreign-financed extractive sector.

D. Countries in which gross investment rates were from 14.0 to 15.9 percent.

E. Countries in which gross investment rates were from 12.0 to 13.9 percent.

F. Countries in which gross investment rates were 11 percent or less.

Modernization of
Industry | Industrialization, 1950–63

Statistical analyses consistently yield marked positive correlations between per capita GNP and the proportion of both employment and national product originating in the industrial sector.[50] There are many reasons for this association between greater industrialization and rising national incomes. Among the most important are the change in composition of consumer demand in favor of domestic production as domestic markets and levels of skill and technology increase, and the growth of intermediate demand for industrial products as consumer-goods industries expand.

The proposition that, historically, industrialization was associated with rising standards of living for the majority has been widely held despite historical evidence of widespread displacement of cottage and handicraft workers together with the creation of a large, poorly paid, unskilled proletariat and a large pool of unemployed during the early stages of industrialization.[51] In contemporary underdeveloped countries, industrialization policies have tended to skew the income distribution by raising the share of profits in national product higher than it would have been under free market conditions.[52] For example, the policy of keeping the terms of trade between agriculture and industry artificially low has benefited primarily industrialists and importers who sell in highly protected domestic markets while paying low wages to labor. The policy of supplying capital to large-scale manufacturing at a price well below its marginal product has raised the capital intensity of production, discriminated against small and medium-scale industry, led to a slower rate of absorption of labor than would otherwise have occurred, and contributed to the maldistribution of income.

To measure the relationship between industrialization and distribution, we have developed a composite indicator of the extent of modernization of production techniques in industry as of about 1961. The indicator of the level of modernization of industry is composed of three principal elements: (1) a rough, quantitative estimate of the relative importance of indigenous, modern power-driven industrial activities compared with that of traditional handicraft production (these estimates were based primarily on judgments from recent country studies and were cross-checked with data on installed capacity of electrical energy per capita[53]); (2) the degree of modernity of machinery and organization in the modern industrial sector, as indicated by the incidence of the most up-to-date large-scale and/or otherwise relatively efficient production methods; and (3) the diversity and range of goods produced in the modern industrial sector. Qualitative information for both (2) and (3) was taken from recent country studies. Doubtful cases were resolved by interviews.

Modernization of industry. The classification scheme for the level of modernization of industry (as of about 1961) groups countries into four broad categories.

A. Countries with industrial sectors that, as of about 1961, were producing a wide variety of domestic consumer and/or export goods and at least some intermediate goods by means of power-driven factory production methods. In addition, these countries had several industries in which the most modern large-scale or otherwise relatively efficient production methods were applied. Finally, all countries had at least 80 kilowatt-hours per capita installed electrical capacity. Although handicraft industry and domestic putting-out systems were still significant in the production of domestic consumer goods in many of these countries, they were less important than factory production for a considerable variety of consumer goods.

B. Countries with industrial sectors that, as of about 1961, were producing a fair variety of consumer and/or export goods by means of power-driven factory production methods and that had several industries in which the most modern large-scale or otherwise relatively efficient production methods were applied to some extent. These countries, however, are differentiated from those in category A by the fact that handicraft industry and/or the domestic putting-out system were relatively more important in the production of domestic consumer goods, taken as a whole, than were modern methods of production. Finally, almost all the countries in this category had from 25 to 80 kilowatt-hours per capita installed electrical capacity. Countries in which the majority but by no means all of the modern production units were in the foreign-financed and -managed sector are classified B−.

C. Countries with industrial sectors in which, as of about 1961, a limited number of domestic consumer and/or export goods were produced by means of small-scale, power-driven factory production methods and in which the most modern large-scale or otherwise relatively efficient production methods, if they existed, were generally confined to production that was foreign-financed and -managed. Countries that had a very limited number of the most modern large-scale or otherwise relatively efficient domestically financed production units are classified C+. In addition, these countries were characterized by the overwhelming predominance in consumer goods production of handicraft industry and/or the domestic putting-out system. Finally, with only a few exceptions, countries in this category had less than 25 kilowatt-hours per capita of installed electrical capacity.

D. Countries in which industrial development, as of about 1961, was very slight and was characterized by handicraft industry and/or the domestic putting-out system. Small-scale factory production was either nonexistent or contributed a negligible proportion of the output of domestic consumer and export goods. The most modern large-scale or otherwise relatively efficient production methods in most instances did not exist; countries that had a single modern foreign-financed large-scale plant are classified *D*+. Finally, in almost all these countries there were less than 10 kilowatt-hours per capita installed electrical capacity.

Our index of the overall change in the degree of industrialization for 1950–63 is a composite of three statistical elements: (1) the average annual rate of change in constant prices in industrial output (mining, manufacturing, electricity, and water) for the period 1950–63; (2) the change for 1950–63 in the proportion of gross domestic product originating in industry; and (3) the change for 1950–63 in the proportion of the total male labor force employed in industry. The first of the three elements, the average percentage increase in the total absolute size of the industrial sector, was the primary one by which countries were grouped into three broad categories. Data on changes in industrial output for about half the countries in the sample are available in the United Nations, *Yearbook of National Accounts Statistics, 1964.*[54] The majority of the remaining countries were classified with respect to this attribute on the basis of judgmental information. The second and third elements in the index, the changes in the relative importance of industrial employment and output, were used to judge the change in the proportionate weight of the industrial sector.[55] Data on both labor force and output in industry were supplemented by qualitative judgments regarding trends for 1950–63, because statistical estimates were either unsatisfactory or entirely lacking for about one-third of the countries in our sample. In fact, one reason for including three measures of the change in degree of industrialization was that data were not sufficient to validate the use of any single measure.

Industrialization, 1950–63. The final classification scheme for our indicator of the change in degree of industrialization for 1950–63 is stated below.

A. Countries that demonstrated a marked change in the degree of industrialization for 1950–63, as indicated by an average annual rate of increase in constant prices in industrial output of over 7.5 percent during a substantial part of the period 1950–63. In addition, these countries showed some increase in the proportion of GDP originating in industry, with the great majority showing an increase of from 4 to 10 percentage points. Practically all those for which data are available also showed a rise in the proportion of the total male labor force employed in industry.

B. Countries that demonstrated a moderate increase in the degree of industrialization for 1950–63, as indicated by an average annual rate of increase in constant prices in industrial output of from 3.0 to 7.5 percent during a substantial part of the period 1950–63. Some but not all of these countries also experienced a moderate increase of a few percentage points in the proportion of GDP originating in industry and/or the proportion of the total male labor force employed in industry. Also included in this category are several countries for which estimates of rates of change in industrial output are not available but in which either (1) data on industrial employment and/or output show an increase in the relative weight of industry or (2) qualitative information indicates a moderate increase in the relative importance of industry.

C. Countries in which there was either no marked change or an actual decline in the degree of industrialization. Countries in which average rates of increase in real industrial output were less than 3 percent for a substantial part of the period 1950–63 and in which there was no significant change in the relative weight of industrial employment or output are classified C. A number of countries for which no statistical data are available are also classified C on the basis of qualitative information indicating that there was no significant change in the degree of industrialization. Countries for which available data and/or qualitative information indicate that there was a decline in the relative importance of the industrial sector since 1950 are classified C−.

Character of Agricultural Organization

An important concomitant to successful industrialization, particularly in countries at low-income levels, is the modernization of the agricultural sector. One aspect of agricultural progress that helps determine the extent of overall economic advancement is the pattern of ownership and management of agricultural land. In this context a great deal has been written about the need of many underdeveloped nations for reform of land tenure systems.[56] One reason for expecting a direct connection between agrarian structure and agricultural income and output is that, under the traditional tenancy systems characteristic of many low-income countries, the proceeds of production increases do not go primarily to those who farm the land, and therefore do not provide sufficient incentives for innovating activity. In addition, however, there is another aspect of agricultural organization, closely related to ownership patterns, that is also important to income distribution, variations in the size of farming units. In particular, the prevalence of individual holdings too small to be economically viable contributes to the skewedness of income distribution within the agricultural sector as well as in the economy as a whole.

Attempts to increase agricultural productivity and output where the distribution of land ownership is extremely unequal tend to further deteriorate the relative and even absolute position of the low-income small farmers.[57] This is because great inequality in the distribution of land holding biases the entire institutional structure within which productivity increases occur in favor of large landowners. Credit, information and research services, the nature of available technology, marketing mechanisms, tax structures, and the terms of trade between industry and agriculture all tend to operate to their benefit.

In view of the acknowledged importance of the character of agricultural organization, we included in our analysis a composite indicator of ownership-management patterns and of the economic viability and orientation of the agricultural sector as of about 1960. In classifying individual countries, we consulted a large number of recent country studies, in addition to a number of regional studies having data on the distribution of types of ownership and tenancy.[58] To resolve doubtful cases we consulted a small number of country experts.

The classification scheme for the indicator of the character of agricultural organization as of about 1960 is summarized below.

A. Countries characterized by the predominance of commercial owner-operated farms that were sufficiently large to be economically viable. Countries in which the remaining part of the agricultural land consisted primarily of commercial farms too small to be economically viable and/or subsistence farms (tenant or owner-operated) on which the marketing of surpluses was incidental are classified A—; all the other countries are classified A. Excluded from this category are all countries in which, as of about 1960, 55 percent or more of the population was in a traditional subsistence sector in which cash-cropping was insignificant.

B. Countries characterized by the predominance of large owner-absentee commercial farms or plantations in which the absentee owners were either expatriate or indigenous. Countries in which the remaining part of the agricultural land was farmed primarily by small, economically viable commercial owner-operated enterprises are classified B+. Those in which the remaining part of the agricultural land was farmed primarily by small subsistence units (owner-operated or tenant) in which marketing of crops was unimportant or in which the size of the unit was too small to be economically viable are classified B—. All other countries are classified B. Excluded from this category are all countries in which, as of about 1960, over 55 percent of the population was in a traditional nonmonetized sector.

C. Countries characterized by the predominance of small owner-operated subsistence farms in which the marketing of surpluses was of incidental importance or in which the size of the farming unit was too small to be economically viable. Countries in which the remaining part of the agricultural land consisted primarily of commercial owner-operated farms (indigenous or expatriate) that were large enough to be economically viable are classified C+. Those in which the remaining part of the agricultural land was farmed primarily by owner-absentee commercial enterprises or plantations are classified C; also classified C are those in which the remaining part of the land was farmed by a combination of these two types. Finally, countries in which the remaining part of the agricultural land consisted primarily of small subsistence tenant farms or communally owned farmland in which cash-cropping was insignificant are classified $C-$.

D. Countries characterized by the predominance of communally owned agricultural lands and/or small subsistence tenant-operated farms in which the marketing of crops was unimportant. Countries in which the remaining part of the agricultural sector consisted primarily of commercial owner-operated farms (indigenous or expatriate) that are large enough to be economically viable are classified $D+$. Countries in which the entire agricultural sector consisted almost exclusively of communally owned lands are classified $D-$. The remaining countries are classified D.

Modernization of Techniques in Agriculture / Improvement in Agricultural Productivity, 1950–1963

The importance of the agricultural sector to economic development as a source of supply of both labor and food to growing urban industrial areas has received a good deal of attention in recent analyses of economic growth.[59] Without improved organization of existing factors and increased application of new techniques in agriculture, supplies of agricultural products are frequently not adequate to meet the increased demand for them that typically accompanies urbanization and industrialization. The resultant rise in agricultural prices, by shifting the terms of trade against industry, can seriously impede the growth of industrial production. In addition, since the process of economic growth for the average underdeveloped country involves a major shift of employment from agriculture to industry, the increased food requirements of the growing population must typically be produced by a relatively smaller agricultural work force. Thus, in general, one would expect countries that are more industrialized and urbanized to have higher levels of productivity in their agricultural sectors than do countries at lower levels of economic development.

Increases in agricultural productivity may shift the distribution of income in favor of or against agriculture, depending upon the nature of income increases both within and outside agriculture, income elasticities of demand for food, and the government's agri-

cultural price policies.* When not preceded by land reform, increases in agricultural productivity tend to benefit large "progressive" farmers disproportionately, thereby deteriorating the distribution of income within the rural sector.[60]

Our indicator of the level of modernization of techniques in
agriculture is a composite variable based upon (1) judgments
regarding the extent of use of mechanical power, fertilizer, and
other modern techniques in agriculture, cross-checked by quantitative data (where available and appropriate) on the use of tractors and fertilizer, and (2) qualitative and quantitative information regarding the relative weights of traditional and modern
agriculture. Since data on employment and product in the traditional and modern agricultural sectors are generally unavailable,
we used estimates of the traditional subsistence sector, together
with qualitative information on the modern agricultural sector,
to obtain a rough indication of the prevalence of modern techniques.[61] Statistical data on the use of tractors and the use of
chemical fertilizers as of about 1961 were drawn primarily from
the Food and Agricultural Organization, *Production Yearbook,
1963.*[62] Qualitative information for preliminary classifications was
taken from a large number of recent country studies. Since we
found, however, that preliminary data in a number of instances
did not provide us with consistent country scores, we consulted
regional and country experts to resolve the doubtful classifications.

Modernization of techniques in agriculture. The classification
scheme presented below groups countries with respect to the level
of modernization as of about 1961.

A. Countries in which the agricultural sector was characterized
by the moderate use of mechanical power and other modern tech-

---

* Mexico illustrates well the case of agricultural breakthrough that adds
to rural income inequalities. See "The Dichotomy of Prosperity and Poverty
in Mexican Agriculture," *Land Economics,* 45 (1969). Taiwan and Japan
illustrate the case of agricultural progress that is successful in narrowing
differentials between the city and the countryside. See Kazushi Ohkawa,
Bruce F. Johnston, and Hiromitsu Kaneda, eds., *Agriculture and Economic
Growth: Japan's Experience* (Tokyo, 1969), and T. H. Lee, *Intersectoral
Capital Flows in the Economic Development of Taiwan, 1895–1960* (Ithaca,
N.Y., 1971).

niques that were not, however, applied exclusively to the production of a single crop. This moderate use of modern methods by these countries was indicated (where appropriate) by the use of more than 1 tractor per 1,000 agricultural population, the use of more than 5 kg of chemical fertilizer (nitrogen, phosphate, potash) per 1,000 agricultural population, and/or significant use of improved pastures, modern breeding practices, and/or modern irrigation systems.

B. Countries that had (1) a relatively important monetized agricultural sector in which there was some significant use of modern techniques (mechanical power, fertilizer, better breeding practices, improved pastures, where appropriate), in addition to (2) a fairly important nonmonetized traditional subsistence sector that in most instances had absorbed more than 25 but less than 55 percent of the total population as of about 1960. Countries in which the monetized sector was only weakly modernized, as indicated by the limited use of primarily small-scale modern techniques, are classified B—. Excluded from this category are countries in which more than 55 percent of the total population was in the traditional subsistence agricultural sector as of about 1960.

C. Countries that had the same characteristics as those in category B, except that their monetized agricultural sectors involved relatively fewer people than did their traditional sectors. In these countries more than 55 percent of the total population was in the traditional subsistence sector as of about 1960. Countries in which the monetized sector was only weakly modernized, as indicated by the limited use of primarily small-scale modern techniques, are classified C—.

D. Countries that were characterized by the almost exclusive use of traditional agricultural methods. In these countries there was no significant use of mechanical power, chemical fertilizers, or other modern agricultural techniques.

In defining an indicator of the degree of improvement in agricultural productivity for 1950–63, we again combined qualitative and quantitative elements. An increase in agricultural productivity was defined as an increase in total agricultural output greater than could be accounted for by additional inputs of the same quality as those prevailing in 1950. We examined statistical series relating to the increased use of tractors and chemical fertilizers but found them unreliable as an indicator of changed techniques for a sufficient number of countries, apparently because of changes in the coverage of the data; therefore, we did not use them systematically to determine boundaries between categories. We relied primarily on qualitative judgments contained in recent country studies and on interviews when grouping countries into four categories with respect to the extent of such improvements as the more extensive use of mechanical power or chemical fertilizers, more modern irrigation systems, better crop rotation, improvement of pastures, and more scientific breeding. It should be noted that we did not consider the fact of increased agricultural output for 1950–63 in itself to be indicative of improved techniques, since in a number of countries, including many African ones, agricultural output increased significantly through the expansion of the area of cultivation by means of existing techniques.

Improvement in agricultural productivity, 1950–63. Following is the classification scheme for our indicator of the degree of improvement between 1950 and 1963.

A. Countries in which there was marked improvement in agricultural productivity in 1950–63, as indicated (where appropriate) by marked increases in the use of chemical fertilizers or mechanical power, the completion of important modern irrigation systems, or marked extensions in the use of other modern agricultural techniques. In addition, these countries generally experienced substantially greater overall growth rates of agricultural output than increases in population.

B. Countries in which there were moderate improvements in agricultural productivity in 1950–63. Among these countries are a number in which cultivable land was expanded through the application of modern irrigation methods or by the use of multicropping techniques.

C. Countries in which there was no significant improvement in agricultural productivity in 1950–63. Included in this category are some countries in which substantial increases in total agricultural output occurred but in which the increases in output were largely due to additional inputs of the same quality as those generally prevailing in 1950.

D. Countries in which agricultural output in about 1963, compared with agricultural output in 1950, remained static or declined because of a reduction in land under cultivation and/or a decline in the average quality of other inputs.

Adequacy of Physical Overhead Capital

Physical overhead capital, particularly in the form of transportation and power networks, is crucial to the development of low-income countries. Power supplies are necessary for the creation of a modern industrial sector, and transportation is essential both to the spread of production for the market and to the expansion of consumer demand for the products of industry and agriculture. Furthermore, investment in both transportation and power tends to be subject to marked pecuniary external economies that, particularly at the lowest level of development, greatly facilitate direct investments in other fields. Finally, the services of neither transportation nor power can as a rule be imported; thus, international trade cannot significantly reduce the size of the investment in physical overhead capital necessary to create national markets and a steadily expanding industrial sector. It is for these reasons that investment in transportation and power plays a central role in theories of the "big push," controversies over balanced or unbalanced growth, and discussions of the role of external economies in the growth process.[63]

The supply of physical overhead capital can also have a major distributional impact, particularly in rural areas. Studies of village development, for example, indicate a clear association between the availability of feeder roads and village income.[64] The indivisibility of irrigation and power schemes affects income distribution by contributing to geographical patterns favoring clusters of large users.[65]

To describe the extent of physical overhead capital in less developed countries, we have defined an indicator of the adequacy of physical overhead capital as of about 1961. Although statistics on transportation and power are better than most data on low-income economies, we found that the only generally useful series for measuring level of adequacy of overhead capital was that of kilowatt-hours per capita installed electrical capacity;[66] this served as a rough guide to intercountry differences in the extent of power installations and tended to be confirmed by qualitative information. In contrast, data on mileage of roads, for example, however deflated, proved unreliable as a measure of adequacy of transportation networks because of the extent of substitutability between various means of transportation and the wide intercountry differences in geography. Therefore, in classifying individual countries, we relied heavily upon qualitative judgments contained in recent country studies on the general adequacy of internal transportation systems (land, water, air, as appropriate) in meeting current requirements for raising economic growth rates. Preliminary classifications that appeared doubtful were resolved through a small number of interviews with country and regional experts.

Our classification scheme for adequacy of physical overhead capital, as of about 1961, was divided into four broad categories.

A. Countries in which internal transportation systems (including roads, rails, and waterways) and power networks were reasonably effective in meeting current requirements for more rapid economic development. Feeder roads to agricultural regions formed a reasonably adequate network for the marketing of agricultural products, and intercity connections were fully established. Inclusion in this category, however, did not require a country's transportation facilities to have been in particularly good condition; the only requirement was for them to have been more or less serviceable. With respect to power facilities, countries in this category had power networks that were, generally speaking, adequate to their current needs, as indicated in part by the fact that almost all had installed electrical capacity of more than 90 kilowatts per capita.

B. Countries in which internal transportation systems and power networks, while generally adequate for the current needs of economic development, suffered fairly marked deficiencies in limited parts of their systems, which were to some extent hindering their further development. For example, some of these countries lacked feeder roads to agricultural areas in significant sections of the country; others were suffering from power breakdowns due to inadequate installations. Excluded from this category are countries in which the major geographical portion of the country was suffering from lack of both transportation and power facilities. Most of the countries in this category had from 25 to 90 kilowatts per capita installed electrical capacity.

C. Countries in which internal transportation and power systems, while serving the commercialized sector of the economy without major deficiencies and bottlenecks, failed to provide a network of continuous services over a major, if not predominant, geographical portion of the country. In particular, widespread lack of feeder roads to agricultural areas hindered the current development efforts of many of these countries, whereas in others lack of power installations hindered the development of industry in important sections of the country. Most of the countries in this category had between 10 and 25 kilowatts per capita of installed electrical capacity.

D. Countries in which transportation and power systems were pervasively inadequate throughout the overwhelming portion of the country and in which this inadequacy constituted a major bottleneck to further economic development. Most of these countries had less than 10 kilowatts per capita of installed electrical capacity, and in addition, many of them had less than 200 miles of paved roads in the entire country.

Effectiveness of the Tax System / Improvement in the Tax System, 1950–1963

The contributions that an effective tax system can make to the economic growth of underdeveloped countries are varied. Taxation above all enables governments to secure control over resources that they can then use to finance the basic investments in physical and social overhead capital necessary to successful development. Taxes are also a major instrument for making the distribution of income more equitable or for altering it in order to promote private savings. Furthermore, taxation is a principal means for avoiding inflation by absorbing the excess of personal incomes over the supply of consumption goods which is typically created by the development process.[67]

Tax systems have not generally been effective in redistributing income in developing countries, in part because they are devised to serve multiple goals.[68] Thus, empirical studies indicate that the pre-tax and post-tax distributions of income are often very similar.[69] Progressive income tax legislation is difficult to enact where wealthy groups have political influence; and indirect taxes are typically regressive, especially when consumer goods are imported and taxes on beverages and tobacco are high.

Preliminary experimentation with measures of the effectiveness of tax systems confirmed the view held by a number of development specialists that no single quantitative measure, such as the ratio of direct tax to total tax revenue, is sufficient for differentiating among the tax systems of less developed countries.[70] We have chosen a multicriteria indicator of the level of effectiveness of tax systems. The ratio of total domestic government revenue to GNP was selected as a broad overall measure of success in raising revenue. The ratio of direct tax revenue to total government revenue was a second element incorporated in the indicator; however, special treatment was given countries in which a single foreign extractive sector provided almost all direct tax revenue. These two statistical elements were combined with qualitative judgments regarding the breadth of the tax base and the efficiency of tax collections.

The sources for the statistical data on tax systems were for the most part publications of the International Monetary Fund and the United Nations.[71] Where available, data on local government revenue were included in the estimates. Qualitative information came from recent country studies and was cross-checked by means of about a dozen interviews with regional and country experts.

Effectiveness of the tax system. The final classification scheme for the indicator of the level of effectiveness of tax systems, as of about 1960, is presented below.

A. Countries that had a moderately effective tax system, as indicated in most instances by (1) a ratio of government domestic revenue to GNP of at least 15 percent and (2) a ratio of direct tax revenue to total government domestic revenue of at least 20 percent. These countries generally were characterized also by the absence of widespread difficulties in either direct or indirect tax collections. Countries in which the direct tax base was relatively broad are classified *A+*.

B. Countries that had tax systems of limited effectiveness, as indicated in most instances by (1) a ratio of government domestic revenue to GNP of at least 15 percent and (2) a ratio of direct tax revenue to total government domestic revenue of at least 10 percent. These countries generally were characterized also by the absence of widespread difficulties in the collection of indirect taxes but often experienced considerable difficulty in collecting direct taxes. Excluded, however, are countries in which revenues derived almost exclusively from a foreign-owned extractive sector and in which tax institutions were rudimentary. Also included in this category and classified *B−* are a few countries with a ratio of less than 10 percent direct tax to government domestic revenue but with a significantly higher ratio than 15 percent government domestic revenue to GNP.

C. Countries that had relatively ineffective tax systems, as indicated in most instances by (1) a ratio of government domestic revenue to GNP of 10–14 percent and (2) a ratio of direct tax revenue to total government domestic revenue of less than 10 percent. The tax systems of these countries generally were characterized also by an extremely narrow tax base and/or widespread difficulties in the collection of taxes. Also included are a few countries in which the ratio of direct tax to government domestic revenue was 10 percent or more but in which the principal form of direct tax was a traditional land tax. Excluded from this category are countries in which tax revenues derived almost exclusively from a foreign-owned extractive sector and in which tax institutions were rudimentary.

D. Countries that had pervasively inadequate tax systems, as indicated by a ratio of government domestic revenue to GNP of less than 10 percent and/or by heavy dependence upon a foreign-owned extractive sector for taxes, combined with rudimentary tax institutions.

To represent the change in effectiveness of tax systems for 1950–63, we used a composite variable of three statistical elements. The change in the ratio of government domestic revenue to GNP was chosen as one broad measure of the change in overall success in raising revenue. A second measure of the extent of overall improvement was the average annual rate of increase in real government domestic revenue. This second measure proved necessary to evaluate countries experiencing rapid rates of growth of GNP during the years after 1950; in some of these, stability in the ratio of domestic revenue to GNP was maintained only through considerable improvement in the coverage and flexibility of their tax systems. The average annual rates of change in total government domestic revenue were deflated where possible by using the implicit GNP deflater calculated from United Nations sources.[72] The third statistical element in our index of improvement in tax systems was the change in the ratio of direct tax to total government domestic revenue, a common indicator of changes in the structure of tax systems.* Since the relevant data for estimating the above measures were lacking for many countries in our sample, qualitative information from recent country studies and interviews with country and regional experts were used where necessary to classify individual countries. The sources used were in general the same as those referred to in our discussion of the level of effectiveness of tax systems.

* It should be noted that for all these statistical series, individual country classifications were often based upon varying subperiods within the 1950–64 period. These subperiods were generally of from eight to ten years. The variations provided one of the reasons for obtaining qualitative cross-checks for the classifications.

Improvement in the tax system for 1950–63. The classification scheme for this indicator is stated below.

A. Countries that showed a marked improvement in their tax systems in 1950–63, as indicated by qualitative judgments and by success in meeting one of the following three criteria: (1) an average annual rate of increase in real government domestic revenue of more than 10 percent; (2) an increase in the ratio of government domestic revenue to GNP of more than 5 percentage points, combined with an average annual rate of increase in real government domestic revenue of more than 5 percent; or (3) an increase in the ratio of government domestic revenue to GNP of more than 10 percentage points. Countries in which marked improvement occurred only after 1961 are excluded.

B. Countries that showed a moderate improvement in their tax systems in 1950–63, as indicated by qualitative judgments and in most instances by both an average annual rate of increase in government domestic revenue of more than 5 percent and an increase in the ratio of government domestic revenue to GNP of more than 2 percentage points. In addition, almost all the countries in this category meet one of the following criteria: (1) an increase in the ratio of direct tax to government domestic revenue of more than 5 percentage points; or (2) a marked improvement in the collection of indirect taxes. Countries excluded from category A because marked improvement occurred only after 1961 are included here.

C. Countries that showed limited improvement in their tax systems in 1950–63, as indicated by qualitative information or statistical measures that give evidence of at least one of the following: (1) success in increasing government domestic revenue at least enough to meet rising government expenditures; (2) moderate improvements in the collection of indirect taxes; or (3) a moderate increase in the ratio of direct tax to total government domestic revenue.

D. Countries that had pervasively inadequate tax systems, as indicated by a ratio of government domestic revenue to GNP of

less than 10 percent and/or by heavy dependence upon a foreign-
owned extractive sector for taxes combined with rudimentary tax
institutions.

Effectiveness of Financial Institutions / Improvement
in Financial Institutions, 1950–1963

A fundamental aspect of the economic performance of a developing country is its success in increasing the proportion of total
domestic resources available for investment, or, in other words,
the extent to which it raises its rate of domestic savings. It is
equally important, however, that the available internal savings be
effectively channeled into productive investment. In the execution
of both these functions, financial institutions (central banks; commercial, savings, and specialized development banks; and, where
they exist, developed monetary exchanges) can play an important
role.[73] At very low levels of income, the volume of voluntary domestic savings entering the banking system tends to be extremely
low, and lending tends to flow mainly to large commercial enterprises, foreign trade, or the modern expatriate sector. The financial
system thus concentrates resources in the hands of the already
wealthy. At the same time, within the predominant traditional
portion of the economy, savings by producers tend to be directly
invested and long-term investment to be financed through local
unorganized money markets at higher interest rates.[74] The financial system thus tends to discriminate in favor of the rich. Countries at higher income levels generally have financial institutions
that are more effective both in attracting savings and in financing
medium- and long-term investment. Financial institutions thus
provide an important mechanism for facilitating both savings and
investment; nevertheless, their positive influence upon economic
development in the short run may vary greatly, according to
whether other social, political, and economic conditions are favorable to economic growth and income redistribution.

Where countries engage in programs of accelerated development, their banking systems typically supply capital at subsidized
rates to large enterprises. By thus encouraging the adoption of

capital-intensive techniques of production, the countries that follow this procedure both contribute to unemployment and tend to distort the income distribution in favor of profit receivers and owners of large enterprises.

We have chosen two indicators to represent, respectively, the long-run level and the short-run improvement in the effectiveness of financial institutions. In each case, we have sought to construct a composite variable combining the success of financial intermediaries in attracting private savings with the extent to which they provided medium- and long-term credit to the major sectors of the economy. Our preference for fairly broad indicators was reinforced by the fact that the use of single statistical measures earlier in our research had not been fruitful. Our indicator of the level of financial institutions as of about 1961 includes two statistical measures of the flow of internal savings through a country's financial system: the gross domestic savings rate and the ratio of the sum of time and demand deposits plus money to GNP. A third element in the index is a judgmental classification based on the extent of the flow of capital from the banking system into medium- and long-term investment in industry and agriculture. The principal sources of the statistical data were publications of the United Nations and the International Monetary Fund, while the judgmental information was taken primarily from recent country studies.[15] Preliminary classifications were then cross checked in about a dozen interviews with country and regional experts.

Effectiveness of financial institutions. The final classification scheme follows

A. Countries in which financial institutions were at least moderately effective in attracting private savings and in which these institutions provided a fairly adequate supply of medium- and long-term credit to both industry and agriculture. All countries that in about 1961 had *both* ratios of time and demand deposits plus money to GNP of more than 30 percent *and* gross domestic savings rates of more than 13 percent are included in the present category; in addition, a number of countries are included which meet only one of these statistical criteria but which nevertheless are considered to have relatively effective financial institutions.

B. Countries in which local financial institutions (including those that were foreign-owned or -directed) were able to attract a small but not insignificant volume of indigenous private savings. In these countries the financial institutions provided at least some medium- and long-term credit for both the industrial and agricultural sectors, although the total amount was small. Included in this category and classified *B—* are countries in which voluntary private savings was negligible but in which the government was able to obtain a flow of compulsory savings, at least part of which was used by government-controlled financial intermediaries to provide medium- and long-term credit to industry and agriculture. Also classified *B—* are countries in which an overwhelming part of voluntary private savings left the country. All countries in the *B* category, as of about 1960, had either gross domestic savings rates of more than 9 percent or ratios of time and demand deposits plus money to GNP of more than 15 percent.

C. Countries where local financial institutions (including those that were foreign-owned or -directed) attracted a negligible volume of indigenous private savings and where the funds for financing medium- and long-term investment in the technologically advanced sectors of the economy stemmed almost completely from foreign capital inflow. In all these countries investment in the agricultural sector (except in the technologically advanced portion) was either self-financed or financed through unorganized money markets. All countries that had both a gross domestic savings rate of less than 9 percent and a ratio of time and demand deposits plus money to GNP of less than 15 percent are included. In addition, a number of countries are included that meet only one of these statistical criteria but that nevertheless are judged to have had very inadequate financial institutions; for example, countries with no branches of their institutions outside the capital city are included here.

Improvement in financial institutions, 1950–63. In choosing a variable to represent the improvement in financial institutions, we sought to classify countries on the basis of statistical measures of the extent of increase in 1950–63 in both the volume of private saving through the banking system and the volume of lending by banks to the private sector. To measure changes in institutional effectiveness in attracting savings, we computed the percentage point change in the ratio of the volume of time and demand deposits to GNP for the period 1950/51–1962/63.* As a rough measure of changes in the extent of institutional lending to private persons and businesses, we calculated the approximate increase in the real value of private domestic liabilities to the banking system during the same period.† For those countries where data for computing these two measures were unavailable, we examined several series of data that were partially indicative of the activities of their financial systems, and classified the countries on the basis of the predominant *direction* of movement in recent years in the several series.‡ The series used were the changes in volume of time deposits, demand deposits, foreign assets held by the banking system, and domestic government and private liabilities to the banking system. Data for all these series were drawn primarily from the publications of the International Monetary Fund.[76]

The definitional scheme for this indicator follows.

A. Countries that demonstrated a marked improvement in the effectiveness of their financial institutions, as indicated by qualitative information and savings and lending activities and, in most instances, by either (1) an increase of more than 5 percentage points in the ratio of time and demand deposits to GNP or (2) a more than fivefold increase in the real value of private domestic liabilities to the banking system. Also included in this category

---

* For a number of countries this had to be based on data covering a shorter subperiod.

† There is, of course, no appropriate price index for deflating data on private domestic liabilities to the banking system or any other financial data. To obtain a rough approximation of real changes, we have used, wherever data permit, the implicit GNP deflator computed from real and money estimates of average rates of change in GNP, taken from the United Nations, *Yearbook of National Accounts Statistics, 1964.* Once again, for a number of countries, data refer to a shorter subperiod than 1950/51–1962/63.

‡ We are grateful to Dr. Richard Goode for his suggestions along these lines.

are some countries for which data to compute (1) and (2) were insufficient but in which there was a marked increase in the real value of both the sum of private and government liabilities to the banking system and the volume of time and demand deposits.

B. Countries that demonstrated a moderate improvement in the effectiveness of their financial institutions, as indicated by qualitative information on savings and lending activities and, for those countries for which the relevant data are available, by either (1) an increase of 2 to 4 percentage points in the ratio of time and demand deposits to GNP or (2) a twofold to fourfold increase in the real value of private domestic liabilities to the banking system. Also included in this category are countries for which data were insufficient to compute (1) or (2) but in which there was a positive (but not marked) increase in the real value of the sum of both private domestic and government liabilities to the banking system, the volume of time and demand deposits, and total foreign assets held by the banking system.

C. Countries that showed no significant improvement in the effectiveness of their financial institutions, as indicated by qualitative information on savings and lending activities and, for countries for which the relevant data are available, by either (1) a negligible increase or a decrease in the ratio of the sum of demand and time deposits to GNP or (2) a negligible increase or a decrease in the real value of private domestic liabilities to the banking system. Also included in this category are countries for which data were insufficient to compute (1) or (2) but in which there was both a decrease in the real value of foreign assets held by the banking system and a decrease in the real value of the liabilities of domestic government to the banking system, the volume of time deposits, and/or the volume of demand deposits.

Improvement in Human Resources

The contribution of education to economic performance has received a good deal of attention in recent years. As discussed in the section on our indicator of the extent of literacy, education tends both to improve the quality of the labor force and to promote sociopolitical integration and modernization.[77] Not unexpectedly, a number of recent cross-sectional studies of economic performance have yielded consistent evidence of a positive association between levels of economic development and the rate of additions to the stock of education (measured by school enrollment ratios).[78]

Educational policy is often a compromise between the political and economic interests of various interest groups.[79] Harbison argues that "the goals of development are the maximum possible utilization of human beings in productive activity and the fullest possible development of skills, knowledge, and capacities of the labor force. If these goals are pursued, then others such as economic growth, higher levels of living, and more equitable distribution of income are thought to be likely consequences."[80]

As a measure of the rate of improvement in human resources, we have incorporated in our analysis Harbison and Myers' composite index of levels of human resource development. However, we interpret this index to refer to the rate of improvement in human resources, since it is a weighted average of secondary and higher-level enrollment ratios rather than an average of the related stocks of education. This index is composed of two elements: enrollment at the second level of education as percentage of age group 15–19 and enrollment at the third level of education as percentage of the appropriate age group, with the latter being given five times the weight of the former.[81] Since this composite index was calculated by Harbison and Myers for only about two-thirds of the countries in our sample, we extended it to the remaining countries in the following manner. First of all, we established four broad categories defined in terms of the Harbison and Myers index. We then obtained, for about 1961, estimates of total enrollment at the second and third levels from the latest UNESCO surveys of education.[82] To obtain estimates of the ratio of enrollment to the total population of the appropriate age group for countries where population data were inadequate, we used rough approximations based on surveys of similar countries whenever possible; we were able to classify some countries in the lowest category without an estimate of the appropriate enrollment ratios because of the extremely low level of total enrollment.[83] We were not able to make adjustments for length of schooling similar to those made by Harbison and Myers, but we considered these to be less important for the broad approximations necessary for our four-way classification than they would have been for point estimates.

The final classification scheme is defined in terms of the Harbison and Myers index described on pp. 31–32 of *Education, Manpower and Economic Growth,* and refers generally to the year 1961.

A. Countries that showed significant rates of increase in their stock of human resources, as indicated by a Harbison composite index number of 40.0 or higher. An *A—* rating is given to countries with index numbers between 40.0 and 45.0. An *A+* rating is given to those countries with index numbers higher than 75.0.

B. Countries that showed moderate rates of increase in their stock of human resources, as indicated by Harbison composite index numbers between 20.0 and 39.9. A *B—* rating is given to countries with index numbers between 20.0 and 25.0. A *B+* rating is given to countries with index numbers between 35.0 and 39.9.

C. Countries that were making slight to moderate additions to their stock of human resources, as indicated by a Harbison composite index number between 6.0 and 19.9. A *C—* rating is given to countries with index numbers between 6.0 and 8.0. A *C+* rating is given to countries with index numbers between 15.0 and 19.9.

D. Countries that were making relatively few improvements in their stock of human resources, as indicated by a Harbison composite index number of less than 6.0. A *D—* rating is given to countries with index numbers less than 2.0. A *D+* rating is given to countries with index numbers between 4.0 and 5.9.

Structure of Foreign Trade

The contribution of international trade to economic growth is a subject of considerable interest to development economists because of the importance of the foreign trade sector in many, if not most, contemporary developing countries.

At the same time, there are disadvantages for an underdeveloped economy of dependence upon export trade. First, there are marked fluctuations in the proceeds from most exports typically produced by less developed countries. These have affected most adversely countries dependent on sales from only one or two major crops or products for export proceeds. Second, there is evidence of relatively low, long-range elasticities of demand for many primary products, particularly foodstuffs, produced by underdeveloped countries. Third, the failure of many low-income countries to alter their structures of production in response to unfavorable export markets, and thus their slowness in diversifying export economies, tends to accentuate the unfavorable consequences of instability of export proceeds and low elasticities of demand for products.[84]

The import substitution policies of underdeveloped countries have aggravated the problems of income inequality by raising the prices of domestic consumer goods above world market prices and by generating economic rents through licensing, tariffs, exchange controls, and overvaluation of the currency.[85]

Our indicator of the structure of trade of underdeveloped countries is a purely statistical composite measure of (1) the extent to which developing countries have shifted from the exporting of primary products and raw materials to the increased exporting of processed and manufactured commodities and (2) the extent to which these countries have diversified their exports. To represent the first of these aspects of trade structure, we used the percentage of total exports accounted for by manufactured goods (SITC categories 3 to 8*) in 1960–62. The degree of diversification in trade structure was measured by the percentage of total exports accounted for by the four leading exports and the two leading exports, respectively, of each country. Data were obtained from the World Bank as well as from the United Nations, *Yearbook of International Trade Statistics* (tables on countries); more recent country studies were used in only a very small number of cases to complete our data for this indicator.

* We exclude, however, raw and uncut diamonds.

The classification scheme for the indicator of the structure of trade in 1960-62 follows.

A. Countries in which manufactured commodities accounted for more than 35 percent of total exports. Countries that showed significant diversification of exports, as indicated by the fact that four leading exports accounted for less than 40 percent of total exports, are classified A+.

B. Countries in which manufactured commodities accounted for between 20 and 34 percent of total exports. Countries that, in addition, showed significant diversification of exports as indicated by the fact that four leading exports accounted for less than 40 percent of total exports are classified B+. Countries in which the two leading exports accounted for over 65 percent are classified B−.

C. Countries in which manufactured commodities accounted for between 10 and 20 percent of total exports. Countries that, in addition, showed significant diversification of exports, as indicated by the fact that their two leading exports accounted for less than 40 percent of total exports, are classified C+. Countries in which the two leading exports accounted for more than 65 percent of total exports are classified C−.

D. Countries in which (1) manufactured commodities accounted for less than 10 percent of total exports and (2) less than 75 percent of total exports came from the four leading commodities. Countries that showed moderate diversification of exports, as indicated by the fact that their two leading exports accounted for less than 50 percent of total exports, are classified D+.

E. Countries in which (1) manufactured commodities accounted for less than 10 percent of total exports; (2) more than 75 percent of total exports came from the four leading commodities; and (3) the two leading commodities made up less than 75 percent of total exports.

F. Countries in which (1) manufactured commodities accounted for less than 10 percent of total exports and (2) extreme concentration of exports existed, as indicated by the fact that the two leading commodities accounted for more than 75 percent of total exports.

*Rate of Population Growth / Country Size and
Orientation of Development Strategy*

It is to be expected that the size of a country's population will
affect its pattern of growth. Particularly at low levels of development, the wider market available to larger countries contributes
to earlier and more rapid industrialization, because it enhances
possibilities for capturing both internal economies of scale and external economies associated with expanding markets.[86] A larger
country is also less inhibited than a smaller one in its growth by
limitations on market size posed by inequality in the distribution
of income. The size of a country's total population is used in the
present study as a proxy for the potential size of its internal market.
The score given each country is the size of its population in millions
according to the latest census data.

Rate of population growth. It has often been argued that the
rate of growth of population is a major contributor to low income
levels and to poor rates of growth of income in developing countries.[87] To the extent that poor households have more children than
rich households, and to the extent that they contribute less to family income than they consume, higher rates of population growth
would also increase the skewness of the distribution of income.

To test this hypothesis we incorporated an index of the rate of
population growth into the analysis of income distribution. The
score given each country is the rate of growth of its population in
percent between 1955 and 1965, as computed from the International Bank for Reconstruction and Development World Tables.

Country size and orientation of development strategy. Countries
vary greatly with respect to basic structural characteristics likely
to affect their development patterns systematically. Cross-section
empirical studies have shown, for example, that there are significant differences in development patterns between countries with
different trade orientations (toward manufacturing or primary
exports) as well as different population sizes.[88] Small industry-
oriented countries, for example, typically import a large share of
their capital goods, and would thus be expected to show the lesser

capital intensity and more equal income distribution likely to characterize predominantly consumers' goods production.

The variable used in this study groups countries into three categories depending on their size and development strategy, along the lines suggested in Chenery and Taylor.[89] All small (populations less than 20 million) primary producing countries are in one group; all small manufacturing-oriented countries are in another group; all large countries (populations over 20 million) are in a third group. This variable is treated as a nominal variable in the analysis.

SUMMARY

The 48 indicators defined in this and the previous chapter represent a wide range of social, political, and economic characteristics of underdeveloped countries. They summarize both leading aspects of the social and economic transformations commonly associated with urbanization and industrialization and important political attributes of the growth of modern nation-states, with stress on influences particularly likely to affect the distribution of income and power. In the selection of variables, the inclusion of numerous narrow measures of socioeconomic and political structure was avoided; rather, an effort was made to choose fairly broad indicators of those features of developing societies most likely to influence economic and political performance. The variables included do not, of course, cover all facets of underdeveloped countries that, a priori, appear significant in the process of economic development. For example, important motivational attributes such as the degree of social approval of economic activity and the extent of achievement motivation are excluded, since they could not be defined with sufficient concreteness to permit reliable classification of individual countries.

CHAPTER THREE

Political Participation
in Underdeveloped Countries

The widening of political participation in underdeveloped countries to include broad segments of the population is a matter of increasing concern to those interested in the welfare of the people for several reasons. Participation in the political process is conceived by many to be an important aspect of social equity and political equality as well as "an essential element of democratic government, inseparable from such other attributes of democracy as consent, accountability, majority rule, and popular sovereignty."[1] Second, participation in political decisions and national planning is often thought to favor the achievement of a more egalitarian distribution of economic and political power. Without the participation of less favored groups, the economic programs of the government—expenditure patterns, tax structures, planning policies, implementation measures—may enrich wealthier elites and large profit receivers. In principle, wider popular participation provides mechanisms through which goals and instruments may be redirected toward improving distribution of the fruits of economic development, although all too often these mechanisms do not achieve this result. Finally, participation by individuals in participant institutions such as labor unions, political parties, and farmers cooperatives is one way to provide them with a sense of personal worth and identity without which the dislocations of economic development tend to produce alienation and anomie.

The difficulties of studying political participation in underdeveloped countries are at least twofold. In the first place, most theories on the subject have little relevance to analyzing the political institutions of underdeveloped countries, because they derive from a body of liberal political philosophy that presumes the existence of "a community with a strong sense of its own solidarity and concern for the public interest, with a generally educated population, and probably with a degree of experience in working the required institutions."[2] Second, efforts to measure political participation have been limited largely to studies of electoral participation. These are particularly inappropriate for underdeveloped countries, where voting rarely takes place with an informed electorate making choices between genuine alternatives. Hence, we had to solve the problem of measuring political participation in a meaningful way before we could proceed with our study of influences affecting participation.

A further difficulty with the state of the literature on political participation for our present purpose is that both theory and empirical work emphasize its nature and consequences rather than its causes. Early political theorists such as Rousseau and Mill stressed the role of participation in government decisions both as a means for protecting private interests and as a mechanism for developing the social and political capacities of the individual.[3] Recently, a number of political scientists have sought to make the concept of political participation operate by constructing typologies for ranking countries along a single spectrum ranging from participant to authoritarian forms. Sigmund Neumann, for example, constructs a typology of party systems with two extreme types, democratic and dictatorial systems.[4] The essential participatory functions, in his view, are the integration of the individual into the political system and his politization. He distinguishes between societies with parties of individual representation and those with parties of social integration on the basis of the solidarity of their elites, the pervasiveness of politics in the society, and the degree of participation available to the citizens. Joseph LaPalombara and Myron Weiner construct a typology of party systems in which the stages of participation are those of repression, mobilization, limited admission, and full admission into the political system.[5] In contrast, Giovanni Sartori proposes a classification based on the workability or unworkability of a party system.[6] He stresses the extent to which parties share their fragment of total political power, and he is less concerned with the composition of parties than with the distribution of power among them, i.e. their coalition and bargaining potential.

A quite different approach to the conceptualization of political participation is taken by writers who stress the psychological dimension and the importance of attitudinal transformations as a measure of the extent of participation. Douglas E. Ashford, for example, views political participation as the extent to which the population accepts the government's goals and policies. This depends on people's awareness of the "process in every nation of seeking a way to bring the activities of the government closer to the people."[7]

Quantitative studies of causes and correlates of societal levels of political participation have concentrated primarily on the relationship between socioeconomic development and representative institutions. Lipset, Cutright, and Smith, among others, have all found significant correlations between the spread of more participant institutions and such influences as industrialization, urbanization, and the spread of literacy, mass communication, and education.[8] Their measures of participation have included length of period during which more or less free elections had been held[9] and composites formed by assigning countries points for such features of their political systems as type of party and franchise requirements.[10] Hagen also finds a close relationship between levels of economic development and political participation, measuring the latter by a classification according to competitiveness of political structure.[11]

Particularly relevant to the present study are recent qualitative studies that have focused on possible causes of the spread of political participation in contemporary underdeveloped countries. Daniel Lerner's classic study of the Middle East, *The Passing of Traditional Society*, stresses the critical causal role of increases in urbanization, literacy, and mass communication in promoting the development of participant societies by contributing to, among other things, psychic mobility, which he views as the essential element in the makeup of modern man.[12] Karl Deutsch emphasizes the causal influence of social change in generating pressures for transformations of political structure and leadership that eventually tend to increase political participation.[13]

Beyond these few quantitative and qualitative studies, the literature on the causes of the spread of participation has been limited largely to qualitative histories,[14] behavioral studies of interpersonal variations in participation in particular countries,[15] and descriptive case studies of contemporary developed and underdeveloped nations.[16] While suggestive, they do not provide an adequate basis for a systematic study of political participation in underdeveloped countries.

The present study investigates sources of intercountry differences in levels of political participation in developing nations during the period 1957–62. A typological measure of political participation is constructed and used to classify 74 noncommunist underdeveloped countries for the period 1957–62. Thirty-nine independent variables are used to represent a wide range of social, economic, and political influences that could be expected a priori to affect levels of political participation. The technique of discriminant analysis is applied to obtain a set of country characteristics that best discriminate among groups of nations having different extents of political participation. The technique is also applied to three subsamples representing successive levels of socioeconomic development, since studies of participation in individual countries suggest that the assumption of linearity for the range of countries in the full sample is inappropriate.

Theory has guided our choice of variables and played a crucial role in interpreting the results. While we have not applied theory to specify fully the discriminant equations, we have used it as a major input in selecting a set of candidate variables. The variables chosen statistically from this set are those that empirically provide the best fit to the domain described by the data. Where the state of theory relevant to our choice of variable has left us in doubt, we have included rather than excluded a variable. We have also included variables where causation might be thought to run in both directions. To exclude variables characterized by interaction with political participation would introduce specification errors due to the exclusion of relevant influences that would be more serious, in our opinion, than biases arising from interactions involving a departure from the assumptions of the statistical model.

As is well known, there is no *statistical* justification for causal interpretations of statistical results. In interpreting our results, we have applied historical knowledge and a priori theory to derive hypotheses regarding the nature and direction of causation between the independent variables and levels of participation. At each step in the discriminant analyses, we have also taken account of information on alternative candidate variables. The use of a priori information is particularly important to the interpretation of cross-section studies, since there is no statistical reason for viewing cross-section results as representing typical paths of change over time. Our approach is thus explicitly empirical or hypothesis-seeking in its use of the discriminant technique even though theoretical considerations have guided selection of the candidate variables.

There are a number of pitfalls to the approach we have selected. First, the variables are crude measures of the influences they are designed to represent, suitable only to an initial investigation of a poorly explored subject. Both data deficiencies and problems of conceptualization arising from the rudimentary state of relevant theories have contributed to their lack of sensitivity. By including them, however, our analysis suffers less from the omission of relevant influences than do studies in which variables are limited to those represented by available numerical series.* Second, the variables with the "best fit" may be proxies for other influences, either closely correlated ones included in the candidate set or ones omitted from the analysis altogether. As discussed below, we have attempted to take account of this pitfall. Last, our approach is exploratory and suitable primarily to study of a domain where a

---

* For a discussion of the reduction in the bias of estimates of observed variables, achieved by including a poor proxy for an unobservable variable without which an equation is misspecified, see Michael R. Wickens, "A Note on the Use of Proxy Variables," *Econometrica*, 40 (1972): 759–61.

priori theory does not provide well-validated, fully specified models for testing. The usefulness of the present study will therefore depend on the nature, range, and fruitfulness of the hypotheses it suggests.

THE TECHNIQUE OF DISCRIMINANT ANALYSIS

Discriminant analysis is one of several fairly powerful statistical techniques for elucidating the structure of complex multidimensional phenomena by means of data reduction.[17] These techniques are of the "analysis of variance" type, and all simplify the geometric structure of the data according to a variety of rules. Underlying their application is a search for an optimum degree of simplicity: in developing a fresh approach to the analysis of such complex and varied interactions as those involved in the spread of political participation, it is desirable to keep the analysis within bounds by reducing the dimensions of the problem and yet to avoid predetermining the results by a priori elimination of possibly relevant variables.

The solution of many theoretical problems in the social sciences requires the development of adequate typologies of societies or of social traits. The techniques of discriminant analysis were evolved specifically to explore problems of classification by highlighting the significant differences among different groups of objects.

Discriminant analysis determines statistically, by an analysis of variance, those linear combinations of country characteristics that best discriminate among various groups of nations. The derived functions represent those linear combinations of traits each of which, given the preceding variables, maximizes the distance remaining between the square of the difference between group means and the variance within groups. The discriminant functions obtained in this manner can then be used with a high degree of reliability to classify countries into groups on the basis of a relatively small number of characteristics.

The particular form of discriminant analysis chosen scans the initial list of variables and then selects those that add most to the explanation of the variance between group means, given the other variables already included. Variables are added successively to the discriminant analysis until no variables can be found that contribute a reduction of variance between group means significant at the 5 percent level.

Once the classification of countries by extent of political participation was prepared, the computation of the discriminant functions was carried out as indicated in Cooley and Lohnes, to which the interested reader is referred for the mathematical and procedural technique.[18] The important points for our present purposes are that (*a*) the discriminant functions are chosen in such a way as to maintain the greatest possible separation between the populations being compared,* and (*b*) the number of independent discriminant functions that can be developed when the number of variables exceeds the number of groups is one less than the number of groups.

The technique of discriminant analysis is particularly well suited to our analysis of sources of intercountry variation in political participation in underdeveloped countries. Our dependent variable classifies countries into a number of discrete groups, thus providing a natural starting point for a discriminant analysis. Stratifying the sample provides for nonlinearity in the relationships among the variables for the full range of countries studied. Hence, the linearity of the discriminant equations is less of a constraint than it would be in a smaller sample.

THE VARIABLES

The Dependent Variables

The concept and measurement of political participation. Our first task in designing a study of political participation in underdeveloped countries was to define the concept so as to compare

---

* More specifically, the discriminant functions are the solutions, X, of the matrix equation $(B - \lambda W)X = 0$, where B and W are the dispersion matrices between and within populations. This matrix equation is derived by maximizing the ratio of the between sum of squares ($X'BX$) relative to the within sum of squares ($X'WX$) on the discriminant function represented by the eigenvalues λ and their associated eigenvectors X. For more detail, see Cooley and Lohnes, pp. 117–18.

one country with another. One basic requirement was that the definition apply to the full range of underdeveloped countries. An important part of the literature on political participation, however, falls into two major divisions.

One segment relates to the growth of parliamentary institutions in the Western democracies[19] and thus concerns, in the words of a standard essay on political participation, "those voluntary activities by which members of a society share in the selection of rulers and, directly or indirectly, in the formation of public policy."[20] But this concept fails to encompass the kind of political participation that typifies the growth of the rudimentary participant institutions characteristic of many countries at very low levels of socioeconomic development, which are very little concerned with rulers and policies.

In contrast to this literature, writings on political participation in contemporary communist countries and in noncommunist countries with single-party political systems exclusively emphasize other forms of political participation. Concepts of participation based on experience in single-party systems were also inadequate for our purpose, since we had to be able to include countries with both multiparty and single-party systems in one classification scheme.

The absence of a suitable model led us first to attempt an a priori conceptualization of political participation suitable to our needs. Next, we studied descriptive data on participation in the 74 underdeveloped countries. This step involved examination of two to three published books and articles on each country. The purpose of this step was to record the basic information and then study how well our initial formulation fit the actual country situations. By studying the gaps between data and concept, we were able to reformulate the concept to fit the real world better, and further published sources were studied to obtain the additional information required. These new data were fitted into the revised conceptual scheme, and further reformulations of the concept undertaken as necessary. When all the countries were classified provisionally, we consulted experts on particular countries in order to confirm or adjust our provisional decisions and obtain further indications of any lack of fit between concept and data. Altogether, we consulted more than 100 experts on particular countries and over 250 published studies. Finally, we were able to classify the 74 underdeveloped countries in our sample on the basis of extent and effectiveness of political participation with reasonable confidence and without forcing them into a Procrustean bed.

Constructing an indicator of political participation. In early investigations of the development process in developing countries, we used several rather narrow indicators of political democracy: strength and competitiveness of the national political party system, freedom of political opposition and of the press, and type of political party system.[21] A major deficiency of this set of variables was its strong emphasis on participation through national political parties. For the present study we therefore broadened the measures to include alternative mechanisms—for example, special interest associations—for influencing national political decisions.

This formulation specified three broad sets of criteria for distinguishing among countries with respect to the extent of political participation: (1) the breadth of representation and extent of choice offered by the national political party system, (2) the variety, political effectiveness, and degree of autonomy of voluntary interest groups having as one of their functions political representation of members with some common socioeconomic or cultural-ethnic identification, and (3) the extent of local political participation through formal, nontribal political institutions and informal associations carrying out political functions.

After the initial criteria were defined, a wide variety of secondary data sources were examined to test whether actual country situations could be classified reasonably successfully under this definitional scheme. It soon became evident that a fair number of countries with quite broadly based national systems of representation did not also have reasonably effective special interest associations and nontribal (modern) local political institutions. It also became clear that our provisional assumption that all multiparty systems could be ranked above single-party systems was not satisfactory. Additional difficulties arose from the scheme's failure to give enough weight to the extent to which participant mechanisms actually influenced political decisions.

Our next step therefore was to reformulate our definitional scheme to distinguish more meaningfully between degrees of participation within countries with two or more national political parties and within those with only one. For countries with multiparty political systems, we decided to differentiate between (1) those in which there were important voluntary special interest associations and local political institutions as well as national political parties, and (2) those in which these nonparty mechanisms were negligible or very weak. We then divided the countries in the first category into two groups on the basis of how well the participant mechanisms represented the major groups in the population and how influential the mechanisms were in national political decisions. We thus obtained, in all, three major categories of political participation for countries with multiparty systems.

Redefining the degrees of political participation in single-party systems proved more difficult. According to a number of African experts, variations among countries in the overall effectiveness of participant mechanisms could not be related primarily to the presence and strength of special interest associations or local political institutions. They felt that the real factor differentiating these was the attitude of the leadership; countries with the more effective mechanisms for involving the population politically were generally those in which the leadership had worked from the top to create a network of participant groups at national and local levels. Our criteria for classifying single-party systems were therefore revised to distinguish (1) countries in which the leadership had successfully taken measures to develop national and local mechanisms for broad popular participation, (2) countries in which the leadership had taken such measures but with quite limited success, and (3) countries in which participant mechanisms either had not been encouraged or had been suppressed.

At this point we still had one important conceptual problem to resolve, that of comparing participation in single-party and multiparty systems.

Our inability to rank participation in multiparty and single-party systems clearly derived from our difficulty in conceptualizing the phenomenon of political participation adequately. The component of participation most consistently associated with the single-party/multiparty dichotomization appeared to be the extent of individual choice among channels for the representation of political interests. The presence of more than one political party seemed in itself to offer more choice than the presence of only one party. But even this generalization turned out to be questionable. Several experts we interviewed pointed out that multiparty systems in which each party had a clear-cut cultural or ethnic identification did not in fact offer individuals with given cultural-ethnic identities any choice between parties. In some countries all political parties catered to the same narrow socioeconomic group so that most of the population had no genuine choice of channel to represent their interests. Furthermore, the extent of actual choice between different types of channels for representation could be considerably greater in a country with a single-party system and active labor unions than in some multiparty countries.

The two other important components of popular political participation—extent and effectiveness of representation of the major cultural-ethnic and socioeconomic groups, and actual participation by the population in the political process—were even less closely related to the multiparty/single-party dichotomization.

The solution to our conceptual problem, we became convinced, lay in a definition of political participation in terms of its basic components rather than of such specifics as the number of parties. Three components appeared to be fundamental: the coverage of representative institutions, degree of choice between mechanisms for representation, and actual political involvement of the population (see Appendix A for more precise definitions). In this formulation, forms of *local* participation were included only when they clearly involved the population, at least indirectly, in *national* political decisions.

The classification schema finally adopted for measuring political participation therefore groups underdeveloped countries in terms of the following broad criteria: *

I. The extent to which the major socioeconomic and cultural-ethnic groups, through participant associations and institutions, have their interests represented in and are able to influence the making of national political decisions affecting them.

II. The extent to which individuals belonging to nationally represented cultural-ethnic and socioeconomic groups can choose between different political channels in seeking national representation of their interests.

III. The extent of actual participation by individuals in the national political process through participation in political parties, special interest groups, or other institutions or associations carrying out political functions, or through voluntary voting between genuine political alternatives.

The 74 countries in the sample were ranked according to these criteria and given a composite score. The results are given in Table A2 in Appendix A. This appendix also presents an abstract of the several categories of the composite indicator, Table A1; the specific characteristics of each category of the composite indicator in terms of the three elements comprising it; and a description of the categories of the overall participation index.

In weighting the three components, primary weight was given to the distinction between countries with at least a minimal degree of actual participation and those without it; that is, no countries were assigned to the higher categories without a likely one-fourth of the adult male population involved minimally in the political process. In differentiating among countries in the higher categories, extent of choice among political channels was weighted more heavily than representativeness of the political system. In contrast, in

* It will be noted that the three criteria do not include explicitly the extent to which participation actually influences national political decisions—a critical component of the concept of popular political participation. The omission was dictated by both overwhelming data deficiencies and serious problems of conceptualization. To rectify this omission would have required intensive case studies and a long process of successive definition starting from a multitude of pairwise country comparisons. This research effort was far beyond our limited resources.

distinguishing among countries with very low levels of actual participation, major weight was given to representation of major socio-economic and cultural-ethnic groups; for without some minimal degree of representation of major groups in the population, wider political choices for the minority having representation are not very meaningful. The crude weights implied by our composite index are thus nonlinear, varying as they do over the spectrum of popular political participation.

A fundamental premise underlying the construction of our measure was that (as in the economic sphere) the capacity of a system to enhance individual welfare depends on its success in transmitting and aggregating the choices of individuals. Extension of the coverage of representative institutions to include all major groups in the population (the first element in the composite) clearly augments the capacity of a political system to provide for participation in the national political arena. An increase in actual individual participation probably broadens people's involvement in national political institutions and associations. A diversity of personal preferences is more likely to be transmitted to national decision makers in a representative manner when people have a variety of associations and institutions (the second element) through which to express their choices.* We recognize that neither the extension of a representative system to accommodate additional cultural-ethnic groups nor expansion in the choice of participant mechanisms necessarily leads immediately to increases in actual political participation. Both developments may nevertheless be expected to expand the capacity of a political system to induce wider individual participation in the political process. This does not mean, of course, that a wider sharing of political power will result.

The Independent Variables

The independent variables include a wide range of economic, social, and political characteristics of underdeveloped countries that a priori reasoning and historical experience indicate either

---

* The view that the capacity of a political system to provide for political participation increases with greater diversity of participant mechanisms is consistent with theories of consumer choice in the economic domain. In

contribute to variations in levels of political participation or interact with participation. Excluded are variables where a priori
knowledge suggests that causation operates uniquely from political
participation to the influence in question. The included variables
summarize characteristics of the countries in the sample during
the period 1957–62 or, in some cases, as of about 1960; a few
measures of rates of change refer to the period 1950–63 (see Chapters 1 and 2).

The political variables describe characteristics of political institutions and political leadership likely to affect the extent of political participation. Five variables describe important characteristics of the national political system: freedom of political opposition
and of the press, competitiveness of political parties, predominant
basis of political party system, political centralization, and political
stability. The strength of the labor movement describes an important nongovernment participant institution. Three variables represent selected aspects of colonial experience of possible relevance
to the development of government: recency of self-government,
type of colonial experience (British, French, or other), and length
of colonial experience. A measure of the extent of administrative
efficiency is also included. Finally, five measures summarize key
characteristics of political leadership: the political strength of traditional elites, the political strength of the military, the political
strength of religious organizations, the extent of leadership commitment to promoting economic development, and the extent of
direct government economic activity.

The economic influences included in the study are those basic
characteristics of economic and technical change most likely to
determine the structure of economic and political power in developing countries: the level and rate of change of per capita GNP,
the level of investment, the character of agricultural institutions,
the level of modernization of industry and rate of industrialization,
modernization of techniques in agriculture, and the adequacy of

---

analyses of consumer behavior, the economic welfare of individuals taken
as a whole is presumed to increase when the variety of goods and services
available expands.

transportation and power networks. Also included are measures of the effectiveness of tax and financial institutions and the rate of improvement of human resources.

Social and socioeconomic influences likely to affect political participation include measures of fundamental structural changes typically associated with the early stages of economic development that determine the life style and opportunities of the vast majority of the population: the spread of commercialized agriculture, the extent of dualism, the extent of social mobility, the size of the indigenous middle class, and the degree of urbanization. Also included are indicators of the spread of literacy, mass communication, predominant type of religion, and more "modern" attitudes characteristic of industrialization and urbanization. An indicator of crude fertility rates also reflects the pace of change in fundamental social attitudes relevant to modernization. Finally, indicators of social tension, national integration, and ethnic and cultural homogeneity summarize key social influences affecting national political institutions.

Although the coverage of these indicators is quite broad, there are some important omissions. Psychological and cultural influences, as well as other attitudinal forces likely to account for inter-country differences in the spread of a sense of personal obligation toward the well-functioning of political institutions, are not included among our indicators because of currently insuperable problems of measurement. Also omitted are some variables that political theory suggests are important to participation, such as the extent of multiple channels for articulating interests In general, however, coverage of the variables is sufficiently broad to suggest the nature of important influences that may not have been explicitly included because of deficiencies of data or problems of conceptualization.

THE STATISTICAL RESULTS

Neither the direction of causation nor its mechanisms can be inferred from statistical associations without the application of a priori knowledge. In the present case, both theory and historical evidence are required to interpret our cross-section results as indicative of "typical" causal relationships among the influences studied. As is usual in cross-country studies, the "unexplained" residuals are interpreted to represent influences specific to the individual countries, in contrast to the "systematic" common influences expressed in the estimated equations.[22]

Theory and a priori evidence are particularly important in interpreting results when a model has not been specified because of the multiplicity of reasonable hypotheses regarding the determinants of the phenomena under study. Where a large set of candidate variables has been included, as in our case, interpretations of the "best fitting" relationships are, of necessity, tentative hypotheses rather than firm conclusions. The contrast with standard econometric work is, however, one of degree rather than substance, since it is rare in econometric research that alternative hypotheses are limited to the single alternative required by statistical theory. Thus even when reasonable hypotheses are ruled out in specifying a model, interpretations of the results of econometric work based on the model remain hypotheses rather than conclusions.

As with all statistical results, our interpretations are valid only for the range of variations represented by the data inputs. The results for the "high" sample, for instance, relate to patterns of change characteristic of the Latin American level of development in the period 1957–62; their applicability to countries at higher levels of development would need to be tested.

The present section is organized as follows. The discriminant results for all 74 countries are examined first. This sample is then divided into three subsamples representing successive levels of socioeconomic development (since individual country studies suggest the likelihood of nonlinearity in the relationships for the full sample).* The discriminant analyses for the three subsamples are then discussed. Finally, the results of test runs are presented in

* For a discussion of the factor analysis on the basis of which the three subsamples were composed, see Adelman and Morris, *Society, Politics, and Economic Development,* chap. 4. The individual country factor scores and the sample makeup are given in Appendix A.

which the separate components of the composite index are the dependent classifications.*

A major problem with stepwise statistical procedures is that the variables selected may be proxies for influences they do not represent directly. Where the range of candidate variables is quite broad, insight into the nature of these influences may be gained by study of the "next best" candidate variables. It will be recalled that, at each step in the analysis, the variable was selected for which the F ratio was highest, given the prior inclusions (see Tables B1 through B4 in Appendix B). The next best variables were also examined at each step to gain more insight into the forces represented by the included variables. A marked drop in the F ratio of an omitted variable after a given step indicates that this variable's relationship with political participation is to some extent represented by the variable included at that step.

Additional insight into the forces represented by the included variables was also gained by calculating simple correlations between included and omitted variables. The net correlations between the omitted variables and political participation at successive steps in the analysis were studied for the same purpose. Finally, to aid in the interpretation, we examined in detail those countries classified in each category of political participation by the successive variables included in the discriminant functions, and we studied the individual country scores on the variables included. The discussion of results draws on all these sources of information.

---

* It should be noted that the dependent groupings of scores on political participation are not identical for the four samples because of differences among samples in the distribution of scores and the need for a minimum number of countries in each group. For the full sample (the only sample with the full range of possible scores), seven groups are used. In the subsamples only three or four groups are used. The groupings are as follows:

Full sample	Low	Intermediate	High
A	D & E	A & B	A
B	G & H	C & D	B & C & D
C & D	I & J	E & F	E & F
E		G & J	G & H & J
F			
G & H			
I & J			

Another problem in the interpretation of our results is that in some of the discriminant equations variables are included that are conceptually very close to components of the concept of political participation as defined here. With any multidimensional composite such as political participation or GNP, it is quite usual for the proximate causes of the phenomenon studied to include some of its major components. The growth rate of GNP cannot be related to the growth of factor inputs, for example, without measuring inputs that are components of GNP. In our case, only one of the three components of political participation is conceptually similar to some of the independent variables: the extent of choice of channels for representation conceptually overlaps strength of the labor movement, freedom of political opposition and the press, and competitiveness of the political party system.

Several points are relevant in judging whether the modicum of overlap between dependent and independent variables detracts from our analysis. First, our measurement procedures for the dependent and independent variables were independent.* Second, the concept of choice of channels for representation is by no means identical to the related independent variables, forming as it does a continuum that has its own distinctive characteristics. Third, the complex of forces represented by the secondary variables in the analyses are considerably broader than those measured by the included independent variables. Indeed, in the discriminant analysis in which the classification by choice of channels is the dependent variable, the most important forces represented in the discriminant analysis are social rather than political.† Hence, the substantive results are by no means limited to relationships with components of political participation.

Results for the Full Sample

The discriminant analysis for the 74-country sample shows that both social and political variables are important in accounting for

---

* Both definitional scheme and country classifications for the independent variables are based on unpublished country reports and interviews made in 1963–64. Those for the dependent variable are based on published country studies and questionnaires obtained in 1968–69.

† See pp. 137–38 below.

the variance in popular political participation among groups of countries (Table B1, Appendix B). The important variables are social mobility, the predominant basis of political parties, and political strength of the traditional elite. Of less importance are the level of per capita GNP, social tension, mass communication, strength of the labor movement, and direct government economic activity.

The *first* variable in the discriminant function, social mobility, is an index primarily of the extent of popular access to middle-class occupations and to education. It is not surprising that differences in this capacity should prove closely related to differences in the capacity for political participation, since a common complex of fundamental socioeconomic and cultural factors affects both. For example, a widening of people's horizons through education leads to efforts to improve economic and social status and to desires to advance personal interests through political channels. The weakening of the attachment of individuals to traditional social organizations leads them to seek substitute political and nonpolitical attachments so as to enhance their sense of identification and achievement. Then, too, the closely related expansion of the more specialized economic opportunities characteristic of industrialization and urbanization, by directly increasing possibilities for upward social movement, leads more people to seek political means for promoting their economic interests.[23]

The extent of social mobility is important not only directly but also as a proxy for a much wider range of influences that indirectly favor the growth of political participation. This is evident from a study of variables whose *F* ratios dropped more than 6 points after social mobility entered the discriminant function. They include such economic characteristics as the relative size of the nonmonetized agricultural sector, modernization of agricultural techniques, modernization of industry, effectiveness of financial institutions, and per capita GNP. They also include such social influences as the nature of social organization, literacy, size of the indigenous middle class, and modernization of outlook. These variables all measure the spread of economic and social participation in the more specialized activities of modernizing societies.[24] They may also be interpreted as standing for the generalized process of "social mobilization," which Karl Deutsch denotes as "a concept which brackets together a number of more specific processes of change, such as changes of residence, of occupation, of social setting, of face-to-face associates, of institutions, roles, and ways of acting, of experiences and expectations, and finally of personal memories, habits and needs, including the need for new patterns of group affiliation and new images of personal identity."[25] Social mobilization is defined, therefore, as "the process in which major clusters of old social, economic and psychological commitments are eroded and broken and people become available for new patterns of socialization and behavior."[26] This process tends to generate pressures for political and administrative reform and for a more general transformation of the political elite, while the "increasing numbers of the mobilized population, and the greater scope and urgency of their needs for political decisions and governmental services, tend to translate themselves, albeit with a time lag, into increased political participation."[27]

The *second* variable to enter the discriminant function is the predominant basis of the political party system. Increases in score on this indicator represent movement through a spectrum from no-party and one-party systems toward multiparty systems with strict cultural-ethnic identifications, then toward multiparty systems with personalistic bases, and finally toward multiparty systems with ideological bases. Increases in this index thus indicate expansion in the meaningful choices people can make among political channels.* An examination of the drop in *F* ratios associated with the entry of this variable reinforces this interpretation. Most im-

---

* It will be recalled that extent of choice between different channels for representation is one of the three components of our measure of political participation. An increase in choice of channels expands the capacity of a system to induce political participation. For an interesting study of the decline in territorial parties and increasing emphasis on functional cleavages cutting across traditional divisions into localities and provinces in the history of Western European politics, see Stein Rokkan, "Electoral Mobilization, Party Competition, and National Integration," in Joseph LaPalombara and Myron Weiner, eds., *Political Parties and Political Development* (Princeton, N.J., 1966), pp. 241–66.

portant are strength of the labor movement, freedom of political opposition and press, and competitiveness of the political party system. Since increases in labor union strength involve reductions in their control by dominant parties and governments, they represent potential alternative channels for political participation.[28] Hence, this complex of variables summarizes influences expanding national capacity for popular participation through increases in both extent of choice among participant institutions and extent of opposition to current government policies permitted within the political system.*

The *third* variable to enter the discriminant function is the political strength of the traditional elite (with a *positive* sign). The explanation for the positive relationship between the presence of strong traditional elites and greater political participation lies in the fact that in countries that have political parties, an important traditional elite usually ensures the presence of a traditional party as well as nontraditional parties. Single dominant parties are almost invariably mass-based and nontraditional. Thus, the presence of a politically influential traditional elite in a country with a representative system (such as Chile during the period studied, for example) usually coincides with more rather than less choice between political parties.

The *fourth* variable, level of per capita GNP, contributes to the correct classification of a very few countries. Most of the common influences promoting both increased political participation and higher per capita GNP, such as growth of literacy and the middle class, are represented by social mobility earlier in the equation. At this step in the analysis, per capita GNP serves rather to correct the classification of a small number of countries at the extremes of the spectrum of political participation for which the po-

---

* It should be noted that the presence of trade unions as a channel for political participation is a component of our measure of political participation, so that there is thus some overlap between the dependent and independent variables. While this is not, strictly speaking, desirable, such overlap is not uncommon in econometric studies; savings rates, for example, are frequently related to levels of income. Since participation through trade unions is only one aspect of one of three components of our participation indicator, the overlap is not very great.

litical variables in the equation provide poor predictors of level of political participation. Level of economic development represented by per capita GNP serves to classify them more accurately than do their political characteristics.

The *fifth* variable to enter the discriminant function is social tension, which contributes to the classification of a handful of countries marked by major ethnic divisions. Our analysis indicates that political participation is less where social tension is very pronounced. This may be because increased social tension contributes to the malfunctioning of the political system; and the failure to achieve broad political participation in turn increases social tension by preventing the articulation of demands within the system.

The *last* three variables in the discriminant function—mass communication (with a negative sign) and strength of labor movement and extent of direct government economic activity (with positive signs) are of very little use in classifying countries, although one can deduce reasons for their entry. The possibly surprising sign of mass communication suggests the role that mass communication media can play in very low income countries in inducing popular support for authoritarian regimes. The role of labor unions has already been discussed and their influence underlined by their importance as a secondary variable in the first step of the analysis. The primary effect of the final variable, direct government economic activity, is to classify correctly a few countries at the very bottom of the scale. Since increases in political participation at low levels of development usually occur only where promoted by government, the inclusion of this variable suggests that government efforts to expand participation through a network of dominant-party local political institutions tend to be accompanied by an active government role in the economic area.

The results for the full sample thus suggest that the most important influences in discriminating among different levels of national political participation are the forces of social mobilization and the extent of choice and freedom of opposition within the political system. The analysis discriminates quite well at the extremes of the spectrum of political participation, but does less well in differentiating among the intermediate categories. In all, it misclassifies 21 countries, of which seven are assigned to a category adjacent to the correct one.

Results for the Low Sample

The results of the discriminant analysis for the low sample (Table B2) gives greatest weight to variables that are political in nature. The discriminant function that best classifies the 28 countries in the sample (leaving five misclassified) has only three variables: strength of the labor movement, length of colonial experience, and modernization of outlook.

The priority of the *first* variable, strength of the labor movement, suggests the importance of development within a reasonably permissive atmosphere of the more specialized political institutions characteristic of modern political systems. This rather broad interpretation rests on an examination of the changes in F ratios of the omitted variables when the index of political strength of labor movements enters the discriminant function. Those variables for which F ratios drop at least four points are freedom of political opposition and of the press, administrative efficiency, competitiveness of political parties, and political strength of the military (with a negative sign). The importance of these variables at this step suggests that labor unions are more likely to induce participation when the political atmosphere provides some significant degree of freedom of opposition and of the press. Increases in labor union strength among countries in the low group typically took place under the aegis of a government dominated by a single political party or in an environment in which the freedom of unions to oppose the government was in some respects significantly limited.[29] The inclusion of administrative efficiency among the variables represented in the discriminant function by strength of the labor movement indicates the importance of the growth of governmental institutions for the expansion of popular political participation. The indicator of competitiveness of the party system suggests the importance of alternative mechanisms for influencing the government, while the inclusion of the military with a negative sign stresses the association of stronger labor unions and more competitive political parties with less authoritarian forms of government.

The *second* variable, length of colonial experience, serves to classify only a few countries for which strength of the labor movement is a poor indicator of the spread of political participation. Given a certain level of administrative capacity expressed by step 1 in the analysis, colonialism may tend eventually to favor higher levels of political participation both by weakening the hold of traditional rulers and by promoting a modicum of governmental expertise favorable to leadership oriented toward economic development.[30] The inclusion among the secondary variables of leadership commitment to economic development and political strength of the traditional elite is consistent with this interpretation.* The analysis indicates, however, that the importance of colonialism in discriminating among extents of political participation in low-level countries is quite small.

The *final* variable, modernization of outlook, ranks countries by the extent to which educated urban groups engage in at least some specialized modern activities and the extent to which programs of political, social, and economic modernization have gained some support among the rural as well as the urban population. It is thus an indirect measure of the growth of attitudes favorable to participation in the more differentiated and specialized institutions typical of modern industrial societies. However, the variable has little variance for this group, with most countries in the sample falling into the lowest category. Hence, it adds little to the correct classification of countries.

The analysis for the low sample distinguishes quite well between countries with least participation and those with intermediate scores. It separates less well those scoring highest for the sample, misclassifying three out of the six countries in the top group. The complex of political variables represented by strength

---

* The inclusion among the secondary variables of recency of self-government (positively related to colonialism and participation) is probably explained by the fact that countries that have never been dependencies have the lowest scores on both recency and self-government and length of colonialism.

of the labor movement is most important in discriminating among countries, while social influences are of little weight in the analysis. Given the lack of high scores on political participation in this sample, the relative unimportance of social variables suggests strongly that these countries are below a threshold at which the forces of social mobilization become sufficiently strong to contribute significantly to the wider spread of political participation. It also implies that, at this level, the primary reason for greater political participation is governmental efforts to foster more effective participant mechanisms from the top.

Results for the Intermediate Sample

The results of the discriminant analysis for the intermediate sample express a more complicated set of relationships than those for either the low or the high samples. Perhaps this is not surprising in light of the fact that the intermediate sample is composed of extremely diverse and rapidly changing societies in which patterns of social, political, and economic change vary greatly.[31] Most of the countries in this group are in a state of transition from traditional oligarchies to what Huntington calls "radical praetorianism."* In political participation the nations in this set span the entire range of the full sample.

The discriminant function that best classifies countries at the intermediate level (see Table B3) includes three variables: freedom of political opposition and of the press, importance of the indigenous middle class, and political strength of the traditional elite.

As for the *first* variable, as Huntington points out, modernization is typically associated with a marked redistribution of power and often requires the mobilization of new social forces into poli-

---

* Praetorianism means the intervention of the military into politics. "Radical praetorianism," according to Huntington, refers to a period in a society's development that marks the political emergence of the middle class. The two most active social forces during this period are the military, on the one hand, and the intelligentsia and students, on the other. For a discussion of praetorianism and political modernization, see Samuel P. Huntington, *Political Order in Changing Societies* (New Haven, 1968), particularly chap. 3, "Political Change in Traditional Politics," and chap. 4, "Praetorianism and Political Decay."

tics. To accommodate economic and social modernization, a political system must be able to assimilate these forces. Such a process is not likely to take place without at least some scope for political opposition to traditional interests, together with some changes in political institutions permitting the representation of more varied interest groups. The significant drops in F ratio of political centralization (with a negative sign) and of the predominant basis of political parties suggest that movements away from centralized authoritarian political forms and toward party systems capable of accommodating specialized interest groups are important features of the institutional changes conducive to increased participation.

To explain the *second* variable to enter the discriminant function, the role of the middle class, we turn again to Huntington. He suggests that political expansion at the intermediate level of development involves extending participation from a small elite to middle-class groups. This expansion is essential to the enlargement of power of the political system (a necessary element in political modernization) and to the shift from traditional ruling monarchies to middle-class praetorianism.[32] The significant drop in the F ratio of social mobility at this step suggests the importance to increased participation by the middle class of expanding social and economic opportunities for advancement.

The *third* variable of importance in the discriminant function is political strength of the traditional elite. The greater its power, the less the extent of political participation. Associated with declines in the importance of the traditional elite are increased political strength of the military and reduced political stability. This complex of variables suggests that the replacement of traditional oligarchies by middle-class-oriented political regimes is often mediated by the military at this development level. The process tends to involve an alliance between middle-ranking officers and the civilian middle class, from which the officers were recruited and whose norms of professionalization and bureaucratization they share.[33] To quote Huntington, "The middle class makes its debut on the political scene not in the frock of the merchants but in the epaulettes of the colonel."[34]

The transition from control by a traditional elite to middle-class political participation is often accompanied by coups d'etat of varying degrees of violence and by increased political instability. The preceding instability arises both because there are no institutional channels for absorbing middle-class pressures into the political system and because of the realignment within the traditional power structure this process requires.

The intermediate results contrast with those for the low analysis in that social as well as political influences are important in distinguishing different degrees of participation, although political characteristics remain foremost. The classification for this sample distinguishes quite well among countries at the upper end of the spectrum of political participation and does least well in classifying countries like Tunisia, Algeria, and Iraq, for which the political and social characteristics included in the discriminant function predict a higher level of political participation than actually occurred during the period studied. Given the diverse paths of social and political change marking this sample as well as the uneven pace of changes within countries, it is not surprising that the analysis leaves six out of 21 countries misclassified, the least good fit of any sample.

Results for the High Sample

The discriminant analysis for the high sample (Table B4) yields the following most important variables: strength of the labor movement, predominant basis of the political party system, rate of improvement in human resources, competitiveness of the political party system, and social mobility.

In interpreting the results of the analysis for the high countries, it is important to recall that the method used to classify countries by extent of participation scores them as highly participant only if they rank high in capacity to assimilate political mobilization in structured political organizations as well as in political mobilization itself. If the desire for political participation in a country has outrun the capacity of the political system to assimilate it, our method of classification does not give it the highest rank. Thus the forces stressed in this analysis are those that are important to the reformist, nonrevolutionary development of a broadly based political system.

The *first* variable for the high sample, strength of the labor movement, is important both in itself and as a proxy for a broader set of socioeconomic and political influences. An increase in the strength of labor unions at the "high" level of development signifies an expansion of participation to include urban industrial groups by the creation of what in effect is a special political party. Labor unions in developing countries are often part of the government's political establishment: their memberships are an economic elite; their leaders are often part of the government bureaucracy; and even at relatively high levels of development they often have been established at government initiative and enjoy state protection.

The leading alternative candidate for this step is the extent of social mobility. As discussed above in connection with the results for the full sample, modernization leads to demands for greater socioeconomic and political participation in the benefits of economic development. Systems that have made upward mobility easier are also likely to provide wider participation in political associations and institutions.

The close relationship between social and political change at this level of development is shown here by some of the variables whose *F* ratios drop significantly with the entry of social mobility into the discriminant function: strength of the labor movement, predominant basis of the political party system, political freedom, and centralization. The socioeconomic influences also associated with social mobility—effectiveness of financial institutions, physical overhead capital, modernization of outlook, and importance of the indigenous middle class—all stress the expansion and increased specialization of economic opportunities conducive to increased social and political participation.

The *second* variable in the discriminant function at this level is the predominant basis of the political party system. As indicated earlier, this variable groups countries along a scale, with the lower end designating absence of political parties or the presence of a single mass-based party and the upper end characterized by competitive political parties articulating class interests, such as those of factory workers and industrialists. The variable is thus indicative of the extent to which the structure of political parties is modern, in Huntington's sense. Its inclusion, then, expresses the interaction between growth in the capacity of a political system to provide for political participation by members of various social groups and changes in the nature of political parties that make them more effective mechanisms for aggregating and expressing politically the more specialized and diverse interests typical of urban industrial societies. The association at a "high" level of development of the nature of the party system with expansion of participation is thus consistent with Huntington's statement that the more modern the political party system, the more able are the political parties to furnish the institutional framework for expanded social mobilization.[35]

The inclusion of improvement of human resources as the *third* variable in the discriminant function suggests the positive contribution of the spread of secondary and higher education in increasing awareness of the potentialities of political action. It also suggests the importance of common influences such as the rise of the middle class (the major secondary variable) in the expansion of both human resource skills and political participation.

The *fourth* variable, competitiveness of the political party system, represents directly the importance of greater choice among channels for the widening of political participation. As Huntington points out, electoral competition between parties in countries at a high level of socioeconomic development tends both to expand political participation and to strengthen party organization, thereby leading to greater political stability. "Party competition of this sort," he says, "enhances the likelihood that new social forces which develop political aspirations and political consciousness will be mobilized into the system rather than against the system."*

* *Political Order*, p. 429. At lower levels of development, interparty competition may merely lead to greater factionalization without increasing participation by new social groups.

The *final* variable in the discriminant analysis, social mobility, serves to classify two countries only: El Salvador, in which both political participation and social mobility are lower than expected, and Turkey, in which they are higher than expected, on the basis of other characteristics of their political structure. These cases reinforce the point made above, that the national capacity to provide political participation is closely related to capacity to provide opportunities for social and economic advancement.

At the "high" level of development, socioeconomic and political forces interact closely in influencing political participation. This is evident from the wide range of socioeconomic influences for which strength of labor movement stands proxy in the first step of the analysis. The importance of social influences is also stressed by the inclusion of both improvement in human resources and social mobility in the discriminant function. It is thus at this level that the impact of the forces of social mobilization in promoting broader political participation becomes fully evident. The discriminant function for this sample provides almost perfect discrimination among countries, leaving only one country incorrectly classified. The close relationship among political and social influences in the "high" sample supports the hypothesis that there is a threshold beyond which social and socioeconomic changes eventually induce wider political participation. Our results suggest that the spread of individual participation in the more specialized economic and social activities of modernizing societies tends finally at this level to be translated into pressures for a larger popular share in the political process.

Discriminant Analyses for the Components of Political Participation

Since our measure of political participation is composed of three components, we made test runs for our full sample with the separate components to see whether the resultant classification functions were broadly consistent with our analysis of the composite index.

The discriminant analysis for *effectiveness of national represen-*

tation of major socioeconomic and cultural-ethnic groups yields the same variables as in the results with the composite index, except that social tension is excluded and literacy included (both with negative signs), but the order of entry is different and interesting. The first variable, labor, and its sociopolitical correlates are the same. The second variable, however, is political strength of the traditional elite with a negative sign and no important secondary variables. This suggests that the political hold of the traditional elite is a foremost impediment to effective national representation of major socioeconomic and cultural-ethnic groups. Per capita GNP, the third variable, serves to classify correctly a small number of countries for which scores on traditional elite are, by exception, poor predictors of extent of representation. The fourth variable, predominant basis of the political party system, classifies only a few countries, suggesting that this dimension of participation is not closely related to extent of representation. The remaining variables classify even fewer countries and may, for the most part, be interpreted as for the composite index. The inclusion of literacy with a negative sign serves to classify a small number of countries for which the representativeness of their political systems is unusually high or low relative to other characteristics of their political structure.

The discriminant analysis for the extent of *choice of channels* for representation includes six variables: literacy, competitiveness of parties, traditional elite, basis of parties, labor, and fertility. These results, while broadly consistent with those for the composite measure, have two marked differences of emphasis. The high *F* ratio of the first variable, literacy, and the weight of social influences among its secondary variables (urbanization, mass communication, modernization of outlook, middle class, and character of agriculture) suggest that the forces of social mobilization are particularly important to the development of more varied political channels for representing the increasingly specialized groups characteristic of modernizing societies. The second variable, competitiveness of political parties, is more important here than in the analysis for the composite index, since it represents a leading mechanism for expanding the capacity of a political system to provide meaningful political choices. The third variable, traditional elite, comes in with an unexpected sign, being positively related to choices of channels for representation. It contributes to the classification of a small number of countries where a traditional elite dominates a narrowly based multiparty system. Since extent of choice among channels ranks countries on choices for that part of the population *with* representation, these countries score moderately well on choice of channels although very low on representativeness of their political systems.

The discriminant analysis for *actual political participation* has only two variables: social mobility with its usual social and political secondary variables, and the predominant basis of political parties with the usual alternative political variables. Since the dependent classification by actual participation distinguishes only two groups of countries, it is to be expected that the discriminant function would include fewer variables. Those included represent the two most important sets of influences in the analysis for the composite index: the forces of social mobilization and those indicative of the modernization of political structure and institutions.

Thus, test runs with the individual components of participation confirm the broad outlines of the analysis for the composite index, while the ways in which they diverge are consistent with the substantive differences among the three dimensions of political participation they represent.

SUMMARY AND CONCLUSIONS

The process of national development in low-income countries involves the emergence of a wide range of diverse interest groups involving large numbers of individuals seeking new patterns of personal commitment to substitute for their weakened attachments to traditional institutions. These countries therefore face the need to accommodate their political systems toward a sharing of political and economic power among the varied contestants in the political arena. The analyses in this chapter point to some of the means whereby this transfer of power may take place, as well as to the serious strains on the polity and society that it provokes.

On the whole, the discriminant analysis for countries at the lowest level of development suggests that the development of participant political institutions requires a political structure that includes specialized political organizations having a modicum of freedom and government efforts to promote participation from the top. The former is indicated by the strength of the labor movement, the growth of the political party system, the negative role of the military, and administrative efficiency. The latter is implied by the nature of positive changes in political participation within the range of scores in this sample.

The essential characteristics summarized by the discriminant analysis for the intermediate group of countries describe the process underlying the breakdown of traditional political systems and the extension of participation to the urban middle class. Along socioeconomic lines, the process involves the rise of the middle class and the decline of the traditional landowning elite; politically, it involves seizure of power by the military and varying degrees of political instability.

The analytical results for countries at the "high" level indicate the capacity of the political system to provide the institutional organization required for assimilating the forces created by higher levels of socioeconomic modernization. The new elements that must be assimilated are the urban workers and the peasants. The organizational structures required for this are modern, competitive political party systems and labor unions; the socioeconomic preconditions are expansion of the system's capacity to provide for upward social mobility and improvements in human resource skills.

Perhaps the principal lesson suggested by the above results is that increases in political participation are by no means automatic consequences of socioeconomic development in underdeveloped countries. The results further suggest several hypotheses regarding typical interactions among the various influences affecting the spread of political participation in underdeveloped countries undergoing social, economic, and political change.

The early stages of social mobilization and economic modernization generate pressures for political and administrative reform as well as a general transformation of the political elite. Economic change typically affects the political system indirectly, however, through related social and institutional transformations that create pressures for political change. For these pressures to lead to viable forms of political participation requires both the institutionalization of socioeconomic interest groups and the evolution of mechanisms for sharing political and economic power among them which are sufficiently equitable to be generally accepted. Success in accommodating these demands on the political system tends to reduce social tensions, but the process of inducing the necessary political changes is fraught with social conflict and often accompanied by violence. If the resultant instability exceeds the capacity of the system to integrate conflicting claims peacefully, authoritarianism and the suppression of incipient participant institutions may postpone indefinitely the development of modern forms of participation.*

* This final generalization with respect to the relationship between political stability and political participation is supported by a set of test runs in which independent variables relating to 1957–62 were used to discriminate among degrees of political participation during the 1963–68 period. In these runs, greater participation during 1963–68 was associated with more political instability during 1957–62. This contrasts with the concurrent relationship between political stability and participation during 1957–62, which associates greater participation with more stability.

CHAPTER FOUR

Who Benefits from Economic Development?

The equitable distribution of income among individuals and households is central to a nation's welfare and has become a major public concern in both developed and underdeveloped countries. Egalitarian philosophies stimulated by the industrial revolutions of Western Europe have produced widespread expectations that economic growth will equalize wealth and earnings opportunities as well as raise the average level of economic welfare.[1] These expectations have not been borne out. Even in economically advanced countries, the persistence of significant hard-core poverty for large minorities in the midst of growing affluence for the majority has contributed to serious social tensions and political conflict.[2] Public concern over income inequality has been heightened by both Marxian and contemporary radical stress on forces in capitalist societies that tend to increase the concentration of wealth and income[3] and by more orthodox studies of conflicts between distributional justice and economic efficiency.[*]

[*] James E. Meade, *Efficiency, Equality, and the Ownership of Property* (London, 1964). There is relatively little disagreement over the proposition that the total economic welfare of a community with marked income inequality can be increased significantly by income transfers from wealthier to substantially poorer persons, given the presence of eventually diminishing marginal utility of commodities as a whole to individuals. This is so even without the assumption that interpersonal comparisons of utility are possible for all persons in an income distribution. The proposition only requires the weaker assumption that the marginal utility of commodities as a whole for persons at the extremes of the income distribution can be *ranked*. For a defense of comparing marginal utilities for the purpose of measuring the effects on welfare of distributional changes, see James E. Meade, *Trade and*

Theories of income distribution usually emphasize explanations of functional income shares and also vary greatly in the distributional patterns they imply.[4] Classical economists combined a subsistence wage theory, a competitive profit model, and the Ricardian rent theory to develop a dynamic analysis of growth and distribution. On this basis they predicted that, as a rule, landlords would benefit at the expense of both capitalists and workers in the course of economic development.[5] Marx, in his model of capitalist accumulation, assumed that continuous labor-saving technical advances would increase the industrial reserve army of unemployed and depress wage levels, resulting in a falling share of wages in total output.[6] In neoclassical theory, relative factor shares are governed by relative marginal productivities that, given the technology, are determined by the relative amounts of factors employed. In this model, relative shares change with both technical changes affecting marginal productivities and changes in the relative amounts of factors employed.[7] More recently, Keynesian behavioral assumptions have produced distributional theories in which differences in the propensity to save between wage earners and capitalists and variations in the rate of investment interact to determine the distribution of income between wages and profits.[8] The implicit assumption of all these theories with respect to the size distribution of income is that individuals possess various quantities of primary factors of production (capital, labor, land, or entrepreneurship) which determine their income shares and that these functional shares determine the distribution of personal incomes.

Little explicit theorizing has been done about the determinants of the size distribution of income among individuals except for a few elegant models in which income distribution is determined by stochastic processes marginally related to basic economic forces.[9] In contrast, empirical studies of income variation have yielded a variety of hypotheses and some sketchy evidence on the impact of such influences as industrialization, level of education, distribu-

---

Welfare (London, 1955), chap. 5. A now classic discussion of interrelationships between economic welfare and income distribution can be found in I. M. D. Little, *A Critique of Welfare Economics*, 2d ed. (Oxford, 1957).

tion of wealth, and taxation, and of such personal characteristics as age, sex, race, family size, and occupation, to mention a few.[10] The results, while interesting, have been scanty and have generally been based on observations over relatively short time periods in a few advanced countries. Comparisons between countries have been few because of insufficient data and conceptual difficulties.[11]

In recent years, interest in the process of economic development has stimulated empirical analyses of the interrelationship between economic growth and distribution of income. Kuznets's work on currently advanced nations indicates that "the relative distribution of income, as measured by annual incidence in rather broad classes, has been moving toward equality—with these trends particularly noticeable since the 1920's but beginning perhaps in the period before the first world war."[12] But other evidence suggests that at low levels of development economic growth tends to induce greater inequality in the distribution of income. Studies of the early years of industrialization in several European countries indicate a relative worsening of the position of low-income groups with, at best, stability in their absolute position.* Little work has been done on growth and distribution in today's underdeveloped countries, but such evidence as there is suggests that in many of them economic growth has led to increased inequality in the distribution of income.†

* Kuznets suggests that relative income inequality may well have widened in England between about 1780 and 1850 and in the United States and Germany between 1840 and 1890. "Economic Growth and Income Inequality," *American Economic Review*, 65 (1955): 18–19. Even the most optimistic estimates for Great Britain during the industrial revolution conclude that little, if any, absolute betterment in workers' standards of living occurred before the 1820's at the earliest. See E. J. Hobsbawm (Part A) and R. M. Hartwell (Part B), "The Standard of Living During the Industrial Revolution: A Discussion," *Economic History Review*, 16 (1963), reprinted in *The Economic Development of Western Europe: The Eighteenth and Early Nineteenth Centuries*, ed. Warren C. Scoville and J. Clayburn LaForce (Lexington, Mass., 1969), pp. 135–69. A recent note on "Trends in Wealth Concentration Before 1860" by Jackson Turner Main indicates that a striking increase in the concentration of wealth took place in the United States between 1780 and 1860 (*Journal of Economic History*, 31 [1971]: 445–47); it may be presumed that greater inequality of income resulted.

† Kuznets conjectured in 1955 that in contemporary underdeveloped countries the cumulative effect of concentration of past savings, combined with

The study of income distribution in currently underdeveloped countries is handicapped by inadequacies of both theory and data and by the importance of nonmarket influences rarely allowed for in theories of distribution. The application of neoclassical functional theories to very low income countries, for example, is greatly complicated by the impact upon earnings differentials of such nonmarket forces as norms set by powerful traditional or expatriate elites, semiarbitrary wage scales for government employees, minimum wage laws that are inconsistent with labor availabilities, and the degree of often premature unionization. Keynesian theories are also not very relevant because nonmarket forces restrict the operation of presumed links among savings, investment, and income. While Marxian theories stressing the impact of property ownership on income distribution have greater relevance, they are (like non-Marxian theories) simplistic in their two-class view of society and in their assumption that materialistic motives dominate economic activity. In underdeveloped countries, it is to be expected that a variety of historical, social, and political influences that are difficult to measure will interact with classical economic considerations in determining the distribution of personal incomes.

This chapter investigates the sources of variations in the distribution of income among contemporary, noncommunist, low-income developing countries. Income distribution data on 43 underdeveloped countries, ranging from those with subsistence economies to those rapidly approaching a developed economy, are used to construct crude measures of various facets of income distribution.* The independent variables used are indexes of economic, political, and social forces that could be expected a priori to influence the dis-

---

the absence of dynamic forces for equalization and of government policies to improve the conditions of the poor, had created "a possibility that inequality in the secular income structure of underdeveloped countries may have widened in recent decades." "Economic Growth and Income Inequality," p. 24. A recent study by Richard Weisskoff indicates that in Puerto Rico, Argentina, and Mexico between 1950 and 1963, the income share of lower-income groups declined while per capita GNP was rising. "Income Distribution and Economic Growth in Puerto Rico, Argentina, and Mexico," *Review of Income and Wealth*, 16 (1970).

* Data were not available for the full sample of 74 countries used in Chapter 2.

tribution of income.* These data are analyzed by a stepwise analysis-of-variance technique (described below) that permits highly nonlinear interactions in order to obtain a "best fitting" statistical representation of the empirical regularities underlying the data.

The methodology is thus overtly empirical rather than theoretical. This approach seems appropriate at present, since theorizing about the subject to date has produced a variety of equally plausible but poorly validated hypotheses that do not provide an adequate basis for the construction of a priori specified models.[13] This is not to say, of course, that we have shunned the use of theory. Theory, as well as historical and comparative evidence, guided our choice of variables and was a major input in the construction of the socioeconomic and political typologies employed as independent variables. It also played an important role in our interpretations of the statistical results. Since the use of cross-sectional data to gain insights into dynamic processes poses well-known problems,[14] interpreting these data as representing changes over time requires major use of theoretical reasoning and historical evidence regarding both the progressions over time suggested by the data and the direction of relationships between closely associated variables.

It should be stressed that this study is exploratory and offers only preliminary and tentative insights into the varied interactions affecting the distribution of income in underdeveloped countries.† Both the income distribution variables and the independent variables are crude indexes appropriate only for the early stages of exploration of the relevant relationships. Nevertheless, this type of exploratory effort is essential both to further research into the conceptualization and measurement of the influences involved and to the design of research in depth on their interrelationships. Indeed, without the kind of preliminary insights provided by exploratory studies such as this one, any major investment of resources

---

* For a detailed discussion of the independent variables used in the present studies, see Chapters 1 and 2.

† We might say with Kuznets ("Economic Growth and Income Inequality," p. 4) that "the trends in the income structure can be discerned but dimly, and the results considered as preliminary informed guesses."

in research on the determinants of variations in the distribution of income in underdeveloped countries is likely to be wasted.

THE ANALYSIS OF HIERARCHICAL INTERACTIONS

Our choice of analytic technique was guided by the need for a statistical method that did not assume linear relationships and that placed as few restrictions as possible on the forms of interactions among variables. Such a flexible technique is desirable because the complex processes influencing income distribution affect different strata of the population in different ways and because the forces inducing changes in income distribution may interact quite differently in countries having different characteristics. For example, one might expect that in heavily agricultural countries, industrialization will decrease the share in total income of the lower 60 percent of the population and increase the income share of the upper 20 percent, while in countries with sizable industrial sectors, further industrialization may shift income distribution in favor of the middle 40 to 60 percent of the population.

The statistical method used here is based on an analysis of variance. As with other analysis-of-variance techniques, the focus is on "explaining" variations in the dependent variable.[15] The analysis selects from a set of independent variables the one that splits the parent sample into two subgroups having the smallest possible combined dependent-variable variance within the subgroups or, alternatively, for which the sum of the squared deviations of the subgroup means from the parent-sample mean is at a maximum. Each of the two subgroups thus obtained is then treated as a new parent sample for which the analysis again selects the independent variable providing the "best" split—that is, the one giving the largest total variance of subgroup means from the parent-sample mean. Each of these subgroups is again treated as a parent sample, and the process is continued through a series of binary splits. The result is an asymmetrical branching process that subdivides the original parent sample into subgroups constructed to facilitate prediction of the value of the dependent variable with the least error.

More specifically, at each step in the analysis, and for each candidate *independent* variable, all possible mutually exclusive partitions of the parent group into subgroups are examined, each of which includes particular (usually successive) values of the *independent* variable. For each possible partition of the relevant independent variable, the variance of the subgroup means from the grand mean is calculated for the dependent variable. The "best" partition is one that maximizes the fraction of the total variance of the dependent variable accounted for by the means of the subgroups—in other words, that maximizes the sum of the squared deviations of the subgroup means from the grand mean weighted by sample size. The proportion of parent-sample variance thus "explained" by the best partition for the relevant independent variable is compared with the best partition for all other candidate independent variables. At each step in the analysis, that independent variable is selected for which the best partition accounts for the largest proportion of the overall variance of the dependent variable. The corresponding partition is then carried out and each subgroup is treated as a new parent sample.*

To ensure statistical significance, groups are candidates for splits only (1) if they contain a number of observations greater than $\overline{N}$ (set equal to 10), and (2) if they include at least a specified proportion of the overall variance (set equal to 10 percent). In

---

* For example, if the independent variable X assumes r distinct values X_r, then the parent group is arranged initially so that all observations that have values $X_r \le X_1$ are in group 1, and all observations that have values $X_2, \ldots,$ X_r are in group 2. The means of the two subgroups are then calculated, as well as the variance from the overall sample means that is due to the group means (the "regression" sum of squares); this latter variance is equivalent to the variance attributable to (or "explained" by) the partition. Next, the partition that places the values of $X_r \le X_2$ in group 1 and the remaining data in the parent group in group 2 is tried and the same calculations are carried out. The process is repeated then for $X_r \le X_3$, $X_r \le X_4$, etc. For each independent variable, that binary partition of the parent group providing the largest reduction in the unexplained sum of squares becomes a candidate for splitting the parent group. The same analysis is carried out for each of the independent variables in turn, and the reductions in the variance provided by the best partitions associated with each independent variable are then compared with one another. At each step of the analysis, that split of the parent group is chosen which maximizes the sum of squares explained by the partition over all possible binary, nonoverlapping partitions and over all the independent variables included in the analysis.

addition, splits that are not statistically significant at the 5 percent level (by an F test) and splits that produce splinter groups (i.e. that contain fewer than five observations) are not carried out in the present analysis.

If the independent variables are ordinal (i.e. are ranked in either ascending or descending order so that X_{r+1} is either greater than or less than X_r), only those splits are permissible that place all values of X_r less than or equal to a certain value, say X_m, in a given group. If an independent variable is only nominal (i.e. is assumed to have no natural order), then the analysis forms the partitions that correspond to all possible combinations of values of X_r taken 2, 3, 4, . . . , $r - 1$ at a time, and selects the partition that performs best. The analysis can therefore accommodate dummy variables, or variables for which the investigator does not wish to specify a ranking beforehand.

It is evident that this particular form of analysis of variance is extremely flexible. In spirit, it is akin to a highly nonlinear type of stepwise multiple regression analysis. Like stepwise regression, this technique finds, at each step, those combinations of values of the independent variables that permit prediction of the value of the dependent variable with the least error. But unlike regression analysis, this branching process admits highly nonlinear interactions. For high values of the dependent variable, the variables, interactions, and coefficients that best "explain" a difference of ΔY in the value of the dependent variable can be quite different from those that are required to account for the same difference at low or intermediate values. Furthermore, unlike regression analysis, the independent variables need not be assumed to be uncorrelated with one another. That is, this statistical technique can accommodate interactions among independent variables. (These interactions, of course, constitute a particular type of nonlinearity.)

This analytical technique is ideally suited, therefore, to studying systematic interactions between a dependent variable and a set of independent variables when the phenomenon to be analyzed may affect different parts of the data differently and when the best principles for stratifying the original sample into subsamples are not known in advance. Indeed, this technique of analysis is very well adapted to indicating the best principles for stratification.

THE VARIABLES

The Dependent Variables: Measuring the Distribution of Income

Since the concept of income distribution is multidimensional, it is susceptible to measurement by a variety of methods, no one of which is valid for all purposes.[16] Summary indexes, such as the Gini coefficient, can be suitable for broad comparisons of distributions with very different degrees of inequality, but they are not adequate for comparing distributions with quite different forms of inequality. For investigating differential impacts of distributional changes on various segments of the population, measures of the relative income shares received by particular quantiles of income recipients can be more appropriate. Yet indexes of relative income shares also have their drawbacks: the choice of appropriate quantile is arbitrary, and variations in the incidence of characteristics of income receivers both within given quantiles in different distributions and between different quantiles in a given distribution complicate comparisons over time and across countries.[17] Finally, it should be stressed that all measures of income distribution provide at best only an ordinal ranking of observations with respect to the underlying aspect of income distribution measured.*

Overwhelming data deficiencies greatly complicate any efforts to measure variations in the distribution of income. It would be desirable, for example, to have income data for family expenditure units adjusted for the number of persons in the family and their stage of participation in the labor force; in addition, income distribution data ideally should refer to secular income levels and

---

* Strictly speaking, it is not correct to use ordinal data with statistical techniques requiring the calculation of means and variances. Sensitivity studies are needed to justify the arbitrary assumption of cardinality. In our treatment of the dependent variable we follow the general practice among econometricians of using index numbers in statistical analyses as if they were cardinal. It should be noted, however, that with respect to the independent variables their ordinality is appropriate to the technique of hierarchical interactions. See pp. 146–47.

should take account of movements of individuals between different income groups over time.[18] Yet income distribution data almost invariably relate to income in a single year, are seldom available by appropriate expenditure units, are frequently unadjusted for number of persons, and rarely take account of mobility between income groups. Furthermore, except for recent years in a few countries, data are usually available for only a small number of broad income groups. Finally, the raw data on incomes received, even in some developed countries, are notoriously unreliable.*

The raw data on incomes in the 43 underdeveloped countries studied here have all the deficiencies just described. In addition they pose several special problems regarding comparability, and adjustments could be made for only a few of them. Three types of sources were used: budget (income and expenditure) studies that sample different strata of the population, income information compiled from national censuses, and tax returns. For some countries, budget data referring to particular segments of the population (e.g. only urban or wage earners) were used in conjunction with national accounts and other income data in order to construct an overall picture of income distribution. For some countries for which basic information was exceedingly coarse, a finer breakdown by class intervals was achieved by fitting the available data to an appropriate empirical or theoretical distribution. If the lowest end of the lowest income class was not available, the minimum income was estimated by fitting with an appropriate curve. And if the average income in the highest class interval was not available, the figure was estimated by selecting a value that would equate the average per capita (or per household) income estimated from the income distribution to the corresponding value estimated from the national accounts (i.e. to per capita national income).

There were other sources of incompatibility in the basic data. Some of the information referred to households, some to individ-

* The deficiency often cited is that the basic income data are usually derived from information supplied by the income recipients themselves, the accuracy of which is a function of the recall of the respondent, his perception of the use to which the information will be put, his veracity about a sensitive subject, etc. Only when income data are based on information reported on tax returns can they be regarded as somewhat more reliable.

uals, and some to active population. When more than one type of information was available, information on households was preferred because they most closely approximate expenditure units. No adjustments of distributions relating to individuals or active population were made because of the difficulties in estimating the appropriate adjustments.

Some of the data are, strictly speaking, not comparable in that they refer to different years in the late 1950's and 1960's. More serious as a cause of incompatibility are differences in the extent of breakdown in the raw data by class intervals. Twenty-eight class intervals are available for Zambia, for example, but only five for other African and some Latin American nations. Other things being equal, a greater amount of detail provides a larger estimate of income concentration.

The basic income distribution data for the study are summarized in Table 1. Three dependent variables were constructed from these data.*

1. The income share of the lowest 60 percent of the population.

2. The income share of the middle quintile of the population (i.e., the 10 percent above and the 10 percent below the median income).

3. The income share of the wealthiest 5 percent of the population.

The Independent Variables

The independent variables used in this study consist of 35 indicators of economic, social, and political influences that could be expected, on theoretical grounds, to affect income distribution. For the most part, they describe country characteristics for the period 1957–62; only the measures of rates of change refer to the longer period 1950/51 to 1962/63. (Descriptions of the indicators, to-

* Initially, four additional dependent variables were used: the concentration (Gini) coefficient, the income share of the poorest 20 percent of the population, the income share of the upper 20 percent of the population, and an index of the point at which the income distribution shifts its slope from less than unity to greater than unity. The results of the three analyses presented here are quite representative of the full range of results for the original seven dependent variables.

TABLE 1
Income Distribution Estimates
(Percentage shares by population groups)

Country	0–40	40–60	0–60	60–80	80–100	95–100
(1) Argentina	17.30%	13.10%	30.40%	17.60%	52.00%	29.40%
(2) Bolivia	12.90	13.70	26.60	14.30	59.10	35.70
(3) Brazil	12.50	10.20	22.70	15.80	61.50	38.40
(4) Burma	23.00	13.00	36.00	15.50	48.50	28.21
(5) Ceylon	13.66	13.81	27.47	20.22	52.31	18.38
(6) Chad	23.00	12.00	35.00	22.00	43.00	23.00
(7) Chile	15.00	12.00	27.00	20.70	52.30	22.60
(8) Colombia	7.30	9.70	17.00	16.06	68.06	40.36
(9) Costa Rica	13.30	12.10	25.40	14.60	60.00	35.00
(10) Dahomey	18.00	12.00	30.00	20.00	50.00	32.00
(11) Ecuador	16.90	13.50	30.40	15.60	54.00	33.70
(12) El Salvador	12.30	11.30	23.60	15.00	61.40	33.00
(13) Gabon	8.00	7.00	15.00	14.00	71.00	47.00
(14) Greece	21.30	12.30	34.10	16.40	49.50	23.00
(15) India	20.00	16.00	36.00	22.00	42.00	20.00
(16) Iraq	8.00	8.00	16.00	16.00	68.00	34.00
(17) Israel	16.00	17.00	33.00	23.90	43.10	16.80
(18) Ivory Coast	18.00	12.00	30.00	15.00	55.00	29.00
(19) Jamaica	8.20	10.80	19.00	19.50	61.50	31.20
(20) Japan	15.30	15.80	31.10	22.90	46.00	14.80
(21) Lebanon	7.20	15.80	23.00	16.00	61.00	34.00
(22) Libya	.50	1.28	1.78	8.72	89.50	46.20
(23) Malagasy	14.00	9.00	23.00	18.00	59.00	37.00
(24) Mexico	10.50	11.25	21.75	20.21	58.04	28.52
(25) Morocco	14.50	7.70	22.20	12.40	65.40	20.60
(26) Niger	23.00	12.00	35.00	23.00	42.00	23.00
(27) Nigeria	14.00	9.00	23.00	16.10	60.90	38.38
(28) Pakistan	17.50	15.50	33.00	22.00	45.00	20.00
(29) Panama	14.30	13.80	28.10	15.20	56.70	34.50
(30) Peru	8.80	8.30	17.10	15.30	67.60	48.30
(31) Philippines	12.70	12.00	24.70	19.50	55.80	27.50
(32) Rhodesia	12.00	8.00	20.00	15.00	65.00	40.00
(33) Senegal	10.00	10.00	20.00	16.00	64.00	36.00
(34) Sierra Leone	10.10	9.10	19.20	16.70	64.10	33.80
(35) South Africa	6.11	10.16	16.27	26.37	57.36	39.38
(36) Sudan	15.00	14.30	29.30	22.60	48.10	17.10
(37) Surinam	22.26	14.74	37.00	20.60	42.40	15.10
(38) Taiwan	14.20	14.80	29.00	19.00	52.00	24.10
(39) Tanzania	19.50	9.75	29.25	9.75	61.00	42.90
(40) Trinidad & Tobago	9.42	9.10	18.52	24.48	57.00	26.60
(41) Tunisia	10.62	9.95	20.57	14.43	65.00	22.44
(42) Venezuela	13.40	16.60	30.00	22.90	47.10	23.20
(43) Zambia	15.85	11.10	26.95	15.95	57.10	37.50

Sources and notes for Table 1 will be found at the end of the notes to this chapter, on pp. 244–48.

gether with country classifications, can be found in Chapters 1 and 2.)

With respect to economic influences, five variables represent, directly or indirectly, the extent of factor endowments: natural resource abundance, adequacy of physical overhead capital, effectiveness of financial institutions, rate of population growth, and improvements in human resources. Indicators of sectoral productivity in agriculture are level of modernization of agricultural techniques, improvements in agricultural productivity, and an index of the institutional structure of agriculture, which combines information on land tenure patterns and the size and viability of farming units. The influences on sectoral productivity in industry are represented by indicators of level of industrial modernization and change in degree of industrialization. Several variables summarize various aspects of the allocation of resources between sectors likely to influence economy-wide productivity: subsistence farming (the size of the traditional agricultural sector), an index of the intersectoral pattern of development (the extent of socioeconomic dualism), and the composition of exports (the structure of foreign trade). A population variable is included to suggest the influence on resource productivity of external economies associated with the size of the market. Finally, two direct measures of overall economy-wide resource productivity were introduced into the analysis—indicators of per capita GNP and of level of socioeconomic development—as well as the rate of growth of per capita GNP and a measure of broad rates of change in total productivity, which indicates the potential for economic development.[19] These economic measures were supplemented by a variable suggestive of the extent of income redistribution through taxation (level of effectiveness of the tax system) and a measure of country size and orientation of development strategy. Indicators of improvements in tax systems and financial institutions were also included.

Sociocultural influences likely to affect income distribution are represented by indicators of urbanization and of literacy as well as of the importance of the indigenous middle class and of social mobility (measured by a composite of educational opportunity, access to membership in the middle class, and racial and cultural barriers to mobility. Also included is a measure of cultural and ethnic homogeneity based on the proportion of the population speaking the predominant language as well as on the extent of ethnic and religious homogeneity.

The political indicators include measures descriptive both of political institutions and of characteristics of political leadership likely to influence the distribution of income. Indicators of the extent of political participation and the strength of the labor movement represent the importance of participant political institutions. Two variables represent selected aspects of colonial experience of possible relevance to the current type of government: a nominal indicator of type of colonial experience (British, French, or other) and a variable scoring countries by the number of years they have been self-governing. (Neither of these variables entered the analysis.) Finally, four measures summarize key characteristics of political leadership: the political strength of traditional elites, the political strength of the military, the leadership commitment to promoting economic development, and direct government economic activity.

The coverage of these independent variables is quite broad. They include most of the political, social, and economic institutional influences stressed in social science literature as important to the shape of income distribution. The coverage of conventional, purely economic variables, however, is noticeably incomplete. There are no measures, for example, of relative abundance or relative prices of capital and labor or of relative propensities to save by different classes. While these omissions were necessary because of inadequate data, we do not regard them as seriously hampering our investigation. Our main interest, after all, is in underlying economic and noneconomic institutional influences that are usually taken as given in economic analyses of income distribution. More serious is the lack of direct measures of the distribution of property. Another omission is any measure of variations in the incidence of such household characteristics as age, sex, occupation, and stage of participation in the labor force. It should be noted, however, that the broader the classes of income considered, the more likely it is that variations in the incidence of household characteristics will cancel out and the less likely it is that they will affect the results systematically.*

Validity of Data

In view of the crudeness of our independent variables, the substantial margin of error, and several sources of incompatibility in our income distribution data, the validity of our data for the present investigation needs to be considered.

A basic characteristic of a valid measure is that it "measures what it purports to measure."[20] Whether it does so or not can be established in two fundamentally different ways; one is a matter of definition† and the other (more relevant for the social sciences) is a matter of empirical connections. "Here," says Kaplan, "the validity of a measurement is a matter of the success with which the measures obtained in particular cases allow us to predict the measures that would be arrived at by other procedures and in other contexts."‡ Valid measurement also requires, of course, that a measure be relatively free of error in its several senses.

Several considerations suggest that our crude data are reasonably valid for the purpose of exploring broad interrelationships between income distribution and the various factors we investigate. With respect to our dependent variables, the consistency of the empirical connections obtained with alternative specifications of income distribution, together with the interpretability of the variation among subsets of results (see the section on statistical results below), suggests their validity for the present analysis.

---

* For example, the lowest quintile usually includes a high incidence of both one person households and large family households. It seems likely that a predominance of the latter will slightly bias the results, since data unadjusted for size of family tend to overstate the share of the lowest income group and understate the share of higher income groups.

† The meaning of a variable may be specified by the measurement procedure itself, as when "national product" is specified by the rules for estimating GNP. There is then no question that, for example, GNP measures "national product." This does not, however, validate the use of GNP to represent theoretical concepts of economic welfare or productive capacity.

‡ Abraham Kaplan, *The Conduct of Inquiry* (San Francisco, 1964), p. 199. To illustrate, the use of GNP as a measure of national productive capacity might be validated by the extent to which it can be used to predict other aspects of productive capacity such as constraints revealed by input-output studies or constraints on consumption revealed by budget studies.

As for our independent variables, earlier statistical studies indicate their relative insensitivity to reasonable alternative specifications of the concepts measured; in addition, the statistical interconnections obtained are interpretable and are broadly consistent with other knowledge and evidence.* Specific empirical associations between measures that are conceptually close yet were obtained by independent procedures also suggest that our methods are reasonably appropriate. For example, our indicator of socioeconomic dualism—close conceptually to extent of socioeconomic inequalities, and based on qualitative evidence—shows a close empirical connection to independent estimates of degree of income inequality (see the section on statistical results). Nevertheless it is evident that the empirical connections obtained and our limited experimentation with alternative specifications of indicators do not fully demonstrate that our data measure what they purport to measure. Extensive testing with alternative specifications using different measurement procedures and other bodies of data would be necessary to evaluate them fully.

Validity of measurement also requires reasonable freedom from error.[21] That is, a measure should be sufficiently reliable, or invariant under repeated measurement; sufficiently sensitive, or able to discriminate between different amounts of the property measured; and sufficiently accurate, or free of systematic error resulting from omitted influences presumed included, *for the purpose at hand.*

With respect to reliability, our resources have not permitted the kind of fieldwork necessary to establish invariance under repeated measurement. Nevertheless our procedures in the construction of the independent variables appear to assure a reasonable degree of reliability for our purpose.† We tried to obtain a variability under repeated measurement that was small enough so that variations

* For a more detailed discussion of the validity of our independent variables, see Chapter 1.

† As described in detail in our discussion of methodological considerations in Chapter 1, the application of the method of successive definition, together with the use of expert opinion to eliminate inconsistencies between preliminary operational definitions and actual observations, seems to have reduced variability to a scale not likely to alter the broad picture of interactions obtained in our statistical results.

in country rankings due to unreliability would be small relative to the broad systematic variations that provide the substance of our statistical results.

With respect to sensitivity, it is clear that the degree of discrimination provided by our income distribution data and by our independent variables is not great absolutely. It would not be sufficient, for example, for the use of much of our data as inputs to policy-planning models. Nevertheless the nature of our results suggests that the degree of discrimination is adequate for exploring the broad interactions we are interested in.* In order to test the impact on our results of the lack of sensitivity of our data, we made test runs replacing the income distribution variables with a set of scores computed by assigning countries to categories having arbitrary numbers that preserved the ordering of countries in the original data (except that partial ordering replaced full ordering). The results were identical for two of the analyses and substantially similar for the third. With respect to the independent variables, it should be stressed that our technique of analysis requires only ranking of observations. These data need not be as sensitive, therefore, as would be desirable with other statistical techniques.

With respect to accuracy, our independent variables do not seem to pose major problems of systematic error due to influences that are omitted though *presumed included.* With our income distribution data, the major possibility for systematic error seems to be a possible tendency to overstate the share of the lowest income groups and to understate that of the highest ones for those countries where data are for households rather than members of the population.†

---

* In selecting the number of categories for our qualitative indicators, we compromised between two desiderata: to obtain sufficient discrimination between our observations, and to obtain categories sufficiently broad so that judgment could be used to reliably classify countries for which point information was unavailable. The extent of discrimination in the income distribution data was dictated by the data that were available.

† While there may be biases in our data, *systematic* bias due to our use of expert opinion and qualitative evidence appears to be absent. We obtained marked and interpretable differences in simple correlations for subsamples

The major problems with our data are the interrelated ones of conceptualization and of the availability of primary data. That is, while the operational definitions do indicate reasonably well what is included and what is omitted from the measures, they suffer from the inadequacy of links between the measures themselves and the often vague and ill-defined social science concepts they are intended to represent. It is for this reason, for example, that we have chosen a battery of income distribution variables to measure income inequality; any one taken alone cannot be presumed to represent adequately the rather imprecise multidimensional concept of income inequality.

Thus, in summary, the variables included in our study provide rough measures of an unusually wide range of potential influences on the distribution of income. While very crude, these measures appear to provide reasonably valid country rankings for exploratory investigations into the broad interrelationships involved in variations in the distribution of income in underdeveloped nations.

THE STATISTICAL RESULTS

Each analysis for the three dependent variables presented here is discussed as follows. First, a diagram of the successive splits obtained by the analysis shows, for each split, (a) the independent variable that "best" splits the sample at that step, (b) the size of the subgroups obtained, (c) the dependent variable means for each of the resultant subgroups, and (d) the percentage of the dependent variable variance "explained" by the differences between subgroup means and parent sample mean. Notes to the diagrams list the "next best" independent variables (that are significant at the 1 percent level), with the percentages of dependent variable variance they account for. Summaries follow of the characteristics (as of about 1961) of the countries in the different subgroups obtained in each analysis (see pp. 164, 168, and 174–75).

representing different levels of development (subsamples were constructed after data preparation was complete); to maintain that there is systematic bias in expert opinions requires the assumption that such bias varies systematically with level of development—a somewhat implausible contention.

The summaries of group characteristics provide typologies that are designed to facilitate the interpretation of the results. It should be stressed that it is these average characteristics of the groups that are important to the analysis rather than individual country comparisons across groups. This is because our statistical results portray average relationships between the dependent variable and those independent variables that best "explain" it empirically. Since the groupings do not explain the full variance of the dependent variable, it is to be expected that there will be divergences between actual country situations and assignments of countries to groups that are determined on the basis of average relationships for the sample as a whole.

In interpreting our results, we apply theoretical reasoning, together with historical and comparative evidence, to gain semiquantitative insights into dynamic interactions between the shape of the income distribution and a wide range of socioeconomic and political characteristics summarized by our data. The pitfalls in using statistical relationships to shed light on causal forces are well known: empirical associations may represent causality in either direction or may result from common forces; an included variable may represent closely related influences not explicitly measured by it, and so forth. In addition, cross-sectional data typically violate the assumption of statistical models that, given correctly specified relationships, the behavior patterns of cross-sectional units are homogeneous except for random diversity and the systematic differences in objective opportunities expressed in the included variables. Nor would time series data give a better view of underlying dynamic relationships, for they violate (again, given correctly specified relationships) the assumption required by statistical models that behavior patterns over time are unchanging except for random variations. Given the respective biases of cross-sectional and time series approaches, it is clearly desirable to make complementary use of both. It is obvious that any firm validation of our findings will require testing our conclusions against other bodies of cross-sectional data and against time series studies of individual countries having different characteristics.

Analysis of Share of Income Accruing to
Poorest 60 Percent of the Population

On the average, over the entire set of 43 countries, the poorest 60 percent of the population receives 26 percent of total income. This is a little over 40 percent of the share they would receive were income evenly distributed throughout the economy. The standard deviation of their income share is 7 percent; the range is from 2 percent (Libya) to 38 percent (Israel).

The results summarized in Figure 1 show that the allocation of income to the poorest 60 percent of the population is "explained," broadly speaking, by the extent of socioeconomic dualism, the level of social and economic modernization, and the expansion of secondary and higher level education. The poorest 60 percent received a relatively large share of total income—on the average, between 30 and 34 percent—under two quite different sets of circumstances: pervasive underdevelopment marked by the predominance of small-scale or communal subsistence agriculture (group 7), and substantial development associated with major efforts to improve human resources (group 9). Their income share was smallest where a sharply dualistic development process had been initiated by well-entrenched expatriate or military elites ideologically oriented to receive most of the benefits of economic development (group 4). The remaining subgroups of countries, in which the income share of the poorest 60 percent ranged from 23 to 26 percent, include both fairly well-developed, moderately dualistic countries (group 8) and sharply dualistic countries that had less dynamic modern sectors and were not under the political control of tradition-oriented expatriate elites (group 5). (See p. 164 for summaries of the common characteristics of the countries in each of these subgroups as of about 1961.*)

In general, the results do not support the hypothesis that economic growth raises the share of income of the poorest segments of the population. On the contrary, the contrast between the

* The source for these and subsequent summaries is chap. 2 of Irma Adelman and Cynthia Taft Morris, *Society, Politics, and Economic Development* (rev. ed.; Baltimore, 1971).

sharply dualistic economies in groups 4 and 5 suggests that economic dynamism at low levels of development worked to the relative disadvantage of lower income groups. In the countries in group 4, per capita money incomes significantly higher than those in group 5 were associated with an income share of only 17 percent to the poorest 60 percent. Thus rising money incomes per capita originating in the rapid growth of narrow modern sectors benefited small, usually expatriate, elites. Inequality in both groups of sharply dualistic economies was in turn much greater than in the low-income, less dualistic countries in group 7, in which economic growth, even narrowly based, had not yet been effectively initiated during the period studied here. As for countries at higher levels of development (group 6), the significant overlap in levels of socioeconomic development between subgroups 8 and 9 suggests that even here economic growth did not necessarily result in benefits to the very poor. Our results suggest rather that this group benefited only when there were also broad-based efforts to improve the economy's human resource base.

Analysis of Share of Income Accruing to
Wealthiest 5 Percent of the Population

In our sample the average share of income received by the top 5 percent of the population is 30 percent—six times as large as their share would be with an even distribution pattern. The standard deviation of this share is quite large, 9 percent. The lowest share is 15 percent, in Japan; the highest is 48 percent, in Peru.

The results presented in Figure 2 indicate that the extent of natural resource abundance and the extent of direct government economic activity account statistically for a substantial part of the variations among countries in the share of income received by the wealthiest 5 percent of the population. The extreme concentration of income, however, is accounted for by the political and economic dominance of expatriate and other ethnically and culturally distinct subgroups in the population.

The average share of the top 5 percent in resource-rich countries (group 3) is almost 50 percent greater than in less well-endowed countries (group 2). Within both resource-rich and re-

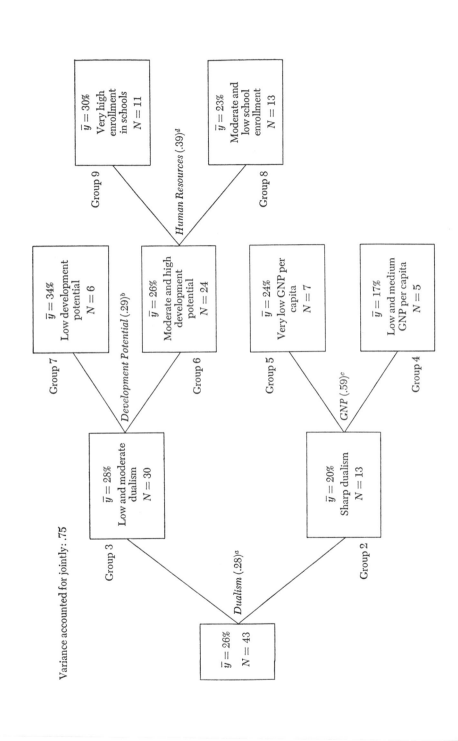

Variance accounted for jointly: .75

Group 9
$\bar{y} = 30\%$
Very high enrollment in schools
$N = 11$

Group 8
$\bar{y} = 23\%$
Moderate and low school enrollment
$N = 13$

Human Resources (.39)[a]

Group 7
$\bar{y} = 34\%$
Low development potential
$N = 6$

Group 6
$\bar{y} = 26\%$
Moderate and high development potential
$N = 24$

Development Potential (.29)[b]

Group 5
$\bar{y} = 24\%$
Very low GNP per capita
$N = 7$

Group 4
$\bar{y} = 17\%$
Low and medium GNP per capita
$N = 5$

GNP (.59)[c]

Group 3
$\bar{y} = 28\%$
Low and moderate dualism
$N = 30$

Group 2
$\bar{y} = 20\%$
Sharp dualism
$N = 13$

Dualism (.28)[a]

$\bar{y} = 26\%$
$N = 43$

Figure 1. Analysis of share of income of the poorest 60 percent of the population.

Notes to Figure 1

GROUP MEMBERS. *Group 5*, Malagasy Morocco, Sierra Leone, Sudan, Tanzania, Tunisia, Zambia. *Group 4*, Gabon, Iraq, Peru, Senegal, South Africa. *Group 7*, Burma, Chad, Dahomey, Ecuador, Niger, Surinam. *Group 8*, Bolivia, Brazil, Ceylon, Colombia, El Salvador, Ivory Coast, Jamaica, Lebanon, Mexico, Nigeria, Pakistan, Rhodesia, Trinidad. *Group 9*, Argentina, Chile, Costa Rica, Greece, India, Israel, Japan, Panama, Philippines, Taiwan, Venezuela.

a The other candidate variables that distinguish well among all 43 countries are the abundance of natural resources (23%), the extent of direct government economic activity (20%), and the political strength of the traditional elite (18%). A higher average share to the lowest 60% is associated with more abun-dance of natural resources, less strength of the traditional elite, and a larger role for the government.

b The next most important candidate variables at this step indicate that a higher average share to the poorest 60% is associated with less ethnic homogeneity (28%), lower scores on the character of agricultural organization (27%), less modernization of industry (23%), less political strength of labor unions (21%), and lower per capita GNP (21%).

c There are no significant alternative candidates at this step. Libya is omitted at this step by reason of a splinter split.

d The other important variable at this step is the structure of foreign trade (35%). The more exports are diversified, the higher the share of the lowest 60% of the population.

A summary of the characteristics of groups 2–9 in about 1961 appears on the next two pages.

Annotation for Figure 1 (*continued*)

Summary of Characteristics (About 1961) of Subgroups in Analysis of Share of Income of the Poorest 60 Percent of the Population

Group 2 ($\bar{y} = 20\%$): 13 sharply dualistic countries
Rich in natural resources (except Senegal and Sudan)
Sharp sectoral or geographic cleavage between an important exchange sector and a predominant, traditional, nonmonetized agricultural sector
Handicraft production more important than modern techniques in the manufacture of consumer goods (except South Africa)
School enrollment ratios less than 40%
Literacy rates less than 35% (except Peru and South Africa)

Group 4 ($\bar{y} = 17\%$): 5 sharply dualistic countries with per capita GNP in 1961 ranging from $175 to $200 (except South Africa, $427)
Income share of upper 20% of population ranging from 64% to 71% (except South Africa, 57%)
Tradition-oriented elites politically strong (except Gabon and Iraq)
At best, moderate development potential (except South Africa)
At best, moderate factor scores on socioeconomic development

Group 5 ($\bar{y} = 24\%$): 7 sharply dualistic countries with per capita GNP in 1961 below $171
Income share of upper 20% of population ranging from 48% to 65%
Tradition-oriented elites *not* politically strong (except Morocco)
Low development potential and low factor scores on socioeconomic development (except Tunisia)

Group 3 ($\bar{y} = 28\%$): 30 countries at most moderately dualistic (except Bolivia and Burma)
Includes two types of countries: those that were not dualistic because there was almost no modern sector, and those that, despite some cleavage between traditional and modern sectors, were characterized by significant interaction between the two

Group 6 ($\bar{y} = 26\%$): 24 moderately dualistic countries (except Bolivia) with moderate or high development potential

Group 8 ($\bar{y} = 23\%$): 13 countries with low or moderate rates of improvement in human resources
Factor scores on the middle two quartiles for the full sample (except Lebanon and Trinidad in upper quartile and Nigeria and Ivory Coast in lower quartile)
Literacy rates less than 55% (except Trinidad, Jamaica, Colombia, and Ceylon)
Per capita GNP under $340 in 1961 (except Trinidad, Lebanon, and Jamaica)

Group 9 ($\bar{y} = 30\%$): 11 countries with *exceptionally* high rates of improvement in human resources
Factor scores on socioeconomic development in the upper third for the full sample (except India and the Philippines)
Literacy rates over 55% (except India and Taiwan)
Per capita GNP over $340 in 1961 (except India, the Philippines, and Taiwan)

(*continued at bottom of next page*)

source-poor countries, the best differentiator for degrees of income concentration is the extent of the direct economic role of the government: the average share of the upper 5 percent is significantly smaller in countries with large public sectors and important government net investments (groups 8 and 6) than in predominantly private enterprise economies (groups 9 and 7). The wealthiest 5 percent receives the smallest share for the entire sample in countries with relatively poor resource endowments in which the government economic role is very important (group 8).

Extreme income concentration at the top is found only in underdeveloped countries with an abundance of natural resources. Group 7, with the highest average share to the wealthiest 5 percent, has rather special characteristics. It combines low-level African countries with countries at the Latin American level of development. The major common characteristic of the group other than resource abundance and income inequality was that the direct economic role of the government was not of major importance.

The African countries in group 7, all in the lowest quartile on socioeconomic development, had either traditional elites that were politically influential or expatriate domination of the middle class, and political participation was very restricted. Their economies were characterized by sharply dualistic growth of a small modern sector and a large relatively backward subsistence agricultural sector. The special traits of these countries suggest that, historically, colonial powers have sought the firmest entrenchment in those poor countries best endowed with natural resources and, further, that the more firmly entrenched the expatriate financial, commercial, and technical elites, the greater the concentration of income

---

Annotation for Figure 1 (*continued*)

Group 7 ($\bar{y} = 34\%$): 6 little or moderately dualistic countries (except Burma) with low development potential

Predominance of either small subsistence farms in which output marketing was marginally important or communally owned and operated lands

Limited industrial sectors in which a narrow range of goods was produced in small factories and rare large-scale production was foreign-financed and -managed

Manufactured commodities less than 10% of exports; marked concentration of exports with more than 75% of exports from the four leading commodities

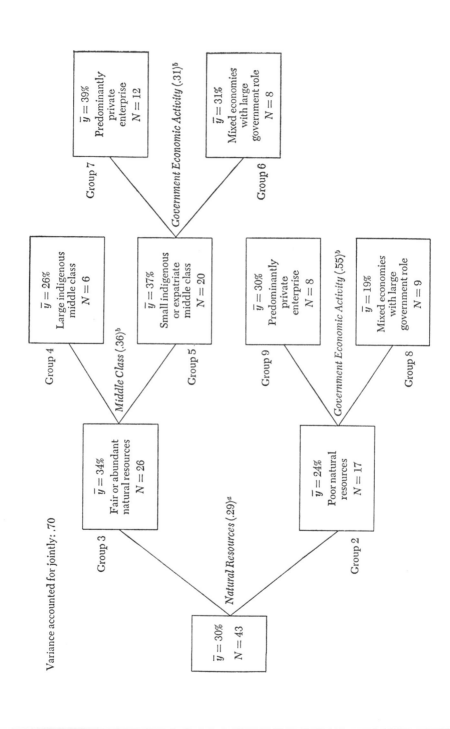

Variance accounted for jointly: .70

Group 7
$\bar{y} = 39\%$
Predominantly
private
enterprise
$N = 12$

Government Economic Activity (.31)[b]

Group 6
$\bar{y} = 31\%$
Mixed economies
with large
government role
$N = 8$

Group 4
$\bar{y} = 26\%$
Large indigenous
middle class
$N = 6$

Middle Class (.36)[b]

Group 5
$\bar{y} = 37\%$
Small indigenous
or expatriate
middle class
$N = 20$

Group 3
$\bar{y} = 34\%$
Fair or abundant
natural resources
$N = 26$

Natural Resources (.29)[a]

$\bar{y} = 30\%$
$N = 43$

Group 9
$\bar{y} = 30\%$
Predominantly
private
enterprise
$N = 8$

Government Economic Activity (.55)[b]

Group 8
$\bar{y} = 19\%$
Mixed economies
with large
government role
$N = 9$

Group 2
$\bar{y} = 24\%$
Poor natural
resources
$N = 17$

Figure 2. Analysis of share of income of the wealthiest 5 percent of the population.

Notes to Figure 2

GROUP MEMBERS. *Group 8*, Ceylon, Chad, India, Israel, Japan, Niger, Pakistan, Sudan, Taiwan. *Group 9*, Dahomey, El Salvador, Ivory Coast, Jamaica, Lebanon, Philippines, Senegal, Surinam. *Group 7*, Brazil, Colombia, Gabon, Iraq, Libya, Malagasy, Nigeria, Panama, Peru, Sierra Leone, Tanzania, Zambia. *Group 6*, Burma, Bolivia, Costa Rica, Ecuador, Morocco, Tunisia, Rhodesia, South Africa. *Group 4*, Argentina, Chile, Greece, Mexico, Trinidad, Venezuela.

^a The two most important alternative candidate variables show that a lower share of income of the top families is associated with greater direct government participation in eco-nomic activity (28%) and broader popular participation in political processes (20%). The remaining significant variables indicate that less concentration of income at the top is associated with more political strength of the labor movement (17%), a less powerful traditional elite (17%), higher per capita GNP (16%), and a higher rate of improvement of human resources (16%). Less dualism of the types characteristic of both very high and very low levels of development is associated with a lower share of income to the top 5% (16%). ^b There are no significant alternative variables at this split.

A summary of the characteristics of groups 2–9 in about 1961 appears on the next two pages.

Annotation for Figure 2 (*continued*)
*Summary of Characteristics (About 1961) of Subgroups in Analysis
of Share of Income of the Wealthiest 5 Percent of the Population*

Group 2 ($\bar{y}$ = 24%): 17 countries not well endowed with natural resources
Having at best either fairly abundant agricultural resources (one acre or more of agricultural land per capita) with no significant mineral resources, or limited agricultural resources (less than one acre of agricultural land per capita) with some but not abundant mineral resources
Spanning the entire range of levels of socioeconomic development and of development policies covered by the sample

Group 8 ($\bar{y}$ = 19%): 9 countries with mixed government–private enterprise economies
Having economies in which the government's direct role was of major importance, as indicated by substantial government investment in infrastructure, health, and education, and by the shares of net investment undertaken by the government, which are often greater than the share of private industry
Spanning all levels of development and full range of development policies

Group 9 ($\bar{y}$ = 30%): 8 countries with predominantly private enterprise economies
Having small public sectors and relatively small contributions of government to net investment (except Senegal, in which the direct role of government was moderately important)
Spanning all levels of development and full range of development policies

Group 3 ($\bar{y}$ = 34%): 26 countries at least fairly well endowed with natural resources
Rich in agricultural resources as well as in either fuel or nonfuel resources (or both)
Spanning the entire range of levels of socioeconomic development and of development policies covered by the sample

Group 4 ($\bar{y}$ = 26%): 6 countries at least fairly well endowed with natural resources, with large indigenous middle classes
In upper quartile on factor scores on socioeconomic development
All but Trinidad in top category on political participation and efforts to improve human resources
In top category on social mobility
With per capita GNP greater than $312 in 1961

Group 5 ($\bar{y}$ = 37%): 20 countries at least fairly well endowed with natural resources, small indigenous or expatriate middle classes
Spanning the lowest three quartiles on factor scores on socioeconomic development
None except Costa Rica and Colombia scoring in top two categories on political participation
None except South Africa and Brazil in the highest group of discriminant scores on development potential

Group 6 ($\bar{y}$ = 31%): 8 countries with small indigenous or expatriate middle classes where the direct economic role of the government was of major importance

(*continued at bottom of next page*)

in the hands of the top 5 percent. Our results are thus consistent with the view of economic backwardness under colonialism held by such political economists as Paul A. Baran, according to which very uneven income distribution is a typical outcome of a narrowly based growth process where natural resources are exploited for the primary benefit of a small class of wealthy, usually expatriate, businessmen.[22]

The remaining countries in group 7 were in the middle third of the full sample of socioeconomic development. In most of them during the period studied, traditional elites were politically influential and major groups in the population were effectively barred from the political process. In addition, their agricultural sectors were characterized by a combination of subsistence agriculture and absentee-owned commercial plantations. These characteristics are also consistent with Baran's thesis that the concentration of control over resources in the hands of a coalition of feudal-type landowners and politically entrenched business elites is a major factor contributing to income concentration at the top.

Concentration was least in those resource-abundant nations at relatively high levels of development where broad-based social and economic advances and intensive efforts to improve human resources were accompanied by the expansion of political participation to include all major groups in the population. Six countries

---

Annotation for Figure 2 (*continued*)
> With important public sectors and large shares of government in net investment
> Spanning the middle two quartiles on factor scores on socioeconomic development

Group 7 ($\bar{y} = 39\%$): 12 countries with small indigenous or expatriate middle classes where the direct economic role of the government was at most moderately important
> In most, the direct economic role of the government not important; in the remainder only moderately important
> In all except Colombia political participation very restricted
> In all except Iraq either the traditional elite influential politically or the middle class dominated by expatriates
> The 7 African countries characterized by sharp dualism (except Nigeria); the remaining countries having agricultural sectors marked by a combination of subsistence and absentee-owner commercial plantation agriculture (except Panama)

with these characteristics split off from the main concentration of the analysis into group 4 by reason of their large indigenous middle classes. In the remaining resource-abundant countries spanning the full range of development levels, the share of the top 5 percent varies systematically with the importance of the government sector. Where the government sector was of major importance, their share was 31 percent compared with 39 percent for the group having greatest concentration. This mild average degree of redistribution appears to be the best that can be achieved without either successful expansion of political participation or broad-based socioeconomic development.

The relationship suggested by our results between economic growth and the income share of the top income group is non-linear. The only way typically available for very low income countries to reduce income concentration at the top appears to be direct economic action on the part of the government. Where either the political influence of traditional elites or the economic dominance of an expatriate middle class prevents expansion of the government economic role, extreme income concentration usually results. For moderately developed countries, broad-based economic growth provides a way to achieve redistribution only where accompanied by social and educational development as well as substantial broadening of political participation. Where these conditions are not met, the extent of a country's resource endowment and the size of the government role, rather than economic growth per se, are the primary forces for redistribution away from the top.

Analysis of Share of Income Accruing to
Middle 20 Percent of the Population

The average share of income accruing to the middle 20 percent of the population in our sample (i.e. the two deciles clustered around the median income) is 12 percent, with a standard deviation of 3 percent. The share ranges from 1 percent for Libya to 17 percent for Israel.* In no country in the sample do middle-

---

* The next highest figures are, respectively, 7 percent for Gabon and 15.8 percent for Japan.

income families get as much as they would with a uniform income distribution.

The portion of income allocated to the middle groups in the income distribution, according to Figure 3, is the only share that appears to vary systematically with level of development. The countries with the highest average share to the middle quintile (groups 6 and 8) are among the more developed in the sample socially and economically, while countries in the group with the smallest average share (group 3) are among the least developed. However, the relationship is nonlinear, since more rapid short-term economic change in the middle range of countries is associated with a smaller share to the middle quintile (group 9) than that received by somewhat lower-level countries undergoing less rapid economic change (group 10).

The primary influence differentiating among countries with respect to the income share of the middle quintile is the extent of socioeconomic dualism.* Thirteen countries with sharp cleavages between a small exchange sector and a large subsistence sector (group 2) had an average share for the middle group of only 9 percent. The remaining countries with an average share of 13 percent (group 1) include those that were less dualistic because of the wider spread of economic growth achieved with higher development levels and those that were less dualistic by reason of rela-

---

* In earlier runs with provisional income-distribution data, the primary variable was the importance of the indigenous middle class—an important next best candidate variable in the present analysis. Not unexpectedly, the results for the middle 20 percent of the population proved more sensitive to final data revisions than did those for the poorest 60 percent or the richest 5 percent (the latter results were substantially unchanged). The reasons are that the range of values is narrower and the cumulation of estimating errors usually greater. Nevertheless, neither the general import of the middle quintile results nor the full set of significant variables has been greatly affected by income data revisions. But the particular primary variables at successive splits are different.

The only independent variable to be revised was the structure of foreign trade. This variable was redefined to give greater differentiation among countries at the upper end of the spectrum. It is undoubtedly for this reason that it gains importance in the present analysis.

For the earlier results see Irma Adelman and Cynthia Taft Morris, "An Anatomy of Income Distribution in Developing Nations," *Development Digest*, 9 (1971): 24–37.

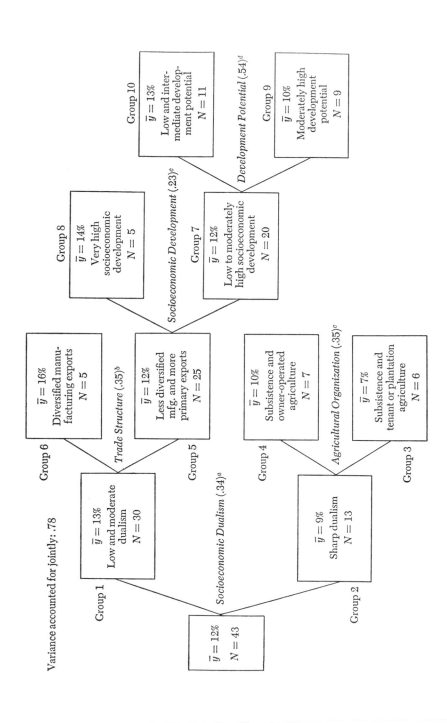

Variance accounted for jointly: .78

Group 1
$\bar{y} = 13\%$
Low and moderate dualism
$N = 30$

Socioeconomic Dualism (.34)[a]

Group 6
$\bar{y} = 16\%$
Diversified manufacturing exports
$N = 5$

Trade Structure (.35)[b]

Group 5
$\bar{y} = 12\%$
Less diversified mfg. and more primary exports
$N = 25$

Group 8
$\bar{y} = 14\%$
Very high socioeconomic development
$N = 5$

Socioeconomic Development (.23)[c]

Group 7
$\bar{y} = 12\%$
Low to moderately high socioeconomic development
$N = 20$

Group 10
$\bar{y} = 13\%$
Low and intermediate development potential
$N = 11$

Development Potential (.54)[d]

Group 9
$\bar{y} = 10\%$
Moderately high development potential
$N = 9$

$\bar{y} = 12\%$
$N = 43$

Group 2
$\bar{y} = 9\%$
Sharp dualism
$N = 13$

Agricultural Organization (.35)[c]

Group 4
$\bar{y} = 10\%$
Subsistence and owner-operated agriculture
$N = 7$

Group 3
$\bar{y} = 7\%$
Subsistence and tenant or plantation agriculture
$N = 6$

Figure 3. Analysis of share of income of middle-income groups (40–60 percent).

Notes to Figure 3

GROUP MEMBERS. *Group 3,* Gabon, Iraq, Libya, Malagasy, Morocco, Tanzania. *Group 4,* Peru, Senegal, Sierra Leone, South Africa, Sudan, Tunisia, Zambia. *Group 6,* India, Israel, Japan, Pakistan, Taiwan. *Group 8,* Argentina, Chile, Greece, Lebanon, Venezuela. *Group 9,* Brazil, Colombia, Costa Rica, Jamaica, Mexico, Nigeria, Philippines, Rhodesia, Trinidad and Tobago. *Group 10,* Bolivia, Burma, Ceylon, Chad, Dahomey, Ecuador, El Salvador, Ivory Coast, Niger, Panama, Surinam.

a Other candidate variables of importance indicate that a higher share of income for the middle quintile is associated with higher development potential (26% of the variance), a higher rate of improvement in human resources (25%), a larger indigenous middle class (24%), a greater extent of political participation (21%), a higher degree of urbanization (20%), greater strength of the labor movement (20%), a

higher level of modernization of industry (19%), and a higher literacy rate (17%).

b The next best candidate variables indicate that the middle sector receives a larger relative income share when the rate of improvement in human resources is higher (26%), and when the level of socioeconomic development is higher (23%).

c There are no significant alternative candidate variables at this step.

d The next most important candidate variables are the level of development of financial institutions (34%) and the extent of leadership commitment to economic development (31%). The share of income of the middle 20% of the population is higher when the level of development of financial institutions is *lower* and leadership commitment to economic development is *less.*

A summary of the characteristics of groups 1–10 in about 1961 appears on the next two pages.

Annotation for Figure 3 (*continued*)

Summary of Characteristics (About 1961) of Subgroups in Analysis of Share of Middle 20 Percent of the Population

Group 1 ($\bar{y} = 13\%$): 30 countries at most moderately dualistic (except Bolivia and Burma)

> Including two types of countries: those not dualistic because of almost no modern sector, and those (despite some cleavage between traditional and modern sectors) with significant interaction between the two

Group 6 ($\bar{y} = 16\%$): 5 countries no more than moderately dualistic, with trade structures marked by a share of manufactured goods in total exports of more than 20% and significant diversification of exports

> With sparse natural resources; none with an abundance of minerals—at most, with some fuel or some nonfuel resources (but not both)

> Giving the government an important direct economic role, as indicated by large public sectors and important shares of government in net investment

> All except Taiwan with leadership showing sustained and reasonably effective commitment to promoting economic development during the period 1957–62

> Demonstrating marked improvement in effectiveness of financial institutions during the period 1950–63

> All with significant indigenous middle classes, although those being fairly small in India and Pakistan

Group 5 ($\bar{y} = 12\%$): 25 countries no more than moderately dualistic (except Bolivia and Burma), with trade structures in most instances marked by a share of manufactured goods in total exports of less than 10% and at most moderate diversification of exports

> In all but five, the share of manufactured goods in total exports being less than 10%; in the majority, over 75% of exports coming from the four leading commodities

> Spanning the full range of levels of socioeconomic development and of short-term economic performance

Group 8 ($\bar{y} = 14\%$): 5 nondualistic countries, having trade structures not marked by significant diversification of exports, at very high levels of socioeconomic development for low-income nations

> With factor scores on socioeconomic development in the upper quartile for the full sample

> Ranking in the highest category on importance of the indigenous middle class

> All but Lebanon ranking in the highest category on rate of improvement of human resources, modernization of industry, and political participation, and all but Chile in the highest category on level of effectiveness of financial institutions

Group 7 ($\bar{y} = 12\%$): 20 countries at most moderately dualistic (except Burma and Bolivia) and characterized by neither significant diversification of exports nor very high levels of socioeconomic development

> All but three (Jamaica, Trinidad, and Panama) having factor scores on socioeconomic development in the lower three quartiles for the full sample

Annotation for Figure 3 (*continued*)
Spanning the full range of scores on most measures of short-term economic performance

Group 9 ($\bar{y} = 10\%$): 9 at most moderately dualistic countries (characterized by neither significant diversification of exports nor very high levels of socioeconomic development) with fairly high development potential
Discriminant scores on development potential in the upper half for the full sample
All but Jamaica and the Philippines having fairly abundant natural resources
All except Nigeria having industrial sectors producing at least a fair variety of consumer and/or export goods by means of power-driven factory production methods
Local financial institutions sufficiently developed to attract at least a small and significant volume of indigenous savings
6 out of 9 having average annual rates of growth of per capita GNP of over 2% during the period 1950/51–1963/64; the remainder having rates of growth of between 1% and 2%

Group 10 ($\bar{y} = 13\%$): 11 moderately dualistic countries (except Bolivia and Burma), characterized by neither significant diversification of exports nor very high levels of socioeconomic development, with low and intermediate development potential
6 out of 11 with relatively sparse natural resources
Industrial sectors with handicraft industry more important in the production of domestic consumer goods than in modern methods, and with the majority of modern production units foreign-managed and foreign-financed
Local financial institutions attracting a negligible volume of private savings
All except Burma and Ecuador having average annual rates of growth of per capita GNP of less than 2% for the period 1950/51–1963/64; 6 out of 11 having rates of growth of less than 1%

Group 2 ($\bar{y} = 9\%$): 13 sharply dualistic countries
Rich in natural resources (except Senegal and Sudan)
Characterized by sharp sectoral or geographic cleavage between an important exchange sector and a predominant, traditional, nonmonetized agricultural sector
Handicraft production more important than modern techniques in the manufacture of consumer goods (except South Africa)
School enrollment ratios less than 40%
Literacy rates less than 35% (except Peru and South Africa)

Group 3 ($\bar{y} = 7\%$): 6 sharply dualistic countries, with a predominance of subsistence agriculture combined with a small commercialized agricultural sector dominated by tenantry, plantation agriculture, or absentee landownership

Group 4 ($\bar{y} = 10\%$): 7 sharply dualistic countries with a predominance of subsistence agriculture combined with a small commercialized agricultural sector characterized by owner-operated farms (except Peru, with a large commercial sector dominated by plantation agriculture)

tive stagnation at low levels of development. The importance of this split is not surprising, since rapid dualistic growth of a narrow modern enclave in countries at low levels of development typically benefited a small expatriate group or a culturally distinct indigenous oligarchy. Furthermore, the carryover of economic growth to the remainder of the economy was usually so restricted that the middle 20 percent of the population counted among the agricultural poor.

Given the narrow spread of economic change in sharply dualistic countries, it is not surprising that the variable best accounting for variations among them in the income share of the middle quintile is the nature of institutional arrangements in agriculture. Specifically, the share of the middle-income group is heavily influenced by the character of commercialized agriculture. A larger share went to the middle quintile in countries where small-scale owner-operated cash-cropping prevailed in the small commercialized sector (group 4). The smallest average share for the entire sample went to those dualistic countries where tenant farming, plantation agriculture, or absentee landownership predominated (group 3).

The influences differentiating best among countries that are at most moderately dualistic are the structure of foreign trade, the level of socioeconomic development, and potential for short-term economic performance. The first two of these splits suggest that two rather different paths of change tend to benefit the middle-income groups in countries that are moderately developed for low-income nations, neither possible where the middle class is dominated by expatriates. One path is represented by the countries in group 6. These countries had rather sparse natural resources and a diversified trade structure based on the export of manufactured goods; they ranked high on the direct economic role of the government, improvements in financial institutions, and leadership commitment to economic development. These associations suggest that in countries at this level where natural resources are not abundant, the diversification of trade structure supported by an active direct role of the government and the growth of financial institutions provides an effective path for increasing the income share of the middle sector. The alternative path available to countries with more generous resource endowments involves broad-based social and economic development simultaneously with quite widespread political participation. This path is represented by the countries in group 8 that rank very high for low-income nations on socioeconomic development, political participation, and efforts to improve human resources.

In interpreting the final split for moderately dualistic countries, it is important to bear in mind that since the countries in group 7 span the lower three quartiles on socioeconomic development, most of their "middle class" falls in the upper, *not* the middle, 20 percent of the population. These countries have not selected either trade diversification supported by government policy or exceptional efforts to improve human resources as their development strategies. The variable accounting best for differences among them in the middle-income share is their development potential (measured by past advances along a broad front), with an *inverse* relationship between the middle income share and development potential. The average share is lower in the group with greater development potential and a higher level of socioeconomic development (group 9). Furthermore, the consistently higher levels of industrial and financial development and the higher rates of economic change in this group suggest strongly that at this level a development strategy stressing even quite broad-based economic change does not, as a rule, improve the relative position of the middle 20 percent of the population unless accompanied by an intensive effort to improve human resources. Rather, in these countries the usual beneficiaries of economic growth appear to have been the upper 20 percent of the income spectrum. This generalization is supported by the fact that the average income of the top 20 percent for this group is 61 percent, compared with 51 percent for the lower-level group with a higher share for the middle quintile (group 10).

ECONOMIC DEVELOPMENT AND THE
DISTRIBUTION OF INCOME

The three cross-sectional analyses of income distribution discussed here suggest a group of multifaceted and highly nonlinear
interactions over time between the dynamic process of economic
development and changes in the distribution of income. Our discussion below depicts the typical path of an underdeveloped country undergoing change that is suggested by our analyses. It is
based on study of the average characteristics of the different country groupings obtained in our results. Individual countries will of
course diverge from this typical path. Our discussion involves a
dynamic interpretation of cross-sectional results. As noted above,
there is no *statistical* justification for interpreting a cross-section
as representative of changes over time. We therefore apply theory
and historical evidence in order to derive the generalizations that
follow. These generalizations should be viewed as a set of hypotheses regarding the dynamics of economic development and income
distribution.

When economic growth begins in a subsistence agrarian economy through the expansion of a narrow modern sector, inequality
in the distribution of income typically increases greatly, particularly where expatriate exploitation of rich natural resources provides the motivating force for growth. The income share of the
poorest 60 percent declines significantly, as does that of the middle
20 percent,* and the income share of the top 5 percent increases
strikingly.

The gains of the top 5 percent are particularly great in very
low income countries where a sharply dualistic structure is associated with political and economic domination by traditional or
expatriate elites. Once countries move successfully beyond the
stage of sharply dualistic growth, further development as such
generates no systematic advantage or disadvantage for the top 5

---

* There is obviously an overlap between the income share of the poorest
60 percent and that of the middle 20 percent. The former measure is of interest when one is concerned with the position of the poorer "majority" of

percent until they reach the very highest level for underdeveloped countries, when broad-based social and economic advances operate to their disadvantage. Instead, their share increases with greater natural resources available for exploitation and decreases with a larger government role in the economic sphere.

As developing nations become less dualistic, the middle-income group is the primary beneficiary under two possible development strategies available to countries that are at least moderately developed. Widely based social and economic advances, combined with consistent efforts to improve human resources and expand political participation and facilitated by a reasonable abundance of natural resources, typically favor the middle sector. Where resources are sparse, the middle sector may nevertheless benefit through the development of a diversified manufacturing export sector supported by an active government economic role and expanding financial institutions. In contrast, when neither of these strategies is followed but rapid and quite widespread economic growth under moderate dualism nevertheless takes place, the relative position of the middle quintile worsens, with the benefits of economic change going rather to the upper 20 percent of the population.*

The position of the poorest 60 percent typically worsens, both relatively and absolutely, when an initial spurt of narrowly based dualistic growth is imposed on an agrarian subsistence economy. Our study suggests that, in an average country going through the earliest phases of economic development, it takes at least a generation for the poorest 60 percent to recover the loss in absolute income associated with the typical spurt in growth. This hypothesis is strongly suggested by a study of Figure 1, analysis for the poorest 60 percent of the population. In the relatively less dualistic subsistence economies of group 7, an average growth rate of per

---

the population. The latter is of most interest to those concerned with the middle groups, which are assumed by political and economic historians to play key roles in national development.

* Our hypotheses about changes in relative income shares are consistent with cross-section regressions of various income shares on per capita GDP. See Appendix C.

capita GNP in the neighborhood of zero percent is associated with an average share to the poorest 60 percent of the population of 34 percent. In the more sharply dualistic economies of group 2, an average growth rate of per capita GNP of about 3 percent is associated with an average income share to the poorest 60 percent of 20 percent. If we hypothesize that the typical path of change is represented by a movement from group 7 to group 2 and assume that the income share of the poorest 60 percent drops from 34 percent to 20 percent, it follows that almost a generation would be needed for the poorest 60 percent in a country with a hypothesized increase in growth rate of 3 percentage points to recover the absolute loss associated with a decline in income share of 14 percentage points.*

Even when growth changes from the sharply dualistic form to one that is more broadly based, the middle sector usually benefits and the poorest 40 percent typically continues to lose both absolutely and relatively. To predict by how much the income position of the poor worsens with given increases in economic growth rates requires assumptions about the nature and the time path of development of a typical country in this transitional phase of economic growth. The most likely transitional path appears to be represented by a move from the less extreme sharply dualistic African countries of group 5 to the moderately dualistic intermediate level countries of group 8 in the analysis for the poorest 60 percent of the population. This move implies a drop of between 2 and 3 percentage points in the share of the poorest 40 percent associated, on the average, with an increment in average per capita economic growth rates of less than 1 percentage point. These comparisons suggest that a period of close to two generations would be required

---

* As stressed above (p. 159), it is the average characteristics of groups that are important for interpreting analyses of hierarchical interactions. Since the inclusion of Ecuador and Surinam in group 7 appeared to us somewhat anomalous, we tested two alternative bases for making the calculations in the text. First, we omitted Ecuador and Surinam. Second, we compared the sharply dualistic countries in group 2 with the four countries in the sample with little dualism because of their small modern sectors (Chad, Dahomey, Malagasy, Niger). The estimated number of years necessary to recoup the implied loss in income share was virtually unaffected in the first case and only a few less in the second.

before the poorest two quintiles recovered their absolute position.*

Even in the last phase of the stage before takeoff, with relatively high levels of development and a capacity for more broadly based economic growth, the poorest segments of the population typically benefit from economic growth only when the government plays an important economic role and when widespread efforts are made to improve the human resource base. These hypotheses are suggested by both the implied gains to the poor in group 9 in Figure 1 (analysis for the poorest 60 percent) and the major losses to the richest 5 percent implied by the characteristics of group 10 in Figure 2 (analysis for the richest 5 percent). They are also consistent with cross-section regressions of the average income of various quintiles of income receivers on per capita GDP (see Appendix C).

Our analysis provides some grounds for speculating about the mechanisms that operate before the takeoff point to depress the standard of living of the poorest 40 percent. In the very earliest stage of dualistic growth, increased wage payments to indigenous workers in modern plantation, extractive, and industrial enterprises tend to be more than offset by concurrent changes in population, relative prices, tastes, and product availability. The lowering of death rates through the introduction of modern health measures such as malaria control accelerates population growth and thus tends to depress the per capita income of the indigenous population. Since increased cash wages are not immediately matched by increased availability of consumers' goods, higher prices erode gains in money income. Subsistence farmers shifting to cash crops are particularly hard hit by rising prices. Typically they suffer both

* Computations from data for countries in groups 5 and 8 give an average share to the poorest 40 percent of 15.7 percent for group 5 and 13.0 percent for group 8. The average growth rate of per capita GNP for group 8 is about 2.0 percent, compared with approximately 1.5 percent for group 5. To regain the implied absolute loss in income share of 2.5 percentage points with an increment in average growth rates of per capita GNP of only 0.5 percentage point requires almost 35 years. It should be stressed that this jump is from countries at the African level of development to countries at the lower end of the Latin American spectrum of development. Our results do not imply an absolute worsening in the position of the poorest 40 percent for, say, a jump from the lower to the upper end of the Latin American range of development levels.

declines in real income and nutritional deficiencies as they become dependent on the market for major necessities previously produced at home.

As the process of economic growth spreads beyond the narrow expatriate enclave, the factors at work to erode the relative and even the absolute positions of the poorest 40 percent appear to be changes in product mix and technology within both agricultural and nonagricultural sectors, rapid expansion of the urban industrial sectors, continued rapid population increases, migration to the cities, lack of social mobility, and inflation.

Regional income inequality typically increases as the concentration of rapidly growing, technologically advanced enterprises in cities widens the gap between rural and urban per capita income. Income inequality also intensifies in the urban sector with the accumulation of assets in the hands of a relatively small number of owners (usually expatriate) of modern enterprises. This concentration is accelerated by the spread of capital-intensive industrial technology through at least three factors—the ease with which owners of modern enterprises obtain capital abroad, the inability of small-scale enterprises to obtain financing, and a growing preference of medium and large entrepreneurs for advanced modern technologies. This labor-saving bias of technological advance, the rapidity of urban population growth, the migration to cities of unemployed rural workers, and the lack of social mobility all tend to swell the numbers of urban impoverished and to decrease the income share of the poorest segments of the urban population.

Several concomitants of the growth process characteristic of the period before economic takeoff also operate to worsen the absolute position of the poor. As agricultural output expands, the inelasticity of international and domestic demand for many agricultural products tends to reduce the real income of agricultural producers. Import substitution policies can raise the prices of consumers' goods above international levels. Simultaneously, mechanization in industry tends to preempt markets formerly supplied by large numbers of artisans and cottage workers. The destruction of handicraft industries acts to reduce incomes and increase unemployment among rural and urban poor. Finally, inflation, the product of investment efforts typically well beyond capacities to save, drives up prices faster than the wages of low-income workers, who have meager bargaining power. At the same time profits tend to rise both absolutely and relatively.

Thus, to summarize, inflation, population growth, technological change, the commercialization of the traditional sector, and urbanization all combine to reduce the real income of the poorest 40 percent of the population in very low income countries in the before-takeoff stage of development. Those middle- and upper-income groups benefit that are better able to finance the application of more advanced capital-intensive techniques of production.

These hypotheses and speculations are, broadly speaking, consistent with other studies, both cross-sectional and time series. Sketchy evidence cited by Kuznets on the early stages of economic growth in currently advanced nations suggests a relative worsening of the position of the poor. (See note, p. 143.) Cross-sectional and time series studies of contemporary underdeveloped countries also lend support to the hypothesis that the initial phases of economic growth increase the inequality of income distribution.[23] It is only very recently, however, that evidence has been brought forward of absolute declines in the average income of the poorest 40 to 60 percent of the population as a consequence of economic growth in these countries.

SUMMARY

The most important variables affecting income distribution are ecological, socioeconomic, and political. Table 2 lists them in the order of the frequency with which they are significant candidates for splitting parent groups into subgroups. The number of times each variable appears as the primary variable in binary splits is also given. The six most important variables associated with intercountry differences in patterns of income distribution, as judged by frequency of significance, are rate of improvement in human resources, direct government economic activity, socioeconomic dualism, potential for economic development, per capita GNP, and strength of the labor movement.

TABLE 2
Summary of Significant Variables

Variable	Frequency of significance	Frequency of appearance as primary variable
Rate of improvement in human resources	4	1
Direct government economic activity	4	2
Socioeconomic dualism	3	2
Potential for economic development	3	2
Per capita GNP	3	1
Strength of labor movement	3	0
Abundance of natural resources	2	1
Factor scores of level of socioeconomic development	2	1
Structure of foreign trade	2	1
Importance of indigenous middle class	2	1
Character of agricultural organization	2	1
Political participation	2	0
Political strength of traditional elite	2	0
Level of modernization of industry	2	0
Literacy	1	0
Degree of cultural and ethnic homogeneity	1	0
Leadership commitment to economic development	1	0
Effectiveness of financial institutions	1	0
Urbanization	1	0

Of the variables of greatest significance in this analysis, the most reliable for increasing the quality of income distribution appear to be the rate of improvement in human resources and direct government economic activity. Increased access to the acquisition of middle-level skills and professional training appears, from our results, to be quite predictable in equalizing effects on the income distribution. The distributional effects of increasing the proportion of government investment in total investment also appear to be favorable to lower- and middle-income recipients. As policy instruments, measures to increase political participation through stronger labor unions are probably less reliable because of their unpredictable impact on the stability of social and political institutions.

While the extent of socioeconomic dualism cannot itself be considered a policy instrument, our results suggest strongly that policies tending to reduce dualism by widening the base for economic growth can be very important for increasing income equality, and particularly for improving the position of the middle-income groups. Instruments having this effect might include providing credit to small, indigenous rural and urban entrepreneurs and expanding technical services to promote the spread of new seeds throughout agriculture.

The consequences for income distribution of increasing the rate of economic growth and improving economic institutions (represented by the development potential variable) are not fully predictable, probably because of the unfavorable effects discussed above. Nevertheless, our results suggest that, once some minimum level of development is reached, a wider coverage of improvements in economic institutions accompanied by either social advances or a shift in trade structure toward more diversified manufacturing exports supported by government policy is likely to increase the share in total income of middle-income groups. Increases in per capita GNP are associated with worsening of the income distribution at low levels of development; only at very high levels for low-income nations is higher per capita GNP associated with a more equal income distribution.

It is quite striking that several variables most closely associated with variations in patterns of income distribution proved to have little importance in our earlier studies of influences on short-term growth rates of per capita GNP. These variables include natural resource abundance, structure of foreign trade, direct economic role of the government, political participation, and even rates of improvement in middle- and higher-level human resources.[24] Yet this study underlines their relevance to differences in the extent of income inequality and thus reinforces the view that the policy instruments that are most effective in improving income distributions are different from those that are best for raising economic growth rates.

CHAPTER FIVE

Social Equity and Economic Growth

The fundamental question raised in this book is the extent to which the benefits of economic growth in underdeveloped countries during the 1950's and 1960's reached those most in need. The basic premise of most national and international efforts to aid low-income nations has been that sustained economic growth leads to higher real incomes for even the poorest segments of the population. The statistical analyses of Chapters 3 and 4 strongly suggest that this optimistic assumption has no basis in fact.

As Chapter 4 shows, inequality of income tends to be greatest where the exploitation of an abundance of natural resources coincides with a concentration of assets in the hands of expatriates; it tends to be least where development strategies stress investment in human resources, greater diversity of manufacturing exports, and expansion of public sector output and investment. In short, our analysis supports the Marxian view that economic structure, not level of income or rate of economic growth, is the basic determinant of patterns of income distribution.*

As Chapter 3 shows, economic modernization has had little direct effect on the sharing of political power. The major forces favoring more participant political structures tend to be social and

---

* As we have seen (p. 171), a country's level of economic development and the income share of the middle 20 percent of its population are only weakly related, although the relationship is statistically significant. The regression analyses presented in Appendix C show weak relationships between income shares and levels of economic development that explain rather little of the variance. We stress again that these and our other conclusions are hypotheses generated by applying a priori knowledge to arrive at dynamic interpretations of cross-section results that are, strictly speaking, timeless.

political rather than purely economic. To be sure, economic modernization is in part responsible for the specialized socioeconomic institutions, the diversified middle class, and the increased educational skills that in turn generate demands for influence on the political process. But such demands tend to go unmet except where the political framework is reasonably permissive.

We also find little warrant for the widespread belief that increased political participation leads to a more equitable distribution of income. This may be because the relationship of income distribution to political power is too complex to be got at by measures of political participation alone. The relationship involves, for example, those effects of the distribution of wealth on political power that provide the basis for the Marxian hypothesis that economic structure determines the structure of political power.

Since the reasoning behind these conclusions is rather complex, we begin the present chapter by summarizing the salient hypotheses that emerge from the analyses of Chapters 3 and 4. In the final pages, after stressing once again the major limitations of our data and our statistical procedures, we discuss the implications of our findings for development policy.

ECONOMIC GROWTH AND INCOME DISTRIBUTION

Short-term economic growth rates are not significantly related to income distribution in our results. Neither are short-term economic improvements such as increases in the effectiveness of tax and financial institutions or increases in agricultural or industrial productivity. The only measure of short-term economic change that we found to be significant, a composite measure of several types of change, is negatively associated with income equality.*

Since no long-term time series on the pertinent data exists for developing countries, we can deduce the impact of longer-term economic change only by comparing the average characteristics of countries at different levels of economic development. In inferring dynamic relationships from cross-section data, of course, we assume in effect that the average country traits associated with

---

* See Chapter 4, pp. 160–62, 172, and 177–78.

successive development levels represent the path of change of a typical underdeveloped country undergoing economic growth.

Our analysis indicates that the relationship between level of economic development and the income share of the poorest 60 percent of the population is asymmetrically U-shaped. Both extreme economic underdevelopment and high levels of economic development are associated with greater income equality; between these extremes a more equal income distribution is generally associated with a lower level of development. This suggests that the process of economic modernization shifts the income distribution in favor of the middle class and upper income groups and against lower income groups. Since levels of industrial development and agricultural productivity show a similar U-shaped relationship to the income shares of the poorest groups, the dynamics of economic development appear to work against the poor.

Only at the very upper end of our sample of less developed nations does greater economic development become positively associated with more equal income distribution. In the absence of specific domestic policy action, only the most highly developed nations during the period studied (Argentina, Chile, Taiwan, Israel) had as even an income distribution as countries that had undergone virtually no development (Dahomey, Chad, Niger).

These results are consistent with the hypotheses advanced by Simon Kuznets and Gunnar Myrdal in the 1950's. Kuznets, working from scanty data on the early stages of industrialization in advanced nations, found evidence that the poorest groups' share of income had decreased. He suggested that the same was true of contemporary underdeveloped countries.[1] Myrdal argued that at very low levels of development upward spirals of economic activity in expanding sectors induced downward spirals in stagnant sectors, leading to marked regional differences in income levels.[*] Our results also tend to confirm Paul Baran's hypothesis that ex-

---

[*] Gunnar Myrdal, *Economic Theory and Under-Developed Regions* (London, 1957), chap. 3. Although our results do not bear directly on regional differences, the importance of the dualism variable in accounting for income inequality has strong regional implications.

treme inequality at the lowest levels of development occurs because the benefits of dualistic growth of a narrow sector exploiting abundant natural resources accrue to ruling coalitions of expatriate businessmen and indigenous property owners.[2] Finally, our analyses are consistent with the distributional implications of dual economy models. These models suggest that the initial spurt of growth of the modern sector in a low-income country worsens the relative income distribution, and that this situation continues until the marginal product of labor in the agricultural sector rises to the level of the institutional wage in the industrial sector.[3]

An even more disturbing implication of our findings is that development is accompanied by an absolute as well as a relative decline in the average income of the very poor. Indeed, an initial spurt of dualistic growth may cause such a decline for as much as 60 percent of the population.* The absolute position of the poorest 40 percent apparently continues to worsen as countries move toward less dualistic growth patterns unless major efforts are made to improve and expand human resources.

Thus our findings strongly suggest that there is no automatic, or even likely, trickling down of the benefits of economic growth to the poorest segments of the population in low-income countries. On the contrary, the absolute position of the poor tends to deteriorate as a consequence of economic growth. We have seen in Chapter 4 that this unhappy phenomenon probably has its roots in the complex of structural changes that typically accompany the early and middle stages of economic development.†

ECONOMIC GROWTH AND POLITICAL PARTICIPATION

In our earlier book we presented hypotheses regarding the most likely causal links between economic development and Western-type political democracy.[4] Our immediate concern was to explain why our "high" sample of countries exhibited both a mild negative short-run association and a significant positive long-run associ-

---

* See Fig. 1, pp. 162–64, and pp. 178ff.
† See the discussion above, pp. 181-83.

ation between economic growth and political democracy.* Clearly the absence of a positive short-run relationship at all levels of development ruled out any possibility that causality runs systematically from type of political system to the economic sphere. We were then left with three possible hypotheses: (1) that increases in political democracy at the "high" level are a result, direct or indirect, of economic growth; (2) that social and economic transformations typically interact to induce increased political democracy; (3) that both increased political democracy and economic growth are typically consequences of a common set of social forces.

The present discriminant analyses permit us to rule out the first hypothesis as unlikely, and lend weight to the second. The close association between our social and economic indicators does not permit us to determine the direction of causality between social and economic influences. But since social variables consistently discriminate better than economic variables in the analyses of political participation, it seems clear that economic influences tend to operate on political systems through social and socioeconomic change rather than directly.

The interactions among economic growth, political institutions, and social structure are so complicated that it may be helpful to list our major findings and the hypotheses they suggest.

1. No significant association between short-term growth rates of per capita GNP and political participation is evident in our discriminant analyses. This result is consistent with our earlier factor analyses.† Our measure of political participation is not only unrelated to changes in per capita GNP, but also unrelated to any

---

* As mentioned above (p. 115), our factor analyses used several rather narrow indicators of political democracy that stressed participation through political parties. The measure of participation used in the present study is considerably broader.

† Irma Adelman and Cynthia Taft Morris, *Society, Politics, and Economic Development* (rev. ed.; Baltimore, 1971), chaps. 5–7. The discriminant analyses of Chapter 3 do not, of course, "test" hypotheses derived from our factor analyses, since the two sets of analyses were carried out with many of the same data. In the factor analyses, there was a very mild negative relationship between growth rates and political democracy at all three levels of development.

of our measures of economic concomitants of GNP changes, including improvements in financial institutions, tax systems, and physical overhead capital as well as the rate of industrialization and improvements in agricultural productivity.

2. Political influences are overwhelmingly important in discriminating among extents of political participation for countries at the lowest level of development. Social and socioeconomic influences as well as political forces are important at the intermediate and "high" levels.

3. Social and socioeconomic variables consistently differentiate better between degrees of political participation than economic variables for countries at the low and intermediate levels of development. Seemingly, then, the chain of causation runs from the social and socioeconomic to the political, rather than from the economic directly to the political or from the political to the economic.

4. In our earlier factor analyses we found a positive relationship between per capita GNP and measures of political democracy only for the "high" sample. Given the absence of a short-run relationship, we hypothesized the existence of a threshold within the range of countries in the high sample below which economic and social forces cannot effectively change the political system of a country.[5] The characteristics of the high sample suggested that above this threshold socioeconomic changes contribute to the establishment of reasonably effective representative institutions when they occur within a fairly permissive political framework.

5. In our discriminant analysis for the intermediate level of development, we found a positive relationship between socioeconomic influences and political participation that contrasts with the mild negative association in our factor-analytic studies of similar measures. This may be because our present measure of political participation takes into account variations not captured by our earlier analysis, namely changes in participation within the framework of a single-party system as opposed to changes involving the development of multiparty institutions.[6]

6. Neither in our factor analyses nor in the present discriminant analyses were our data sufficient to permit measures of short-run

social change. Hence we cannot directly locate the threshold at which social changes begin to interact with or contribute significantly to the spread of political participation. Clearly, however, the relationship between differences in socioeconomic influences and differences in political participation is weak in the low sample and stronger in the intermediate sample. Thus we hypothesize that social and socioeconomic influences begin to contribute to or interact with increases in political participation at the upper end of the low spectrum or the lower end of the intermediate spectrum. These increases, however, do not typically lead to the full establishment of reasonably effective representative institutions that is characteristic of the high sample.

The preceding propositions suggest another hypothesis: that the primary connection between higher levels of political participation and higher levels of economic development is through social modernization. That is to say, countries that have introduced changes in social structure conducive to greater individual upward mobility are also likely to have generated some channels for expanded individual participation in political associations and institutions. In the short run, however, increases in social mobility unfortunately occur at the expense of higher rates of growth of per capita GNP.[7]

THE PROBLEM OF DEVELOPMENT STRATEGIES

The frightening implication of the present work is that hundreds of millions of desperately poor people throughout the world have been hurt rather than helped by economic development. Unless their destinies become a major and explicit focus of development policy in the 1970's and 1980's, economic development may serve merely to promote social injustice.

In the pages that follow we shall discuss possible ways of reorienting development policy and planning. The fundamental values on which our recommendations are based are (1) that a major goal of development policy and planning should be to guarantee social justice to those in need, and (2) that any pattern of economic growth is unjust that fails to improve the standard of living of major segments of the population. These value judgments, which are consonant with more than one social philosophy,* are based on our conviction that anything contributing to extreme inequality in standards of living is morally unacceptable.

Before proceeding further, we must emphasize again those key limitations of the present study that significantly affect our policy recommendations.† First, inferences regarding the relationships between wider economic and political participation and the processes of socioeconomic and political change can be developed from cross-section analyses only by applying a priori reasoning and historical evidence regarding likely time paths of change and likely directions of causality. As we have frequently stressed, these inferences must be made with caution since cross-section results are, strictly speaking, timeless. For this reason, the generalizations on which our policy prescriptions are based must stand as hypotheses rather than established propositions.

Second, our variables do not capture the full range of possible policy instruments. Our measures of political participation do not include qualitative aspects of political institutions or the full range of educational and communications policies. Our measures of income distribution do not take adequate account of institutional measures for redistributing assets or government instruments for influencing factor and commodity markets. Even the instruments that are included are represented crudely. For example, the direct economic role of the government reflects grossly the net importance of quite varied instruments of public policy, and the rate of improvement of human resources suggests only the magnitude, not the quality, of efforts to expand the educational system.

Nevertheless, the implications of our results seem to us suffi-

---

* They follow, for example, from John Rawls's idea of justice as fairness (*A Theory of Justice*, Cambridge, Mass., 1971, chap. 1). In Rawls's view, the idea of social justice involves a set of principles regarding rights, duties, and the division of social benefits that would be accepted by rational men in an initial (hypothetical) situation of equality and freedom. For other views of social justice consonant with ours, see Morris Ginsberg, *On Justice in Society* (Ithaca, N.Y., 1965), and R. H. Tawney, *Equality*, 4th ed., rev. (New York, 1965).

† For earlier caveats, see pp. 4ff, pp. 121ff, pp. 149ff, and pp. 159ff.

ciently strong and self-consistent to warrant our making at least tentative recommendations for development policy. In the discussion that follows, we shall first consider instruments for improving the distribution of income, indicating which appear to be effective and which do not. We shall next consider instruments for promoting wider political participation. Finally, we shall discuss the significance of our results for development planning.

INSTRUMENTS FOR IMPROVING INCOME DISTRIBUTION

Measures to reduce the extent of socioeconomic dualism appear to be overwhelmingly important in achieving income equality at the lowest level of development. We found one group of sharply dualistic countries in which abundant natural resources are exploited by expatriate or culturally distinct indigenous elites and income inequality is extreme.* No policy instruments systematically improve the income position of the very poor, and only the spread of small-scale commercial agriculture proves helpful to the middle-income groups. Instruments that contribute to greater equality in higher level countries typically benefit the richest 20 percent in countries at the low level. The only hope of significantly improving the income distribution in these countries lies in a transformation of the institutional setting. If a country is to avoid stagnation at a low level of development, it must not only eliminate expatriate or neo-colonial elites but replace them with indigenous entrepreneurs and administrators† who are quite widely spread throughout the country.

At the intermediate and "high" levels of development, strategies stressing human resources promote greater income equality, whereas those based on the exploitation of natural resources or

---

* See Chapter 4, pp. 160–64 and 171–75.

† Our results for less dualistic countries at the lowest level of development suggest no effective mechanisms for improving the position of the poor. These countries split off into groups having greater equality by reason of stagnation at low levels of development or low rates of economic change. See pp. 160–61 and 177–78. The only policy instrument significantly affecting the income distribution for low-level countries is increasing the extent of the government's role, a measure that tends to reduce the share of the upper 5 percent.

capital-intensive industrialization tend to shift the income distribution against the lower income groups. The poor benefit not from the expansion of educational systems as such, but from a combination of educational improvements and expanding employment opportunities.

Another way of improving the income distribution in countries at the intermediate and "high" levels is by expanding the direct economic role of the government. Increases in the size of the public sector and the government's share in net investment appear to favor middle-income groups and to reduce the share of upper income groups, but do not improve the relative position of the poor. The leveling effect at the top seems to be essentially ideological rather than a consequence of the efficiency or disinterestedness of the bureaucracy; that is, countries with large government sectors are typically socialist countries and therefore opposed to the accrual of large profits in the hands of upper income groups.

Development strategies that stress the growth of more diversified manufacturing exports also tend to have favorable distributional effects. They lead to higher incomes for the middle 20 percent of the population, and in socioeconomically advanced countries may even improve the position of the poor.

A number of policy instruments proved in our analyses to be unimportant or less important than expected for improving income distribution. Improvements in tax systems that included increases in direct taxes produced insignificant results. The reasons are complex, but they probably include the inefficiency of tax-collecting agencies and difficulties with the structure of political power. Recent studies of Latin America show that neither tax structures nor government expenditure patterns typically favor a larger share of income for the poorest groups in the population.[8] It would appear, then, that any taxation policy designed to improve income distribution must place considerable explicit emphasis on measures that favor the poorest 40 percent.

Financial institutions are also less important than one might expect. Their unimportance is consistent with the hypothesis that the functioning of financial systems reflects closely the power structure of an underdeveloped country. If this is so, our more direct measures of power structure, such as the political strength of the traditional elite and the importance of the indigenous middle class, may reflect some of the impact of financial institutions. At all events, our findings do not rule out the possibility that changes in financial institutions unaccompanied by changes in the power structure might significantly improve the income distribution.

The relative unimportance of agricultural structure and technology in our results was also unexpected. With respect to land reform, the reason is probably that redistribution of land favors higher incomes for the agricultural poor only when supported by measures to maintain the productivity of the redistributed land. Where such supportive measures are absent, as they often are, the relationship expected a priori does not occur.

Since improvements in agricultural productivity also have an insignificant effect on income distribution, it would appear that the introduction of improved techniques, new seeds, and fertilizers primarily benefits middle-income and rich farmers. Not only do the agricultural poor rarely benefit from such improvements, but backwash effects from their introduction on large farms can undermine the position of small farmers by reducing prices, putting pressure on tenancy arrangements, and restricting access to credit and other resources. It would seem to follow that agricultural policies should stress rural development rather than technological innovation.

Finally, industrialization is less important in our results than one might expect. Short-term increases in industrialization are not significantly associated with changes in income distribution. But plotting the means of groups of countries with successively higher levels of industrialization against the income shares of the poorest 60 percent yields an almost perfectly U-shaped relationship. This finding is consistent with Kuznets's hypothesis cited above (p. 188). It suggests that policies promoting industrialization actually worsen income distribution except in developing countries at a high level of development.

In general, the policy implications of our results are depressing.

For countries at the lowest level of development, one looks in vain for policy instruments that will systematically improve the position of the poor. The only clear alternative to expatriate domination of the socioeconomic structure is economic stagnation. Neither the expulsion of expatriates nor indigenous revolution appears likely to lead to economic growth unless accompanied by a wider spread of institutional and administrative capabilities than is usually found in countries at this level.

For countries at the intermediate and higher levels of development, the picture is somewhat brighter. Improvements in human resources within a context of expanding employment, more socialistic government economic programs, and stress on diversified manufacturing exports all have promise as strategies for improving income distribution. Even for these countries, however, the effective policy instruments appear more likely to benefit the middle-income groups than the poorest 40 percent of the population.

INSTRUMENTS FOR INCREASING POLITICAL PARTICIPATION

Wider political participation may be sought either as a desirable end in itself or as a way to obtain greater economic equality. As we have seen, hopes on the latter score get little support from our findings. If this seems surprising, the reason may be our tendency to equate political participation with political power. Increased power may correlate with increased income, but since it cannot be demonstrated that participation implies power, the case for increased political participation must rest on its benefits in spheres other than the economic. The following discussion of instruments for promoting political participation must be read in this light.

For countries that are poorly developed socioeconomically and politically, the best policy is to establish independent political structures (parliamentary institutions, bureaucracies, and specialized political organizations such as labor unions) and institutional means of expanding political awareness and political involvement. Their effectiveness will be greater where political freedom prevails. Participant institutions at this stage of development are of course very fragile, as we learn from the recent political history in sub-Saharan Africa.

In the transitional group of countries (e.g. from Burma to Syria), increasing political participation involves incorporating the middle class and its aspirations into the political system. This requires a shift in political power from traditional ruling elites and authoritarian political structures to middle-class-oriented political regimes and party government. This shift is typically accompanied by violence. Indeed, political instability may well be a sine qua non of the process by which greater political participation is achieved at this level of development.

At the highest level of development for underdeveloped countries, political participation is most effectively increased by strengthening the political party system and increasing social mobility. One way of strengthening a party system is to speed the transformation of personalistic parties into structures for aggregating and articulating the preferences of socioeconomic groups, especially urban workers and peasants. Another is to strengthen multiparty institutions and labor unions.

At the highest level of development, the way to increase political participation is to expand education and correspondingly broaden employment opportunities in a program carefully designed to keep the availability of newly trained personnel in phase with the availability of appropriate jobs.

In conclusion, our results suggest that the most important instruments for increasing political participation in underdeveloped countries are those that involve fundamental changes in socioeconomic and political structure as well as a basic reorientation of development strategies. The establishment of reasonably permissive and effective party systems, the expansion of the political role of the middle class, and the growth of socioeconomic institutions of the type that favor participant systems all require a set of concurrent structural changes that can be achieved only with a broad systems approach to modernization and development.

Thus the path to social justice through greater political participation is no less thorny than the path to social justice through improving the distribution of income.

IMPLICATIONS FOR DEVELOPMENT PLANNING

The record of economic intervention in underdeveloped countries, good as it is in terms of economic growth, has been dismal in terms of social justice. Indeed, economic growth, whether planned or unplanned, has only made things worse. Since there is apparently no simple way of changing things for the better, some radical reorientation of both ends and means is apparently in order.

With respect to ends, the minimum short-run goal that we consider acceptable from the viewpoint of social justice is to increase the average income of the poorest 40 percent at least as fast as the average income for the nation as a whole. (A much faster relative rate of increase is necessary in the longer run to eliminate the current gross inequalities.) Most development planning has emphasized economic criteria for choosing between alternative plans and projects, notably contribution to the rate of growth of per capita GNP. But this criterion is tantamount to an equal weighting of all units of income. And since, on the average, the richest 20 percent of the population receive about 50 percent of the income while the poorest 20 percent receive only about 5 percent, increases in the income of the wealthy are effectively given ten times the weight per capita as income increases for the poor. What is needed, then, is a more egalitarian planning criterion.

One approach[9] is to weight the percentage income improvement on a per capita basis: thus, with current income shares a unit increase in the income of the poorest quintile might be given ten times the weight of the same increase in the income of the richest quintile. Other approaches may involve weighting of income, utility, or such elements of welfare as education, health, housing, and jobs. For any such approach, of course, interpersonal comparisons are needed. Such comparisons are easily enough managed, despite their distastefulness to economists; indeed, they are implicit in all governmental taxation and expenditure policies, as well as in the use of income itself as a measure of welfare.

A reorientation of planning targets toward achieving greater social equity is not enough. We need not only new targets but new instruments for achieving them, new institutions to supplement or supplant the market and nonmarket agencies that have served the rich so well and the poor so badly. Piecemeal policies are unlikely to benefit the poor significantly unless accompanied by fundamental institutional reform.

Planning institutional reform involves a thorough knowledge of the social and institutional setting as well as of the complex interrelationships among the society, the bureaucracy, and the economy. The planners' model must explicitly include interactions among all of these elements. Our results suggest that four interaction processes in particular need to be incorporated: (1) how economic modernization leads to changes in social structure; (2) how social transformations affect the economy and how they generate pressures on the political system for the articulation of special interests and for a share in the benefits of modernization; (3) how the political system translates (or fails to translate) these pressures into public policies; and (4) how these public policies affect the strategy and processes of economic modernization. Only by closing the analytic circle can planners take into account the totality of the indirect effects of a given plan, and guard against the possibility—a very real one with respect to income distribution—that the indirect effects will outweigh the direct effects and reverse their intended direction.

Development planning must have three further characteristics if it is to increase income equality. First, it must focus on the question, Who benefits? This requires careful monitoring of the micro-effects of planning policies. Neither aggregative models nor conventional regional or sectoral models offer a fine enough description of economic behavior to permit a useful analysis of their distributional effects. New planning approaches and mechanisms will have to be devised for this purpose.

Second, full account must be taken of the interdependencies within the economic system. The distribution of income is determined by an interaction among what is produced, how it is produced, and what is consumed, all modified by the social and institutional structure of the nation. Partial equilibrium approaches focusing on only one of these factors (e.g. the choice of technique) cannot give adequate guidance to the formulation of distribution-oriented development strategies, since they inevitably ignore secondary and higher-order effects.

Finally, planning models should be dynamic. The intergenerational transmission of wealth and skills and of access to their acquisition plays a fundamental role in shaping patterns of income distribution over time and has significant social equity implications for any given income distribution.

CONCLUSION

Anyone concerned with the welfare of the world's underprivileged people must recognize that business cannot continue as usual in the development community. Development policies that ought in principle to have made for a more equitable distribution of income have served merely as additional instruments for increasing the wealth and power of existing elites. Even more serious, new elites, many of whom owe their power to development programs, have become adept at manipulating economic and political institutions to serve their private ends.

We have found that increases in political participation do not predictably lead to a more equitable distribution of income, probably because only a major redistribution of political power is likely to affect income distribution significantly. Since our sample does not include any countries in which a revolution transformed the power structure of society before or during the period studied, we cannot assess the potential effectiveness of revolution in increasing the absolute incomes of the poor. Historical evidence, however, offers little basis for optimism on this score.

The only policy instruments that offer some hope for significant improvements in the standard of living of the poor require a basic reorientation in development strategy. In our opinion, the only acceptable strategy for the decades ahead is development of the people, by the people, and for the people. Without new institutions and policies specifically designed to improve the lot of the poor, there is no realistic chance of social justice in the underdeveloped world in our time.

Appendixes

Classification Scheme for Political Participation

The following definitional scheme groups countries by the extent and effectiveness of *national* popular political participation as judged by the following broad criteria:

I. The extent to which the major socioeconomic and cultural-ethnic groups have their interests represented in, and are able to influence, the making of national political decisions affecting them through participant associations and institutions.

II. The extent to which individuals belonging to cultural-ethnic and/or socioeconomic groups that have some form of national political representation can choose between different political channels in seeking national representation of their interests.

III. The extent of actual participation by individuals in the national political process through participation in political parties, special interest groups, and/or other institutions or associations carrying out political functions, or through voluntary voting between genuine political alternatives.

For each of the 74 underdeveloped countries, a composite score for the extent of popular political participation is derived from the rankings of that country with respect to the three criteria listed above. Table A1 specifies the characteristics of the several categories of the composite indicator in terms of the three elements composing it. The precise makeup of the composite is determined by a priori judgments regarding the relative importance of the different aspects of political participation represented. Below is the detailed explanation of the symbols contained in Table A1. Finally, a brief literary description of the categories of the overall participation index completes the presentation of the classification scheme for the participation indicator.

I. Effectiveness of National Political Representation of the Major Cultural-Ethnic and Socioeconomic Groups in the Population

1. In this category are countries characterized by reasonably effective national political representation. These are indicated by the pres-

TABLE A1

Definition of Indicator of Popular Political Participation
in Terms of Its Three Component Elements

Categories of popular political participation (composite)	National political representation	Choice of channel for representation	Actual participation
A	1	1	1
B	2	1	1
C	3	1	1
D	1	2	1
E	2	2	1
E—	2	3	1
F	3	2	1
F	4	1	1
F—	3	3	1
G	1 or 2	2	2
G—	1 or 2	3	2
H+	3 or 4	1	2
H	3 or 4	2	2
H—	3 or 4	3	2
I	4	3	2
J	5	1 or 2	2
J	5	3	1
J—	5	3	2

ence of political institutions and associations (such as political parties, voluntary interest groups or traditional associations carrying out political functions, and local political institutions*) through which the major socioeconomic and cultural-ethnic groups are represented and through which they influence to some significant extent national political decisions directly affecting their interests. Countries are excluded if socioeconomic and/or cultural-ethnic groups probably comprising over 10 percent of the population are excluded from the system of representation.†

* For the purpose of this classification, traditional non-Western-type groupings or associations are considered part of the system of national representation, providing they operate at national level as direct (not necessarily formal) channels for influencing national political decisions.

† Exclusions from the national political process based upon literacy requirements for voting are considered a defect in representation for the purpose of this classification, if they result in the exclusion of major identifiable

2. Countries in which national political representation of the major cultural-ethnic and socioeconomic groups in the population is defective in one *but not both* of the following respects:

(*a*) Political associations and institutions fail to represent some major socioeconomic and/or cultural-ethnic group(s) of the population which, however, probably amount to between one-tenth and one-third of the population, or

(*b*) Most political associations and institutions that are potentially key channels for representation of major groups in the population fail in practice to significantly influence national political decisions directly affecting their members. This subcategory also includes one-party systems used almost exclusively as channels for one-way communication from above.

3. Countries in which national political representation is defective in both of the respects listed in category 2. Excluded from this category, as from category 2, are countries in which the socioeconomic or cultural-ethnic groups without national representation probably amount to more than one-third of the population.

4. Countries in which major cultural-ethnic and/or socioeconomic groups in the population probably constituting more than one-third, but not more than two-thirds, of the population are without formal national political representation. Also included in this category are countries in which a system of parliamentary representation was set up during the period but had not led by the end of the period to the development of political parties or formal political pressure groups.

5. Countries in which major cultural-ethnic and/or socioeconomic groups in the population probably constituting over two-thirds of the population are without formal national political representation.

II. Extent of Choice of Channels for National Political Representation
(for Groups in Population Having Some Form of Representation)

1. Countries in which, for members of socioeconomic and cultural-ethnic groups with national political representation, there is significant choice of channels for political representation of their interests; specifically, significant choice exists both between different channels of a given type (such as national parties with organizational networks covering an important part of the country) and between different types of channels (such as political parties with organizational networks cov-

socioeconomic and/or cultural-ethnic groups to a degree described by the various categories of this scheme. Exclusions of foreigners count as a defect if the foreign residents are permanent immigrants to the country.

ering an important part of the country and labor unions). Included in this category are countries meeting its criteria in which one of two or more independent national political parties dominates the political scene.

2. Countries in which, for members of socioeconomic and cultural-ethnic groups with national political representation, there is little or no choice between different channels of a given type for political representation of their interests (such as political parties with organizational networks covering an important part of the country); there is, nevertheless, significant choice between different types of channels for political representation (such as political parties and labor unions and/or traditional tribal or other channels of representation that actively and directly influence national politics). The countries meeting these criteria are of three different types.

(a) Countries with multiparty political systems in which there is little or no choice between political channels of any given type, because each channel is accessible exclusively to individuals of a specific cultural-ethnic or socioeconomic identification.

(b) Countries with single-party (or multiparty) political systems in which there is little or no choice between political channels of any given type because all national channels are dominated by the ruling political party; excluded are countries in which, for all practical purposes, special interest groups are units of the dominant political party and thus do not provide alternative channels for representation.*

(c) Countries with multiparty systems in which the party system as a whole is relatively unimportant compared with traditional channels for influencing national political decisions, but in which choices among different types of channels for representation are quite varied when both Western-type and traditional channels are taken into account.

3. Included in this category are two types of countries in which individuals in the major socioeconomic and cultural-ethnic groups in the population have little or no choice of channel for political representation of their interests. Included in this category are:

(a) Countries in which there is either no representative political system or a negligible one. Also included in category (3a) with a plus

---

* The kinds of choices available in a one-party system include (1) choices between candidates in parliamentary elections; (2) the wider choices possible in elaborated systems of branch, district, regional, and national elections; and (3) choices between subchannels for various interest groups (labor unions, unions of cooperatives, women's unions, youth leagues, agricultural federations).

score are countries with choices between two or more political parties which were, however, poorly established or newly established and operated almost exclusively in urban centers involving less than 20 percent of the population (other channels of representation, including traditional ones, are negligible). In addition, included in (3*a*) with a plus score are countries without formal political parties or alternative representative channels such as labor unions, but nevertheless with significant choice between individual candidates to a national parliament existing for at least half the period (other channels of representation are negligible).

(*b*) Countries with a single-party political system in which there are very few or no channels for political expression other than the various units of a single dominant national political party. Also included in (3*b*) with a plus score are countries in which special interest groups are so thoroughly integrated into the national party that they are, for all practical purposes, units of the dominant party rather than alternative channels.

III. Extent of Actual Participation by the
*Adult Population in the National Political Process**

1. Countries in which it is probable that at least one-quarter of the adult population participates in some minimal way in political groups, associations, or institutions representing their interests at national level (by voluntary voting between genuine alternatives, or membership, or other even marginal forms of participation).†

2. Countries in which it is probable that less than one-quarter of the adult population participates in some minimal way in political groups, associations, or institutions representing their interests at national level (by voluntary voting between genuine alternatives, or membership, or other even marginal forms of participation).

---

* Political participation in tribal or other traditional organizations and groupings is only counted as actual national political participation for the purpose of this definition if these organizations and groupings actively and directly influence national political decisions. If tribal leaders participate in such groupings but ordinary members do not, only the leaders are considered to "actually participate."

† "Genuine alternatives" in voting means that there are candidates from at least two national political parties under independent control operating on a countrywide basis. "Marginal forms of participation" would include attendance at political rallies or informal public meetings or membership in unions or cultural-ethnic associations working to influence national political decisions. Membership in units of traditional religious, tribal, clan, etc. groupings is only counted if it explicitly involves influencing national politics.

Classification Scheme for Composite Index
of National Political Participation

The following category definitions are brief literary equivalents of Table A1. More detailed specifications can be derived by the combined use of Table A1 and the detailed definitions of the three elements included in the present composite index summarized in Table A1.

A. Countries in which national political representation of the major socioeconomic and cultural-ethnic groups in the population is reasonably effective and in which there is significant choice for given individuals belonging to these groups between a variety of channels for national political representation. Excluded from this category are countries in which it is probable that less than one-quarter of the adult population participate in some minimal way in the national political process.

B. Countries in which, first, national political representation is defective because *either* (a) some major group of the population probably amounting to not more than one-third of the population is without national political representation, or (b) representative organs fail to significantly influence national political decisions. Second, there is significant choice (for individuals belonging to groups having political representation) between a variety of channels for national political representation. And third, countries are excluded if it is probable that less than one-quarter of the adult population participate in some minimal way in the national political process.

C. Countries in which national political representation is defective in both the respects listed under the first criterion for category B, but which meet the second and third criteria for category B. Also included in category C are countries meeting all the criteria of category B for the predominant part of the time period but which were without a representative system for a subperiod of from one and one-half to two years.

D. Countries in which national political representation is reasonably effective but in which there is little or no choice for individuals belonging to groups having political representation between political channels of any given type (although there is choice between different types of channels). This category includes both single-party systems and multiparty systems that have reasonably effective national political representation; the multiparty systems are those in which each party is accessible exclusively to individuals of a given socioeconomic or cultural-ethnic identification. Excluded from this category are countries in which it is probable that less than one-quarter of the adult population participate in some minimal way in the national political process.

E. Countries in which national political representation is defective *either* because some major group(s) in the population probably amounting to not more than one-third of the population are without national political representation or because representative organs fail to significantly influence national political decisions. With respect to choice of channels for political representation and actual political participation, the criteria for the present category are the same as those for category *D*.

F. Countries that meet *one* of the following two sets of criteria. (1) National political representation is defective both because some major group(s) in the population probably amounting to not more than one-third of the population are without national political representation and because representative organs fail to significantly influence national political decisions; at the same time, there is little or no choice for individuals belonging to groups having political representation between political channels of any given type (although they do have choice between different types of channels). Or (2) national political representation is substantially defective in that major socioeconomic or cultural-ethnic groups in the population probably amounting to more than one-third, but not more than two-thirds, of the population are without formal national political representation; however, for individuals in those groups with representation, there is significant choice between a variety of channels for national political representation. Excluded from the present category are all countries in which it is probable that less than one-quarter of the adult population participate in some minimal way in the national political process.

G. Countries in which it is probable that less than one-quarter of the adult population participate in some minimal way in the national political system, but in which national political representation of the major groups in the population either is reasonably good or involves, at the very least, no cultural-ethnic or socioeconomic exclusions of more than one-third of the population. In most of the countries in this category there is some significant choice between different types of channels for representation; countries in this category with no significant choice between different channels are classified *G—*.

H. Countries in which it is probable that less than one-quarter of the adult population participate in some minimal way in the national political process and in which national political representation is defective because of either of the two following reasons. (1) Major groups in the population probably consisting of more than one-third, but not more than two-thirds, of the population are without formal national political representation. Or (2) major groups in the population probably consisting of less than one-third of the population are without formal

TABLE A2
Country Classifications with Respect to the Three Components of the
Composite Index of Popular Political Participation, 1957–62

| Country | Category | Country classification with respect to | | |
		National representation	Choice of channel	Actual participation
Afghanistan	J—	5	3a	2
Algeria	J	5	1	2
Argentina	A—	2	1	1
Bolivia	D	1	2b	1
Brazil	F	4	1	1
Burma	C	2	1	1
Cambodia	I	4	3b	2
Cameroun	H	4	2a	2
Ceylon	B	2a	1	1
Chad	J—	5	3b	2
Chile	A	1	1	1
China (Taiwan)	E	2a	2b	1
Colombia	B	2a	1	1
Costa Rica	A	1	1	1
Cyprus	E	2a	2a	1
Dahomey	G	1	2b	2
Dominican Republic	J—	5	3b	2
Ecuador	F	4	1	1
El Salvador	F	3	2	1
Ethiopia	J—	5	3a	2
Gabon	H	4	2—	2
Ghana	E	2b	2a	1
Greece	A	1	1	1
Guatemala	F	4	1	1
Guinea	E	2b	2b—	1
Honduras	C	3	1	1
India	B+	2a	1	1
Indonesia	E	2b	2a+	1
Iran	H	4	2a	2
Iraq	J—	5	3a	2
Israel	A	1	1	1
Ivory Coast	E	2b	2b	1
Jamaica	A—	1	1—	1
Japan	A	1	1	1
Jordan	J—	5	3a	2
Kenya	H	4	2a	2
Korea (South)	F	3	2b+	1
Laos	J—	5	3a	2
Lebanon	D+	1	2a	1
Liberia	J—	5	3b	2
Libya	J—	5	3a	2

TABLE A2 (*continued*)

Country	Category	National representation	Choice of channel	Actual participation
		Country classification with respect to		
Malagasy	H	3	2a	2
Malawi	H	3	2a	2
Mexico	A–	1	1	1
Morocco	H	4	2b	2
Nepal	J–	5	3a	2
Niger	J–	5	3b	2
Nigeria	E	2a	2a	1
Nicaragua	H	4	2a	2
Pakistan	J–	5	3a	2
Panama	F	4	1	1
Paraguay	G–	2b	3b	2
Peru	F	4	1	1
Philippines	B	2b	1	1
Rhodesia	J	5	1	2
Senegal	G	1	2b	2
Sierra Leone	H	3	2a	2
Somali Republic	D	1	2a+	1
South Africa	J	5	1	2
Sudan	J–	5	3a	2
Surinam	A	1	1	1
Syria	E	2b	2b	2
Tanganyika	D–	1	2b	1
Thailand	J–	5	3a	2
Trinidad	D+	1	2a	1
Tunisia	G	2b	2b	2+
Turkey	B–	2a	1	1
Uganda	H	3	2a	2
United Arab Republic (Egypt)	H	3	2b	2
Uruguay	A	1	1	1
Venezuela	A	1	1	1
Vietnam (South)	J–	5	3b	2
Yemen	J–	5	3a	2
Zambia	D	1	2a	1

national political representation and in addition representative organs fail to significantly influence national political decisions. A score of *H+* is given to countries in the present category in which, for given individuals with representation, there is significant choice between a variety of channels for national political representation. A score of *H* is given to the countries in the present category that are characterized by little or no choice for given individuals belonging to groups having political representation between political channels of any given type (although

TABLE A3
Grouping of Countries by Level of Socioeconomic Development

Lowest group

Country	Factor Score	Per cap. GNP 1961
Afghanistan	−1.02	$ 70
Cambodia	−.55	101
Cameroun	−1.34	86
Chad	−1.70	40
Dahomey	−1.54	40
Ethiopia	−.99	44
Gabon	−.83	200
Guinea	−1.47	60
Ivory Coast	−.98	184
Kenya	−.53	80
Laos	−1.06	60
Liberia	−1.01	159
Libya	−.68	204
Malagasy	−1.31	75
Malawi	−1.57	40
Morocco	−.57	150
Nepal	−1.36	53
Niger	−1.86	40
Nigeria	−.91	82
Senegal	−.52	175
Sierra Leone	−1.39	70
Somali Republic	−1.35	40
South Vietnam	−.49	89
Sudan	−.64	94
Tanganyika	−1.22	59
Uganda	−1.22	68
Yemen	−1.35	90
Zambia	−.89	170

Intermediate group

Country	Factor Score	Per cap. GNP 1961
Algeria	.18	$281
Bolivia	−.35	113
Burma	−.41	58
Ceylon	.35	137
Ecuador	.54	182
Ghana	−.01	199
Guatemala	.35	175
Honduras	.26	207
India	−.28	80
Indonesia	−.40	83
Iran	.09	211
Iraq	−.03	194
Jordan	.16	184
Pakistan	−.08	79
Philippines	.56	117
Rhodesia	.14	215
South Africa	.62	427
Surinam	.54	310
Syria	.57	152
Thailand	.50	97
Tunisia	−.18	161

Highest group

Country	Factor score	Per cap. GNP 1961
Argentina	1.91	$379
Brazil	.79	186
Chile	1.39	453
Colombia	.66	283
Costa Rica	.78	344
Cyprus	1.08	416
Dominican Republic	.81	218
El Salvador	.71	220
Greece	1.47	431
Israel	1.77	814
Jamaica	1.06	436
Japan	1.63	502
Lebanon	1.44	411
Mexico	.75	313
Nicaragua	.88	213
Panama	.84	416
Paraguay	.97	130
Peru	.68	181
South Korea	.85	73
Taiwan	1.05	145
Trinidad	1.15	594
Turkey	.88	193
United Arab Republic (Egypt)	.73	120
Uruguay	1.59	450
Venezuela	1.37	692

Source: Irma Adelman and Cynthia Taft Morris, Society, Politics, and Economic Development: A Quantitative Approach (rev. ed., Baltimore, 1971), pp. 167–70.

they do have a choice between different types of channel). Countries are classified $H-$ if, for all practical purposes, all representative channels are units of the dominant party.

I. Countries meeting the same criteria as those given for categories *G* and *H* with respect to actual political participation and national political representation. With respect to the extent of choice of channels for political representation, the countries in the present category are characterized by little or no choice either between political channels of any given type or between different types of political channel; specifically, they have single-party political systems in which there are very few or no channels for political expression other than the various units of the national political party.

J. Countries in which major groups in the population probably consisting of over two-thirds of the population are without formal national political representation and in which it is also probable that less than one-quarter of the adult population participate in some minimal way in groups, associations, or institutions representing their interests at the national level. Of the countries meeting these criteria, those countries having systems of national representation for groups probably consisting of less than one-third of the population in which there is at least some limited choice of channels of representation are classified *J*; those countries with little or no choice of political channels are classified *J*−.

Table A2

The country classifications listed in Table A2 relate, for most countries, to the period 1957 through 1962. However, for some countries in which the end of 1962 is clearly a poor termination date, the end point may range from 1961 to 1964. Where appropriate, it is chosen to coincide with a major change in government or other important event such as independence. If the resulting classification period is nevertheless characterized by markedly nonhomogeneous subperiods, the classification is based upon the characteristics of the predominant subperiod, as judged by the length of time involved, with a plus or minus adjustment where appropriate for the characteristics of the shorter subperiod.

Results of Discriminant Analysis

TABLE B1

Results of Discriminant Analysis for Political Participation,
Entire Sample, 1957–62

Step and variable	F ratio	Step and variable	F ratio
1 *Social mobility*	17.6	Political strength of the	
Literacy	15.7	traditional elite	6.9
Predominant basis of the		Effectiveness of financial	
political party system	13.2	institutions	6.6
Strength of the labor		Socioeconomic dualism	6.6
movement	12.0	Effectiveness of the tax system	5.4
Per capita GNP in 1961	11.5	Gross investment	5.1
Extent of mass communication	11.4	Crude fertility rate	4.6
Importance of the indige-		Political strength of religious	
nous middle class	10.8	organization	3.7
Modernization of outlook	9.7	Political stability	3.4
Size of the traditional agri-		Change in degree of indus-	
cultural sector	9.5	trialization	3.0
Improvement in human		Social tension	2.9
resources	9.4	Political strength of the	
Freedom of political opposi-		military	2.9
tion and the press	9.2	Length of colonial experience	3.0
Modernization of techniques		Recency of self-government	2.7
in agriculture	8.7	Leadership commitment to	
Administrative efficiency	8.7	economic development	2.5
Character of agricultural		*Coefficient to step 1, +.21*	
organization	8.6		
Modernization of industry	8.2	2 *Predominant basis of the*	
National integration and sense		*political party system*	7.0
of national unity	8.0	Strength of the labor move-	
Adequacy of physical over-		ment	6.3
head capital	7.6	Political strength of the tradi-	
Urbanization	7.4	tional elite	5.4
Competitiveness of political		Freedom of political opposi-	
parties	7.4	tion and the press	4.7

TABLE B1 (*continued*)

Step and variable	F ratio	Step and variable	F ratio
Competitiveness of political		5 *Social tension*	3.0
parties	4.5	Mass communication	2.9
Political strength of religious		Strength of the labor move-	
organization	4.0	ment	2.4
Per capita GNP in 1961	4.0	Political stability	2.3
Administrative efficiency	3.9	*Coefficient to step 5, −.03*	
Political strength of the			
military	3.8	6 *Mass communication*	3.0
Mass communication	3.0	Strength of the labor move-	
Literacy	2.9	ment	2.5
Length of colonial experience	2.9	*Coefficient to step 6, −.08*	
Political stability	2.4		
Coefficient to step 2, +.14		7 *Strength of the labor move-*	
		ment	2.5
3 *Political strength of the tra-*		Direct government economic	
ditional elite	5.3	activity	2.5
Strength of the labor move-		Competitiveness of political	
ment	4.1	parties	2.4
Per capita GNP in 1961	4.0	*Coefficient to step 7, +.14*	
Administrative efficiency	3.4		
Political strength of the		8 *Direct government economic*	
military	3.1	*activity*	2.4
Mass communication	2.5	Competitiveness of political	
Political stability	2.5	parties	2.3
Social tension	2.4	Modernization of industry	2.3
Coefficient to step 3, +.07		*Coefficient to step 8, +.04*	
4 *Per capita GNP in 1961*	4.1	Constant, −24.1	
Strength of the labor move-		Number of countries incor-	
ment	2.9	rectly classified, 21	
Social tension	2.4		
Political stability	2.3		
Coefficient to step 4, +.01			

TABLE B2
Results of Discriminant Analysis for Low Countries, 1957–62

Step and variable	F ratio	Step and variable	F ratio
1 *Strength of the labor movement*	14.3	2 *Length of colonial experience*	6.2
Freedom of political opposition and the press	10.3	Modernization of outlook	5.6
Political strength of religious organization	10.0	Leadership commitment to economic development	5.1
Administrative efficiency	10.0	Political strength of the traditional elite	5.0
Political strength of the military	8.8	Political strength of the military	4.3
Length of colonial experience	8.2	Recency of self-government	4.0
Political strength of the traditional elite	7.2	Social mobility	3.4
Recency of self-government	6.8	*Coefficient to step 2, +.29*	
Competitiveness of political parties	6.2	3 *Modernization of outlook*	5.2
Modernization of outlook	5.3	*Coefficient to step 3, +.11*	
Social mobility	5.1		
Mass communication	4.2	Constant, −10.9	
Coefficient to step 1, +.12		Number of countries incorrectly classified, 5	

TABLE B3
Results of Discriminant Analysis for Intermediate Countries, 1957–62

Step and variable	F ratio	Step and variable	F ratio
1 *Freedom of political opposition and the press*	6.1	Political strength of the military	5.1
Importance of the indigenous middle class	5.7	Political strength of the traditional elite	4.8
Political strength of the military	4.6	Political stability	4.7
Centralization of political power	4.5	Effectiveness of financial institutions	3.9
Crude fertility rate	4.5	Social mobility	3.3
Effectiveness of financial institutions	4.2	Crude fertility rate	3.3
Rate of growth of real per capita GNP	3.6	*Coefficient to step 2, +.44*	
Predominant basis of the political party system	3.5	3 *Political strength of the traditional elite*	5.4
Coefficient to step 1, +.33		Political strength of the military	4.7
2 *Importance of the indigenous middle class*	5.7	Political stability	3.4
		Coefficient to step 3, −.15	
		Constant, −.29	
		Number of countries incorrectly classified, 6	

TABLE B4
Results of Discriminant Analysis for High Countries, 1957–62

Step and variable	F ratio	Step and variable	F ratio
1 *Strength of the labor move-*		National integration and sense	
ment	16.6	of national unity	5.4
Social mobility	13.6	Improvement in human re-	
Modernization of industry	12.5	sources	5.4
Predominant basis of the		Modernization of industry	4.7
political party system	11.4	Character of agricultural	
Centralization of political		organization	3.9
power	11.3	Administrative	
Administrative efficiency	10.1	efficiency	3.6
Competitiveness of political		Urbanization	3.4
parties	8.7	Mass communication	3.2
Character of agricultural		Centralization of political	
organization	8.7	power	3.1
Adequacy of physical over-		Cultural and ethnic homo-	
head capital	8.2	geneity	3.1
Size of the traditional agri-		*Coefficient to step 2, +.77*	
cultural sector	7.9		
Freedom of political opposi-		3 *Improvement in human re-*	
tion and the press	7.7	*sources*	5.8
Mass communication	7.5	Competitiveness of political	
Effectiveness of financial insti-		parties	4.7
tutions	7.4	National integration and sense	
Importance of the indigenous		of national unity	4.1
middle class	6.8	Mass communication	3.7
Per capita GNP	6.6	Social mobility	3.5
Modernization of outlook	6.2	Importance of the indigenous	
Political strength of the		middle class	3.4
military	6.1	*Coefficient to step 3, +.53*	
Literacy	5.8		
Improvement in human		4 *Competitiveness of political*	
resources	5.2	*parties*	4.4
Modernization of techniques		National integration and sense	
in agriculture	4.7	of national unity	4.0
National integration and sense		Social mobility	3.3
of national unity	4.5	*Coefficient to step 4, +.27*	
Effectiveness of the tax system	3.2		
Political stability	3.2	5 *Social mobility*	3.8
Coefficient to step 1, +.63		Character of agricultural	
		organization	3.7
2 *Predominant basis of the po-*		Administrative efficiency	3.6
litical party system	8.4	*Coefficient to step 5, +.49*	
Competitiveness of political			
parties	7.5	Constant, −116.8	
Social mobility	6.6	Number of countries incor-	
		rectly classified, 1	

A Digression on Regression

We shall now show that cross-section regression analyses performed with our data are consistent with the results of our analyses of hierarchical interactions. However, the former suffer all the deficiencies of data, conceptualization, and statistical procedures discussed in Chapter 4, and in addition are less reliable than the latter. Regression analysis is more dependent on and more sensitive to the accuracy of data inputs than is hierarchical analysis, since it requires that measurements be cardinal. In contrast, hierarchical analysis is based on variance comparisons involving averages for relatively homogeneous groups and is therefore much less sensitive to errors of measurement in individual country observations. Furthermore, the level of measurement required of the independent variables is only ordinal. The seriousness with which one takes the regression results, therefore, depends upon one's faith in the consistency they show with the interrelationships suggested by the cross-group comparisons of Chapter 4. We discuss the regressions here in spite of our low degree of confidence in them to avoid their presentation elsewhere without appropriate cautions and caveats.

The dependent variables in the regressions below are the income shares and per capita income of the poorest 40 percent, the poorest 60 percent, the richest 20 percent, and the richest 5 percent of the population.

For the principal independent variable we use World Bank estimates of gross domestic product per capita in 1964 prices for the same year as the income distribution data.* These data pose serious index number

* In the studies of Chapters 3 and 4, where our purpose was to rank countries by GNP per capita as a proxy for level of economic development, we used data for 1961 provided by the Agency for International Development (see Chapter 2, p. 73). Here we could not use the GNP series because we required the absolute value of per capita income for the same year as the income distribution data, not just a value that would rank countries by per capita income. This information was available only in the form of per capita GDP, not per capita GNP.

TABLE C1

Cross-Section Regressions of Relative Income Shares
on GDP per Capita

(T-ratios given in parentheses)

Constant	GDP per capita	GDP per capita squared	Improve-ment in human resources	Direct government economic activity	$\bar{R}^2$
Relative Income Share, Lowest 40 Percent					
21.5	−.06	.00007			.26
(10.7)	(3.9)	(3.6)			
20.2	−.06	.00007	.04		.27
(10.4)	(4.1)	(3.7)	(1.4)		
19.2	−.05	.00005		.02	.25
(7.6)	(3.2)	(2.8)		(1.0)	
19.1	−.05	.00006	.04	.01	.26
(7.6)	(3.3)	(3.0)	(1.1)	(.7)	
Relative Income Share, Lowest 60 Percent					
35.1	−.08	.0001			.21
(11.9)	(3.6)	(3.6)			
32.4	−.09	.0001	.11		.29
(11.8)	(4.3)	(4.0)	(2.5)		
29.9	−.06	.00007		.05	.23
(8.2)	(2.6)	(2.5)		(1.7)	
29.9	−.08	.00009	.1	.03	.29
(8.5)	(3.4)	(3.1)	(2.0)	(1.1)	
Relative Income Share, Upper 20 Percent					
44.9	.10	−.0001			.25
(11.8)	(3.8)	(3.9)			
48.9	.12	−.0001	−.16		.34
(14.1)	(4.6)	(4.4)	(2.8)		
52.6	.07	−.0001		−.08	.28
(11.3)	(2.6)	(2.8)		(2.0)	
52.6	.10	−.0001	−.14	−.05	.35
(11.9)	(3.5)	(3.5)	(2.3)	(1.3)	
Relative Income Share, Upper 5 Percent					
23.9	.06	−.00009			.10
(6.1)	(2.1)	(2.4)			
28.2	.07	−.00008	−.16		.18
(7.8)	(2.7)	(2.5)	(2.6)		
34.3	.02	−.00003		−.11	.20
(7.5)	(.6)	(.8)		(2.9)	
34.4	.04	−.00005	−.12	−.09	.26
(7.8)	(1.5)	(1.4)	(1.9)	(2.2)	

problems as well as other well-known measurement difficulties in that their use involves simultaneous intertemporal and intercountry comparisons. A nonlinear form of this variable was used because our analyses of Chapter 4 indicated significant nonlinearities in the relationship between income shares and level of economic development. Of the various nonlinear forms tested, a function of GDP + GDP² provided the best fit.

Three other independent variables were included in various combinations: rate of improvement in human resources, extent of the direct

TABLE C2

Cross-Section Regressions of Absolute Income Shares
on GDP per Capita

(T-ratios given in parentheses)

Constant	GDP per capita	GDP per capita squared	Improve-ment in human resources	Direct government economic activity	Rate of growth of per capita GDP	$\bar{R}^2$
		Per Capita Income, Lowest 40 Percent				
30.3	.06	.00035				.76
(1.7)	(.5)	(2.1)				
18.3	−.02	.0004	.59			.79
(1.1)	(.2)	(2.7)	(2.2)			
17.0	.11	.0003		.13		.77
(.8)	(.9)	(1.8)		(.7)		
16.8	−.02	.0004	.58	.02		.78
(.8)	(.1)	(2.3)	(2.0)	(.1)		
30.6	.08	.0003			−.80	.76
(1.7)	(.6)	(2.0)			(.3)	
18.7	−.02	.004	.59		−.57	.78
(1.1)	(.1)	(2.6)	(2.2)		(.3)	
		Per Capita Income, Lowest 60 Percent				
30.9	.11	.0005				.86
(1.7)	(.9)	(2.8)				
15.9	.02	.0005	.70			.87
(1.0)	(.2)	(3.4)	(2.6)			
8.5	.20	.0003		.23		.86
(.4)	(1.5)	(2.0)		(1.2)		
8.3	.05	.0004	.65	.10		.87
(.4)	(.4)	(2.7)	(2.3)	(.6)		
31.6	.14	.0004			−1.6	.86
(1.8)	(1.0)	(2.5)			(.6)	
16.5	.03	.0005	.70		−.86	.87
(1.0)	(.2)	(3.1)	(2.6)		(.4)	

TABLE C2 (*continued*)

Constant	GDP per capita	GDP per capita squared	Improvement in human resources	Direct government economic activity	Rate of growth of per capita GDP	$\bar{R}^2$
		Per Capita Income, Upper 20 Percent				
−133.0 (2.2)	4.3 (9.7)	−.002 (4.0)				.94
−70.0 (1.2)	4.5 (10.8)	−.002 (4.5)	−2.5 (2.7)			.95
−27.5 (.4)	3.8 (8.8)	−.002 (3.0)		−1.0 (1.6)		.94
−26.9 (.4)	4.3 (9.2)	−.002 (3.7)	−2.2 (2.3)	−.59 (.9)		.95
−133.6 (2.1)	4.3 (9.1)	−.002 (3.8)			1.4 (.2)	.94
−70.1 (1.2)	4.5 (10.4)	−.002 (4.4)	−2.5 (2.6)		.26 (.03)	.95
		Per Capita Income, Upper 5 Percent				
−407.1 (1.6)	10.5 (5.9)	−.007 (3.2)				.79
−175.5 (.7)	10.7 (5.9)	−.007 (3.0)	−7.2 (1.8)			.80
42.6 (.1)	8.4 (4.6)	−.004 (1.9)	−4.1 (1.6)			.79
44.3 (.1)	9.7 (4.8)	−.005 (2.2)	−5.8 (1.4)	−3.0 (1.1)		.80
−400.5 (1.6)	10.7 (5.7)	−.008 (3.1)			−15.6 (.4)	.79
−101.2 (.7)	10.9 (5.8)	−.007 (3.0)	−7.1 (1.8)		−19.9 (.6)	.79

economic role of the government, and rate of growth of per capita GDP for the longest available period prior to the year of the income distribution data. The first two were included because of their frequent importance in our analyses of hierarchical interactions; the growth rate was included for its conceptual interest.

The regressions indicate rather weak nonlinear relationships between relative income shares and per capita GDP (see Tables C1 and C2). Up to about $350 to $400 per capita (1964 prices), the relative shares of the poorest 40 and 60 percents of the population are negatively related to per capita GDP, and above this level these shares are positively related to it. The relative shares of the upper 20 and 5 percents show the reverse relationship, tending to rise first and decline thereafter. Proportions of variance explained are quite low, ranging from 20 to 30 percent for the lower income shares, to as little as 5 to 10 percent for the upper income shares. Regressions of absolute income shares on per capita GDP alone show positive associations between GDP and all the absolute shares. As would be expected, the proportions of variance explained are quite high, ranging from 75 to more than 90 percent.

In general, the inclusion of either the rate of improvement of human resources or direct government economic activity in the equations improves the fit. These variables are always positively related to the relative and absolute income shares of the poorest quintiles and negatively related to those of the upper income groups. Short-term growth rates are not significantly related to income shares in any of the equations. In the regression of absolute per capita income of the poorest 40 percent on per capita GDP alone, the coefficient relating them is positive. With the addition of rate of improvement of human resources as a second independent variable, the relationship between income of the poor and average GDP shifts from a positive to a net negative one. The shift is understandable statistically, since per capita GDP and rate of improvement of human resources are significantly correlated. We interpret the shift to have substantive meaning in part because of its consistency with the results of the hierarchical analyses.

The regressions of the average absolute income of the poorest 40 percent on per capita GDP express the same somewhat complicated set of relationships discussed in Chapter 4. It will be recalled that the net relationship between the absolute position of the poorest 40 percent and levels of per capita income suggested by the cross-group comparisons in Chapter 4 is negative up to a very high level of development for low-income nations. Only for countries where intensive efforts to improve human resources have been made and widespread socioeconomic advances achieved is the relationship positive.* Similarly, in the cross-section regressions, the inclusion of both per capita GDP and the rate of improvement of human resources as independent variables yields a *net* negative association between the average income of the poorest two quintiles and per capita GDP. As in any regression analysis that includes more than one independent variable, the coefficients express the relationship between a given independent variable and the dependent variable net of interactions with the remaining independent variables. We therefore interpret the results described here to mean that increases in per capita GDP per se, unaccompanied by a higher rate of

* See pp. 178–81 above.

human resources development, are associated with lower average income for the poorest two quintiles of the population. Since per capita GDP and human resources development are significantly correlated, however, it should be stressed that this interpretation rests on external information including that obtained in the analyses of Chapter 4.

The regression results, when examined in their entirety, are thus entirely consistent with the hierarchical analyses, but they rest on a weaker statistical foundation.

Notes

Notes

INTRODUCTION

1. Albert Fishlow, "Brazilian Size Distribution of Income," *American Economic Association Papers and Proceedings*, 62 (1972): 391–402.

2. Irma Adelman and Cynthia Taft Morris, *Society, Politics, and Economic Development* (rev. ed.; Baltimore, 1971).

CHAPTER ONE

1. The discussion in this section owes much to H. Wold, "Nonlinear Iterative Partial Least Squares (NIPALS) Modelling—Some Current Developments," to appear in P. R. Krishnaiah, ed., *Multivariate Analysis, III* (New York, 1973), and is elaborated in I. Adelman and C. T. Morris, "Analysis of Variance Techniques for the Study of Economic Development," *Journal of Development Studies*, 8 (1971): 99–106.

2. Gerald M. Meier, *Leading Issues in Development Economics* (New York, 1964), pp. 53–54, 68–69.

3. John C. H. Fei and Gustav Ranis, "Agrarianism, Dualism, and Economic Development," in Irma Adelman and Erik Thorbecke, eds., *Theory and Design of Economic Development* (Baltimore, 1966), p. 23.

4. Abraham Kaplan, *The Conduct of Inquiry* (San Francisco, 1964), pp. 77–78; italics added on sentence.

5. For a discussion of various types of error, see *ibid.*, pp. 198ff.

6. See Karl Marx, *Capital, The Communist Manifesto, and Other Writings* (New York, 1932), pp. 324ff.; Werner Sombart, "Capitalism," *Encyclopaedia of Social Sciences*, III (New York, 1930); R. H. Tawney, *Religion and the Rise of Capitalism* (New York, 1926); Alexander Gerschenkron, *Economic Backwardness in Historical Perspective* (Cambridge, Mass., 1962); and John E. Sawyer, "Social Structure and Economic Progress: General Propositions and Some French Examples," *American Economic Review*, 41 (1951): 321–29.

7. See United Nations, *Compendium of Social Statistics, 1963* (New York, 1963), Table 8.

8. Bruce M. Russett et al., *World Handbook of Political and Social Indicators* (New Haven, 1964), Table 50.

9. Recent country studies were our principal sources of qualitative information. A few interviews were made to resolve doubtful cases.

10. See, in particular, *African Labour Survey* (Geneva, 1958); *Labour Survey of North Africa* (Geneva, 1960); K. C. Doctor and Hans Gallis, "Modern Sector Employment in Asian Countries: Some Empirical Estimates," *International Labour Review*, 90 (1964): 544–67; and by the same authors, "Size and Characteristics of Wage Employment in Africa: Some Statistical Estimates," *International Labour Review*, 93 (1966): 149–73.

11. For discussion of the importance of urbanization to economic growth, see "The Role of Cities in the Economic Development of Underdeveloped Countries," in B. F. Hoselitz, *Sociological Aspects of Economic Growth* (Glencoe, Ill., 1960), pp. 159–84.

12. See the discussion in Joan M. Nelson, *Migrants, Urban Poverty and Instability in Developing Nations* (Harvard University Center for International Affairs, Occasional Papers, no. 22, 1969).

13. *Ibid.*

14. Technical Bulletin no. 43 (Washington, D.C., 1966), Table III.

15. United Nations, *Compendium of Social Statistics, 1963*, Tables 68 and 69; United Nations, *Demographic Yearbook, 1964* (New York, 1964), Table 10.

16. The principal sources of qualitative information were recent country studies and, for African countries, G. H. T. Kimble, *Tropical Africa* (New York, 1960).

17. For the sources of this information, see the references listed for the indicator of the size of the traditional agricultural sector in notes 7–10 above.

18. For a discussion of the various aspects of opportunities for social mobility, see Gino Germani, "The Strategy of Fostering Social Mobility," in UNESCO, *Social Aspects of Economic Development in Latin America* (New York, 1963), I, pp. 211–30.

19. Russett, *World Handbook*, Table 63.

20. Arthur Banks and Robert Textor, *A Cross-Polity Survey* (Cambridge, Mass., 1964), raw characteristic number 45 (political leadership).

21. For a detailed description of the indicator that included the openness of access to leadership, see our article "A Factor Analysis of the Interrelationship between Social and Political Variables and Per Capita Gross National Product," *Quarterly Journal of Economics*, 79 (1965): 558–59.

22. Daniel Lerner, *The Passing of Traditional Society* (Glencoe, Ill., 1958), pp. 61ff.

23. Russett, Table 64.

24. See, for example, the essays in Lucian W. Pye, ed., *Communications and Political Development* (Princeton, N.J., 1963), as well as Wilbur Schramm, *Mass Media and National Development* (Stanford, Calif., 1964), and Lerner, *The Passing of Traditional Society*, chap. 2.

25. See, for example, Daniel Lerner, "Communication Systems and Social Systems: A Statistical Exploration," *Behavioral Science*, 2 (1957): 267.

26. Russett, Figure B-1, p. 300.

27. The data as well as the case deciles are presented in Table 31 (daily newspaper circulation per 1,000 population) and Table 35 (radios per 1,000 population), *ibid.*

28. See Clifford Geertz, "The Integrative Revolution, Primordial Sentiments and Civil Politics in the New States," in Clifford Geertz, ed., *Old Societies and New States* (New York, 1963), pp. 109ff.

29. Russett, Table 39.

30. Raw characteristic number 18 (linguistic homogeneity). We relied more heavily on Russett, however, because we preferred an index of speakers of a dominant language rather than one of speakers to whom the dominant language was their mother tongue.

31. Raw characteristics number 16 (religious homogeneity) and number 17 (racial homogeneity). Banks and Textor's estimates of racial composition were not sufficiently gradated for our purpose, so a good deal of supplementary information was necessary. We introduced their index of religious homogeneity with only a few changes and additions.

32. See Geertz, "The Integrative Revolution, Primordial Sentiments and Civil Politics in the New States."

33. Raw characteristics number 31 (political enculturation) and number 32 (sectionalism).

34. See United Nations, Department of Social Affairs, Population Division, *The Determinants and Consequences of Population Trends* (New York, 1958), p. 77.

35. See the *Demographic Yearbook, 1962, 1963,* and *1964.*

36. W. E. Moore, "Theory, Ideology, Non-Economic Values, and Politico-Economic Development," in Ralph Braibanti and Joseph J. Spengler, eds., *Tradition, Values and Socio-Economic Development* (Durham, N.C., 1961), p. 5.

37. Lerner, *The Passing of Traditional Society*, pp. 48–49.

38. Raw characteristics number 20 (westernization) and number 23 (political modernization periodization).

39. Max Weber, *The Protestant Ethic and the Spirit of Capitalism* (New York, 1958).

40. R. H. Tawney, *Religion and the Rise of Capitalism.*

41. See selections and references in Gerald D. Nash, ed., *Issues in American Economic History* (Boston, 1964), section 1.

42. Morris David Morris, "Values as an Obstacle to Economic Growth in South Asia: An Historical Survey," *Journal of Economic History*, 27 (1967): 588–607, and the references cited therein.

43. Raw characteristic no. 15 (religious configuration).

44. For a discussion of various measurement attempts, see Nancy Baster, ed., *Measuring Development: The Role and Adequacy of Development Indicators* (London, 1972).

45. This is the approach taken by the United Nations, *International Definition and Measurement of Standards and Levels of Living* (New York, 1961).

46. Irma Adelman and Cynthia Taft Morris, *Society, Politics, and Economic Development* (rev. ed.; Baltimore, 1971).

CHAPTER TWO

1. The following references are only a few of the many that might be cited: G. I. Blanksten, "Transference of Social and Political Loyalties," in B. F. Hoselitz and W. E. Moore, eds., *Industrialization and Society* (Paris, 1963); Phillips Cutright, "National Political Development: Measurement and Analysis," *American Sociological Review*, 28 (1963): 253–64; S. M. Lipset, "Some Social Requisites of Democracy: Economic Development and Political Legitimacy," *American Political Science Review*, 53 (1959): 69–105; Max F. Millikan and Donald L. M. Blackmer, eds., *The Emerging Nations* (Boston, 1961); and A. F. K. Organski, *The Stages of Political Development* (New York, 1965). See also G. A. Almond and J. S. Coleman, eds., *The Politics of the Developing Areas* (Princeton, N.J., 1960).

2. "A Functional Approach to Comparative Politics," in Almond and Coleman, pp. 3–64, and especially p. 18. For a somewhat similar view of political development, see F. W. Riggs, "Bureaucrats and Political Development: A Paradoxical View," in Joseph LaPalombara, ed., *Bureaucracy and Political Development* (Princeton, N.J., 1963), pp. 122–23. See also Cutright, p. 257.

3. Millikan and Blackmer, p. 74.

4. See Blanksten, pp. 177ff.

5. See the discussion of the degree and cultural and ethnic homogeneity for the sources of this information, p. 32.

6. See G. A. Almond in the introductory chapter to Almond and Coleman, p. 58.

7. Organski makes this point in *The Stages of Political Development*, chap. 2.

8. Arthur Banks and Robert Textor, *A Cross-Polity Survey* (Cambridge, Mass., 1964): raw characteristics number 28 (representative character of current regime), number 30 (freedom of group opposition), number 46 (leadership charisma), number 47 (vertical power distribution), and number 48 (horizontal power distribution).

9. *Ibid.*, raw characteristics number 13 (freedom of the press) and number 30 (freedom of group opposition).

10. *Ibid.*, raw characteristics number 42 (party system: qualitative) and number 44 (personalismo).

11. Clark Kerr, "Changing Social Structures," in Wilbert E. Moore and Arnold S. Feldman, eds., *Labor Commitment and Social Change in Developing Areas* (New York, 1960), pp. 351–52.

12. See, for example, Val R. Lorwin, "Working Class Politics and Economic Development in Western Europe," in Val R. Lorwin, ed.,

Labor and Working Conditions in Modern Europe (New York, 1967), pp. 58–72.

13. For a review of this controversy, see Adolf Sturmthal, "Unions and Economic Development," *Economic Development and Cultural Change*, 8 (1960): 199–205.

14. See Walter Galenson, ed., *Labor and Economic Development* (New York, 1959); Walter Galenson, ed., *Labor in Developing Economies* (Berkeley, Calif., 1962); E. M. Kassalow, ed., *National Labor Movements in the Postwar World* (Evanston, Ill., 1963); M. P. Troncoso and B. G. Burnett, *The Rise of the Latin American Labor Movement* (New York, 1960); and B. H. Millen, *The Political Role of Labor in Developing Countries* (Washington, D.C., 1963).

15. See B. F. Hoselitz, "Tradition and Economic Growth," in Ralph Braibanti and Joseph J. Spengler, eds., *Tradition, Values, and Socio-Economic Development* (Durham, N.C., 1961), pp. 83–113.

16. Edwin Lieuwen, *Arms and Politics in Latin America*, rev. ed. (New York, 1961); Manfred Halpern, *The Politics of Social Change in the Middle East and North Africa* (Princeton, N.J., 1963); Banks and Textor, raw characteristics number 45 (political leadership) and number 53 (character of bureaucracy).

17. L. W. Pye, "Armies in the Process of Political Modernization," in J. J. Johnson, ed., *The Role of the Military in Underdeveloped Countries* (Princeton, N.J., 1962), pp. 73ff; see also Millikan and Blackmer, pp. 31–37.

18. Lieuwen, p. 155.

19. Raw characteristic number 54 (political participation by the military).

20. Johnson, *The Role of the Military*.

21. See Sidney A. Burrell, ed., *The Role of Religion in Modern European History* (New York, 1964), pp. 5ff.

22. See J. J. Spengler, "Bureaucracy and Economic Development," in LaPalombara, *Bureaucracy and Political Development*, pp. 225–26.

23. Quoted in "An Overview of Bureaucracy and Political Development," in LaPalombara, p. 10.

24. For a discussion of these problems, see Albert Waterston, *Development Planning: Lessons of Experience* (Baltimore, 1966), chap. 1.

25. Peter Wiles makes these points in his review of Jan Tinbergen's *Central Planning* (New Haven, 1964), *American Economic Review*, 55 (1965): 910.

26. See, for example, H. W. Broude, "The Role of the State in American Economic Development, 1820–1890," in H. G. J. Aitken, ed., *The State and Economic Growth* (New York, 1959), pp. 4–25.

27. For a brief discussion of reasons for the large contemporary economic roles of governments in low-income countries, see Edward Shils, *Political Development in the New States* (The Hague, 1962), p. 27.

28. Alexander Eckstein, "Individualism and the Role of the State in Economic Growth," *Economic Development and Cultural Change*, 6

(1958), reprinted in D. E. Novack and Robert Lekachman, eds., *Development and Society* (New York, 1964); see especially pp. 424–25.

29. See J. G. Williamson, "Public Expenditure and Revenue: An International Comparison," *Manchester School of Economic and Social Studies*, 29 (1961): 43–56; and Alison Martin and W. A. Lewis, "Patterns of Public Revenue and Expenditure," *Manchester School of Economic and Social Studies*, 24 (1956): 203–44.

30. Bruce M. Russett et al., *World Handbook of Political and Social Indicators* (New Haven, 1964), Tables 11, 13, 15, and 17.

31. In addition, we consulted some 30 regional experts. U.N. data were collected from the 1963 *Statistical Yearbook* on countries for which a breakdown between private and government fixed capital formation was available.

32. For a review of many aspects of these controversies, see the articles by Rupert Emerson and D. K. Fieldhouse on colonialism in the *International Encyclopaedia of the Social Sciences*, 3 (New York, 1967): 1–13. See also G. H. Nadel and L. P. Curtis, Jr., eds., *Imperialism and Colonialism* (New York, 1964). For a variety of views on the avowed purposes of colonial development, see D. K. Fieldhouse, ed., *The Theory of Capitalist Imperialism* (London, 1967).

33. See the article by Emerson, *ibid.*, and Nadel and Curtis, pp. 12–22. See also the excerpt by Margery Perham in the latter book, especially pp. 145–46.

34. This point is made by W. E. Moore, "The Social Framework of Economic Development," in Braibanti and Spengler, pp. 68–69.

35. Russett, Table 29.

36. Raw characteristics number 27 and number 43.

37. See I. M. D. Little, *A Critique of Welfare Economics* (2d ed.; Oxford, 1957), p. 6.

38. William Nordhaus and James Tobin, "Is Growth Obsolete?" Paper prepared for National Bureau of Economic Research Colloquium, Dec. 10, 1970 (mimeo.).

39. For discussion of the deficiencies of national income as a measure of differences among countries in levels and rates of change in economic welfare, see E. E. Hagen, "Some Facts About Income Levels and Economic Growth," *Review of Economics and Statistics*, 42 (1960): 62–67, and D. C. Paige et al., "Economic Growth: The Last Hundred Years," *National Institute Economic Review*, July 1961, Appendix II, pp. 42–49. For references to the theoretical literature on the conceptual difficulties involved in measuring gains in welfare, see Little, chaps. 6 and 7.

40. For discussion of the difficulties associated with the use of national income as a measure of total productive capacity and changes in productive capacity, see G. W. Nutter, "On Measuring Economic Growth," *Journal of Political Economy*, 65 (1957): 51–63.

41. Agency for International Development, Statistics and Reports Division, "84 Underdeveloped Countries—Two Thirds World Population Grouped According to Estimated Annual per Capita Income (U.S. Dollar Equivalent), 1961" (Washington, D.C., 1963).

42. For a detailed discussion of the views of the classical economists on the relationship between natural resources and standards of living, see Edwin Cannan, *A History of the Theories of Production and Distribution from 1776 to 1848* (3d ed.; London, 1917), chap. 5. John Stuart Mill gives a more optimistic view than did earlier writers of the possibility that technological progress may successfully offset diminishing returns in agriculture and mining; see his *Principles of Political Economy*, ed. W. J. Ashley (rev. ed.; London, 1909), Book I, chap. 12.

43. The *World Mark Encyclopaedia of the Nations: Americas*; the *Oxford Regional Economic Atlas: The Middle East and North Africa*; and the *Oxford Economic Atlas of the World*.

44. For a survey of capital stock adjustment theories of economic growth, see H. J. Bruton, "Contemporary Theorizing on Economic Growth," in Hoselitz, ed., *Theories of Economic Growth*, chap. 7.

45. William R. Cline, *Potential Effects of Income Redistribution on Economic Growth: Latin American Case* (New York, 1972).

46. See the earlier sections on social and political indicators for references to the rapidly growing literature on noneconomic influences upon economic development.

47. See, for example, the essays in Jan Tinbergen *et al.*, *Investment Criteria and Economic Growth* (New York, 1961).

48. United Nations, *Yearbook of National Accounts Statistics, 1964*, country tables; and AID, various internal documents.

49. P. N. Rosenstein-Rodan, "International Aid for Underdeveloped Countries," *Review of Economics and Statistics*, 43 (1961), Table 3-A, pp. 127ff.

50. See, for example, H. B. Chenery, "Patterns of Industrial Growth," *American Economic Review*, 50 (1960): 624–54, esp. the references cited on pp. 653–54. See also Simon Kuznets, "Quantitative Aspects of the Economic Growth of Nations, II: Industrial Distribution of National Product and Labor Force," *Economic Development and Cultural Change*, 5 (1957), Supplement, pp. 3–111.

51. For reference to the scanty literature on the impact of the early stages of industrialization on the income distribution in currently advanced economies, see Simon Kuznets, "Economic Growth and Income Inequality," *American Economic Review*, 45 (1955): 18–19.

52. For an excellent discussion of this point, see Stephen R. Lewis, Jr., "Notes on Industrialization and Income Distribution in Pakistan," Research Memorandum No. 37, 1970 (Center for Development Economics, Williams College, Williamstown, Mass., mimeo.).

53. The primary source of data on installed capacity of electrical energy in 1961 was the United Nations, *Statistical Yearbook, 1963*, Table 131. Population estimates for 1961 were taken from Russett, Table 1.

54. United Nations, *Yearbook of National Accounts Statistics, 1964*, Table 4B, pp. 373ff.

55. Data on percentage of the active male labor force in industry are from the United Nations, *Compendium of Social Statistics, 1963*,

Table 69, pp. 396ff (included in "industry" were SITC categories 1–5); the United Nations, *Demographic Yearbook, 1964,* Table 9; and in a few instances, the International Labour Organization, *International Labour Yearbook, 1964.* Data on the proportion of gross domestic product originating in industry are primarily from the United Nations, *Yearbook of National Accounts Statistics, 1964,* Table 3, pp. 364ff.

56. See, for example, J. W. Mellor, "The Process of Agricultural Development in Low-Income Countries," *Journal of Farm Economics,* 44 (1962): 704; and Doreen Warriner, *Land Reform and Development in the Middle East* (2d ed.; New York, 1962), pp. 6–7.

57. See, for example, Carl H. Gotsch, "The Distributive Impact of Agricultural Growth: Low-Income Farmers and 'The System' " (Harvard Center for International Studies, 1971, mimeo.); and Uma J. Lele and J. W. Mellor, "Jobs, Poverty, and the 'Green Revolution,' " *International Affairs,* 1972, pp. 20–32.

58. Particularly useful were U.S. Department of Agriculture, Economic Research Service, *Changes in Agriculture in 26 Developing Nations, 1948 to 1963* (Washington, D.C., 1965); and J. P. Powelson, *Latin America—Today's Economic and Social Revolution* (New York, 1964).

59. For references to this literature, see B. F. Johnston and J. W. Mellor, "The Role of Agriculture in Economic Development," *American Economic Review,* 51 (1961): 566–93; and J. W. Mellor, "The Process of Agricultural Development in Low-Income Countries," *Journal of Farm Economics,* 44 (1962): 700–716.

60. William J. Staub and Melvin G. Blase, "Induced Technological Change in Developing Agricultures: Implications for Income Distribution and Agricultural Development." Paper No. 15, University of Hawaii, East-West Center, 1972, mimeo.

61. Estimates of wage employment in the modern sector are available for some countries in the studies of the International Labour Organization referred to in Chapter 1, note 10.

62. FAO, *Production Yearbook, 1963.* The relevant tables were 100, 101, 102, 103, and 104. Estimates of total agricultural population were from Table 4A. For countries having no direct data on total agricultural population, we used data on total population contained in Russett, Table 1, together with estimates of the proportion of the population in the agricultural sector; for the sources of the latter estimates, see Chapter 1, notes 7–8.

63. See, for example, P. N. Rosenstein-Rodan, "Notes on the Theory of the 'Big Push,' " together with the comments of Celso Furtado and Ragnar Nurkse, in the International Economic Association's *Economic Development for Latin America,* H. S. Ellis and H. C. Wallich, eds. (New York, 1963), chap. 3; the selections on "Growth—Balanced or Unbalanced?" in G. M. Meier, *Leading Issues in Development Economics* (New York, 1964), pp. 250–66, and the references cited on pp. 283–84; and Tibor Scitovsky, "Two Concepts of External Economies," *Journal of Political Economy,* 62 (1954): 143–51.

64. Irma Adelman and George Dalton, "A Factor Analysis of Modernization in Village India," *Economic Journal*, 81 (1971): 563–79.

65. See Staub and Blase, "Induced Technological Change in Developing Agricultures."

66. The source for data on electrical capacity was the United Nations, *Statistical Yearbook, 1963*, Table 131. Population figures for adjusting to a per capita basis were from Russett, Table 1.

67. For discussion of the contributions of taxation to economic development, see U. K. Hicks, *Development Finance: Planning and Control* (New York, 1965), pp. 67ff.; and the chapters by Nicholas Kaldor and V. L. Urquidi in Organization of American States, *Fiscal Policy for Economic Growth in Latin America* (Baltimore, 1965).

68. See R. Bird and O. Oldman, eds., *Readings on Taxation in Developing Countries* (Baltimore, 1967).

69. See, for example, Charles E. McLure, Jr., "The Incidence of Taxation in Colombia," in Malcolm Gillis, ed., *Fiscal Reform for Colombia: The Final Report and Staff Papers of the Colombian Commission for Tax Reform* (Cambridge, Mass., 1971).

70. See, for example, Richard Goode, "Reconstruction of Foreign Tax Systems," *Proceedings of the Forty-fourth Annual Conference of the National Tax Association, 1951* (Sacramento, Calif., 1952).

71. More specifically, the sources were the United Nations, *Yearbook of National Accounts Statistics, 1964*, country tables; United Nations, *Statistical Yearbook, 1963*, Table 181; United Nations, ECAFE, "Design of Fiscal Policy for Increasing Government Saving," *Economic Bulletin for Asia and the Far East*, 13 (December 1962), Table 7; U Tun Wai, "Taxation Problems and Policies of Underdeveloped Countries," *IMF Staff Papers*, 9 (November 1962): 428–48; and A. Abdel-Rahmen, "The Revenue Structure of the CFA Countries," *IMF Staff Papers*, 12 (March 1965): 73–118. Also useful in classifying Latin American countries was R. Desai, "Fiscal Capacity of Developing Economies," in Organization of American States, *Fiscal Policy for Economic Growth in Latin America*, chap. 2, Table 2.

72. United Nations, *Yearbook of National Accounts Statistics, 1964*.

73. For discussion of the functions of financial institutions in promoting economic development, with special reference to contemporary underdeveloped countries, see Edward Nevin, *Capital Funds in Underdeveloped Countries: The Role of Financial Institutions* (New York, 1961), chap. 4; and Hicks, *Development Finance*, pp. 51ff. Other general treatments of domestic financing of economic development are E. M. Bernstein, "Financing Economic Growth in Underdeveloped Economies," in W. W. Heller et al., *Savings in the Modern Economy* (Minneapolis, Minn., 1953), chap. 16; and United Nations, Department of Economic Affairs, *Domestic Financing of Economic Development* (New York, 1950).

74. See, for example, U Tun Wai, "Interest Rates Outside the Organized Money Markets of Underdeveloped Countries," *IMF Staff Papers*, 6 (November 1957): 80–142.

238 Notes to Pages 97–103

75. Sources for estimates of average gross domestic savings rates for the period 1957–62 were the United Nations, *Yearbook of National Accounts Statistics, 1964,* country tables; United Nations, Conference on Trade and Development, *Economic Growth and External Debt— An Analytical Framework,* March 1964, Table 9, titled "Some indicators of Economic Growth"; and recent country studies. The sources for data on the volume of time and demand deposits and money were the International Monetary Fund, *International Financial Statistics,* October 1965, country tables, and the *Supplement to International Financial Statistics, 1965/66;* for these data, an average was taken for the years 1957–62. GNP estimates came from the same IMF sources; the United Nations, *Yearbook of National Accounts Statistics, 1964;* and recent country studies. Where possible, an average of GNP estimates for the 1957–62 period was taken, but for some countries only a point estimate for 1960 or 1961 was available.

76. See the references in note 75 above. It should be noted that private and government liabilities to the banking system are listed in the country tables under "domestic credit" as "claims by banks on the private and government sectors."

77. Our indicator of the extent of literacy is discussed on pp. 27–28. See Daniel Lerner, *The Passing of Traditional Society* (Glencoe, Ill., 1958), pp. 61ff., and Russett, Table 64.

78. See, for example, the United Nations, *Report on the World Social Situation with Special Reference to the Problem of Balanced Social and Economic Development* (New York, 1961); Frederick Harbison and C. A. Myers, *Education, Manpower and Economic Growth* (New York, 1964); and Walter Galenson and Graham Pyatt, *The Quality of Labour and Economic Development in Certain Countries* (Geneva, 1964).

79. Samuel Bowles, "Class Power and Mass Education: A Study of Social Structure and Resource Allocation in Schooling" (Harvard Center for International Studies, 1971, mimeo.).

80. Frederick H. Harbison, *Human Resources as the Wealth of Nations* (London, 1973), Preface.

81. Harbison and Myers, chap. 3.

82. UNESCO, *World Survey of Education* (New York, 1961–66), III and IV, country tables.

83. Estimates of total population for 1961 are from Russett, Table 1. The United Nations demographic yearbooks were used to obtain the breakdown of population by age group where available.

84. See the United Nations, *Instability in Export Markets of Underdeveloped Countries* (New York, 1952); A. C. Harberger, "Some Evidence on the International Price Mechanism," *Journal of Political Economy,* 65 (1957): 506–21; and the chapters by Gottfried Haberler ("Terms of Trade and Economic Development") and T. W. Schultz ("Economic Prospects of Primary Products") in Howard S. Ellis and Henry C. Wallich, eds., *Economic Development for Latin America* (New York, 1963).

85. See Derek T. Healey, "Development Policy: New Thinking About an Interpretation," *Journal of Economic Literature*, 10 (1972), especially sections III and VI, and references cited therein.

86. See Hollis B. Chenery and Lance Taylor, "Development Patterns: Among Countries and Over Time," *Review of Economics and Statistics*, 50 (1968): 391–416.

87. For summaries of population theory, see papers appearing in "New Economic Approaches to Fertility," *Journal of Political Economy*, Supplement 81, March/April 1973, and references cited therein.

88. See Chenery and Taylor.

89. *Ibid.*

CHAPTER THREE

1. Herbert McClosky, "Political Participation," *International Encyclopaedia of the Social Sciences*, 12: 253.

2. George H. Sabine, *A History of Political Theory* (3d ed.; New York, 1961), p. 753.

3. See, for example, J. J. Rousseau, *The Social Contract*, translated by M. Cronston (Baltimore, 1968); and J. S. Mill, *Considerations on Representative Government* (ed. Currin V. Shields; Indianapolis, 1958). For a general discussion, see Carole Pateman, *Participation and Democratic Theory* (Cambridge, Eng., 1970).

4. Sigmund Neumann, "Toward a Comparative Study of Political Parties," in Harry Eckstein and David E. Apter, eds., *Comparative Politics, A Reader* (New York, 1963).

5. "The Impact of Parties on Political Development," in Joseph LaPalombara and Myron Weiner, eds., *Political Parties and Political Development* (Princeton, N.J., 1966).

6. Giovanni Sartori, "The Typology of Party Systems: Proposals for Improvement," in Erik Allardt and Stein Rokkan, eds., *Mass Politics: Studies in Political Sociology* (New York, 1970).

7. Douglas E. Ashford, *National Development and Local Reform* (Princeton, N.J., 1967), p. 10.

8. Seymour Martin Lipset, "Some Social Requisites of Democracy: Economic Development and Political Legitimacy," *American Political Science Review*, 53 (1959): 69–105; Phillips Cutright, "National Political Development: Measurement and Analysis," *American Sociological Review*, 28 (1963): 253–64; Phillips Cutright and James A. Wiley, "Modernization and Political Representation: 1927–1966," in *Studies in Comparative International Development* (Rutgers University), 5, no. 2 (1969–70); and Arthur K. Smith, Jr., "Socio-Economic Development and Political Democracy," *Midwest Journal of Political Science*, 13 (1969): 95–125.

9. Lipset, in "Some Social Requisites of Democracy," uses this criterion in differentiating between democracies and dictatorships in Latin America.

10. Cutright uses a measure of this type in both the articles cited in note 8.

11. Everett E. Hagen, "A Framework for Analyzing Economic and Political Change," in Robert E. Asher et al., *Development of the Emerging Countries: An Agenda for Research* (Washington, D.C., 1962), p. 2.

12. Daniel Lerner, *The Passing of Traditional Society* (Glencoe, Ill., 1958), chap. 2.

13. Karl W. Deutsch, "Social Mobilization and Political Development," *American Political Science Review*, 55 (1961): 493–514.

14. See, for example, James B. Bryce, *Modern Democracies* (2 vols.; London, 1921); Alexander Brady, *Democracy in the Dominions: A Comparative Study in Institutions* (Toronto, 1947).

15. McClosky in "Political Participation" surveys the literature on the causes of interpersonal differences in levels of political participation, stressing differences in social and political environment and psychological variables.

16. There is an extremely large number of case studies of political structure in individual developed and underdeveloped countries. See, for example, John Kie-Chiang Oh, *Korea: Democracy on Trial* (Ithaca, N.Y., 1968), or Richard L. Sklar, *Nigerian Political Parties: Power in an Emergent African Nation* (Princeton, N.J., 1963).

17. The technique of discriminant analysis is explained in C. R. Rao, *Advanced Statistical Methods in Biometric Research* (New York, 1952), chaps. 7–9; and in W. W. Cooley and P. R. Lohnes, *Multivariate Procedures for the Behavioral Sciences* (New York, 1962), chaps. 6–7.

18. Cooley and Lohnes, chaps. 6, 7.

19. "Citizen Participation in Political Life," *International Social Science Journal*, no. 1 (1960): 12. The whole issue is devoted to the topic.

20. McClosky, p. 252.

21. Irma Adelman and Cynthia Taft Morris, *Society, Politics, and Economic Development: A Quantitative Approach* (rev. ed.; Baltimore, 1971), chap. 2.

22. See, for example, Hollis B. Chenery and Lance Taylor, "Development Patterns: Among Countries and Over Time," *Review of Economics and Statistics*, 50 (1968): 391–92.

23. For a discussion of the close association between increased social mobility and the growth of varied participant institutions in nineteenth-century Europe, see Eugene N. Anderson and Pauline R. Anderson, *Political Institutions and Social Change in Continental Europe in the Nineteenth Century* (Berkeley, Calif., 1967), pp. 9ff. For a variety of case studies of the relationship between social stratification, social mobility, and the distribution of political power, see Reinhard Bendix and Seymour Martin Lipset, eds., *Class, Status, and Power: Social Stratification in Comparative Perspective* (2d ed.; New York, 1966).

24. For a discussion of the manner in which social and socioeconomic changes in the industrializing countries of nineteenth-century Europe contributed to the breakdown of absolute forms of government and to increased participation by middle-class and professional groups

in politics, see Anderson and Anderson, chaps. 1, 8–10. For discussion of the strong contemporary influence of social environment, particularly education and occupation, on political participation, see McClosky, pp. 256–57. For findings of significant quantitative associations between national representative institutions and urbanization, literacy, and agricultural employment for a sample of developed and underdeveloped countries, see William Flanigan and Edwin Fogelman, "Patterns of Political Development and Democratization: A Quantitative Analysis," in John V. Gillespie and Betty A. Nesvold, eds., *Macro-Quantitative Analysis: Conflict, Development and Democratization* (Beverly Hills, Calif., 1971), pp. 441–73. See also Cutright, "National Political Development," pp. 253–64, for similar results.

25. Deutsch, "Social Mobilization and Political Development," p. 493.

26. *Ibid.*, p. 494.

27. *Ibid.*, p. 499.

28. W. W. Rostow in his recent study, *Politics and the Stages of Growth* (Cambridge, Eng., 1971), stresses the role of organized labor as a key indicator of the extent to which concentration of economic and political power is constrained politically for social welfare and distributional purposes; see chap. 4. Anderson and Anderson, chaps. 8–9, describe the gradual expansion of suffrage and increased participation in political parties as a consequence of the growth of a working class and of the political activities of working-class organizations. For a series of case studies of labor in contemporary underdeveloped countries, suggesting that unions typically operate as channels for influencing the political process, see Walter Galenson, ed., *Labor and Economic Development* (New York, 1959).

29. For case studies of the role of labor unions in underdeveloped countries, see the references cited in Chapter 2, note 14.

30. For discussion of positive and negative aspects of longer colonial rule, see C. E. Black, *The Dynamics of Modernization* (New York, 1967), pp. 102–3.

31. Adelman and Morris, *Society, Politics, and Economic Development*, chap. 6.

32. There is a considerable literature on the role of the middle class in the development of participant institutions in nineteenth-century Europe. See, for example, Anderson and Anderson, chap. 10; and J. Hovde, *The Scandinavian Countries, 1720–1865: The Rise of the Middle Classes* (Boston, 1943), especially chaps. 7 and 13. For discussion of the political role of the middle class in countries largely falling within the present intermediate sample, see Manfred Halpern, *The Politics of Social Change in the Middle East and North Africa* (Princeton, N.J., 1963), chap. 4.

33. Manfred Halpern discusses these interactions with respect to several Middle Eastern countries in the present sample. See his "Middle Eastern Armies and the New Middle Class," in J. J. Johnson, ed., *The*

Role of the Military in Underdeveloped Countries (Princeton, N.J., 1962).

34. Samuel P. Huntington, *Political Order in Changing Societies* (New Haven, 1968), p. 201.

35. *Ibid.* See also Huntington's discussion in chap. 7, "Parties and Political Stability."

CHAPTER FOUR

1. See R. H. Tawney, *Equality* (New York, 1964), for a well-known statement of egalitarian philosophy. See Herman P. Miller, *Rich Man, Poor Man* (New York, 1964), chap. 4, for a discussion of the common "myth" that recent economic growth in the United States has led to more equal income distribution. For an excellent discussion of the various rationales for income equality, see Michael Lipton, *Assessing Economic Performance* (London, 1968), pp. 85ff.

2. See, for example, Michael Harrington, *The Other America: Poverty in the United States*, rev. ed. (Baltimore, 1971), *passim.*

3. See, for instance, Stephan Michelson, "The Economics of Real Income Distribution," *Review of Radical Political Economics*, Spring 1970.

4. For a survey of recent theories of the functional income distribution, see Tibor Scitovsky, "A Survey of Some Theories of Income Distribution," in National Bureau of Economic Research, *The Behavior of Income Shares: Selected Theoretical and Empirical Issues* (Princeton, N.J., 1964), pp. 15ff. See also Martin Bronfenbrenner, *Income Distribution Theory* (Chicago, 1971).

5. John Stuart Mill, *Principles of Political Economy*, new ed., ed. W. J. Ashley (New York, 1961), Book 4, chap. 3, esp. pp. 720–24.

6. Karl Marx, *Das Capital, The Communist Manifesto, and Other Writings*, ed. Max Eastman (New York, 1932), esp. pp. 141–46 and 161–82.

7. See, for example, John Bates Clark, *The Distribution of Wealth* (New York, 1956), esp. chap. 2, and J. R. Hicks, *The Theory of Wages*, 2d ed. (London, 1964), chap. 6.

8. Nicholas Kaldor, "Alternative Theories of Distribution," *Review of Economic Studies*, 23, no. 2 (1956): 83–100.

9. D. G. Champernowne, "A Model of Income Distribution," *Economic Journal*, 63 (1953): 318–51, and Benoit Mandelbrot, "Stable Paretian Random Functions and the Multiplicative Variation of Income," *Econometrica*, 29 (1961): 517–43. An exception is J. E. Stiglitz, "Distribution of Income Wealth Among Individuals," *Econometrica*, 37 (1969): 382–97, in which the impact of alternative assumptions about savings, reproduction, inheritance policies, and labor homogeneity are analyzed within the framework of a simple model of capital accumulation. For a summary of a variety of hypotheses that have been put forth to explain the skewedness in the size distribution of income, see Stanley Lebergott, "The Shape of the Income Distribution," *American Economic Review*, 49 (1959): 328–47.

10. See Simon Kuznets, "Economic Growth and Income Inequality," *American Economic Review*, 65 (1955): 1–28; Gary S. Becker and Barry R. Chiswick, "Education and the Distribution of Earnings," *American Economic Association Papers and Proceedings*, 56 (1966): 358–69; Robert J. Lampman, *The Share of Top Wealth-Holders in National Wealth* (Princeton, N.J., 1962); Roger A. Herriot and Herman P. Miller, "Who Paid the Taxes in 1968?" (paper prepared for a meeting of the National Industrial Conference Board, New York, March 18, 1971, mimeo.) for an attempt to measure the total tax burden (federal, state, and local) by income levels. The results in this latter study indicate very little progressivity in the U.S. tax structure below the very highest income levels. For an interesting application of the technique used in the present chapter to "explain" differential changes in money income for a sample of 1,274 family units in terms of the characteristics of heads of families, see James D. Smith and James N. Morgan, "Variability of Economic Well-being and Its Determinants," *American Economic Association Papers and Proceedings*, 60 (1970): 286–95.

11. See, however, H. T. Oshima, "The International Comparison of Size Distribution of Family Incomes with Special Reference to Asia," *Review of Economics and Statistics*, 44 (1962): 439–45, and Irving B. Kravis, "International Differences in the Distribution of Incomes," *Review of Economics and Statistics*, 42 (1960): 408–16.

12. Kuznets, "Economic Growth and Income Inequality," p. 4. This generalization is based on data for the United States, Great Britain, and Germany; data on Norway and Sweden also show the same broad pattern, according to the same author in *Modern Economic Growth: Rate, Structure, and Spread* (New Haven, 1966), pp. 206ff. For further data supporting this generalization, see Irving Kravis, *The Structure of Income: Some Quantitative Essays* (Philadelphia, 1962), chap. 7, and Simon Kuznets, assisted by Elizabeth Jenks, *Shares of Upper Income Groups in Income and Savings* (New York, 1953). A recent study indicating a slight positive effect of growth in equalizing incomes is Andrew F. Brimmer, "Inflation and Income Distribution in the United States," *Review of Economics and Statistics*, 53 (1971): esp. 40–41.

13. For a more detailed discussion of empirical approaches to the use of quantitative techniques, see Irma Adelman and Cynthia Taft Morris, "Analysis-of-Variance Techniques for the Study of Economic Development," *Journal of Development Studies*, 8 (1971): 99–106.

14. For an analysis of the biases of cross-sectional statistical analyses, see Edwin Kuh, "The Validity of Cross-Sectionally Estimated Behavior Equations in Time Series Applications," *Econometrica*, 27 (1959): 197–214.

15. For a description of the technique, see John A. Sonquist and James N. Morgan, *The Detection of Interaction Effects* (Ann Arbor, Mich., 1964). The only applications of the technique that have come to our attention are two papers by James N. Morgan and James D. Smith: "Measures of Economic Well-offness and Their Correlates,"

American Economic Association Papers and Proceedings, 59 (1969): 450–62, and "Variability of Economic Well-being."

16. For discussions of various measures of income distribution, see, among others, James N. Morgan, "The Anatomy of Income Distributions," *Review of Economics and Statistics*, 44 (1962): 270–83; Kuznets, "Economic Growth and Income Inequality," esp. pp. 12–16; and Anthony B. Atkinson, "On the Measurement of Inequality," *Journal of Economic Theory*, 2 (1970): 244–63.

17. See Irving Kravis, *The Structure of Income*.

18. For a detailed discussion of desiderata for income distribution data, see Kuznets, "Economic Growth and Income Inequality," pp. 1–3.

19. For a description of this measure, see Irma Adelman and Cynthia Taft Morris, "Performance Criteria for Evaluating Economic Development Potential: An Operational Approach," *Quarterly Journal of Economics*, 82 (1968): 261–62. For individual country scores, see Table 5 of that article, pp. 278–79.

20. Abraham Kaplan, *The Conduct of Inquiry* (San Francisco, 1964), p. 198.

21. This discussion follows Kaplan's in *The Conduct of Inquiry*, pp. 199–201.

22. See Paul A. Baran, "On the Political Economy of Backwardness," in A. N. Agarwala and S. P. Singh, eds., *The Economics of Underdevelopment* (New York, 1958), pp. 75–92.

23. For time series studies, see Subramanian Swamy, "Structural Changes and the Distribution of Income by Size: The Case of India," *Review of Income and Wealth*, Series 2 (June 1967), pp. 155–74; Richard Weisskoff, "Income Distribution and Economic Growth in Puerto Rico, Argentina, and Mexico," *Review of Income and Wealth*, 16 (1970); and the references cited on p. 305 of the latter article. For examples of cross-sectional studies, see T. Morgan, "Distribution of Income in Ceylon, Puerto Rico, the United States and the United Kingdom," *Economic Journal*, 43 (1953): 821–35, and Oshima, "International Comparison."

24. See Irma Adelman and Cynthia Taft Morris, *Society, Politics, and Economic Development* (Baltimore, 1971), chaps. 5–7.

Sources and Notes to Table 1, p. 152.
Numbers in parentheses correspond to row numbers in the table.

(1) Argentina, households (1961): United Nations, Economic Commission for Latin America (subsequently abbreviated as UN, ECLA), "Economic Development and Income Distribution in Argentina," E/CN.12/802 (New York, 1969), p. 102.

(2) Bolivia, households (1968): National Secretariat of Planning, prepared for AID, 1969 (allocation between 0–40% and 40–60% estimated on basis of distribution in similar countries in Latin America having about the same share for 0–60%; share of 80–100% interpolated by curve fitting).

(3) Brazil, population (1960): William R. Cline, "Income Distribution Data for Argentina, Brazil, Chile, Colombia, Mexico, and Venezuela," prepared for AID, 1969 (shares of 0–40% and 40–60% estimated by curve fitting).

(4) Burma, households (1958): Central Statistical and Economics Department, Government of the Union of Burma, "Report on the 1958 Survey of Household Expenditure in Rangoon" (adjusted on the basis of National Account data to reflect the distribution of rural income; shares of 0–40%, 40–60%, and 60–80% estimated by curve fitting).

(5) Ceylon, population (1963): Central Bank of Ceylon, Department of Economic Research, "Survey of Ceylon's Consumer Finances, 1962" (Colombo, 1964), p. 66.

(6) Chad, population (1958): Christian Morrisson, *La Répartition des Revenus dans les pays du Tiers-Monde* (Paris, 1969), pp. 194, 205 (division of income between 0–60% and 60–80% estimated on the basis of classification by concentration of income 1A on p. 194; share of 0–40% estimated by curve fitting).

(7) Chile, households (1968): Cline, p. A3 (shares of 40–60% and 95–100% interpolated by curve fitting).

(8) Colombia, households (1964): Cline, p. A5.

(9) Costa Rica, households (1969): UN, ECLA, *Economic Survey of Latin America, 1969* (New York, 1970), Fig. 35, p. 366 (share of 0–40% interpolated by curve fitting).

(10) Dahomey, population (1959): Morrisson, pp. 194, 205 (allocation between 0–60% and 60–80% estimated on basis of classification by income concentration 2A on p. 194; 0–40% estimated by curve fitting).

(11) Ecuador, population (1968): Alianza Para el Progreso *Evaluación del Plan General de Desarrollo Económico y Social del Ecuador* (August 1961), National Development Plan, 1964–73, p. 62 (distribution between 0–40%, 40–60%, and 60–80% estimated on basis of distribution in other Latin American countries having same share to 0 80%).

(12) El Salvador, households (1965): UN, ECLA, *Economic Survey of Latin America, 1969*, p. 378 (share of 40–60% interpolated by curve fitting).

(13) Gabon, population (1960): Morrisson, pp. 194, 205 (allocation between 0–60% and 60–80% estimated on basis of classification by income concentration 6B on p. 194; 0–40% estimated by curve fitting).

(14) Greece, population (1957): Jean Crockett, "Consumer Expenditures and Incomes in Greece" (University of Pennsylvania and Center of Planning and Research, Athens, 1967), p. 96 (share of 95–100% adjusted using UN national accounts data on property income and ILO labor estimates by skill).

(15) India, households (1956–57): P. D. Ojna and V. V. Bhatr, "Patterns of Income Distribution in an Underdeveloped Country: A Case Study," *American Economic Review*, 54 (1964): 714.

(16) Iraq, population (1956): Morrisson, pp. 194, 205 (allocation

between 0–60% and 60–80% estimated on basis of classification 5B by income concentration on p. 194; share of 0–40% estimated by curve fitting).

(17) Israel, population (1957): Haim Ben-Shahar and Moshe Sandberg, "Economic and Institutional Effects on Income Distribution: The Case of Israel," *Public Finance*, 22 (1967): 244 (adjusted using UN national accounts data on property income).

(18) Ivory Coast, population (1959): Morrisson, p. 205 (shares of 0–40% and 40–60% estimated by curve fitting).

(19) Jamaica, households (1958): A. Ahiram, "Income Distribution in Jamaica, 1958," *Social and Economic Studies* (Institute of Social and Economic Research, University of the West Indies), 13, no. 3 (1964): 337.

(20) Japan, households (1962): Tadao Ishizaki, "The Income Distribution in Japan," *The Developing Economies*, 5, no. 2 (1967): 356.

(21) Lebanon, households (1955–60): Morrisson, p. 205 (share 60–80% estimated on basis of similar distributions having about the same income share to the 0–80% group; share of 0–40% interpolated by curve fitting).

(22) Libya, households (1962): Sami W. Dajani, "Family Budget Survey in Tripoli Town, 1962" (Tripoli: United Kingdom of Libya, Ministry of National Economy Central Statistics Office); adjusted with data from *Yearbook of National Accounts* (United Nations, 1968), p. 410; and *Compendium of Social Statistics*, Series K, no. 2 (United Nations, 1963).

(23) Madagascar, households (1960): Morrisson, pp. 159, 204 (allocation between 0–40%, 40–60%, and 60–80% estimated on basis of similar distributions and interpolations by curve fitting).

(24) Mexico, households (1963): Cline, Appendix A.

(25) Morocco, population (1965): Abderrazaq, "Les Salaires dans le Revenu National de 1955 à 1966," *Bulletin économique et social du Maroc*, 19, nos. 106–7 (1967) (share of 0–60% adjusted by estimates of agricultural income and population from UN national accounts and demographic data; shares of 0–40% and 95–100% estimated by curve fitting, with the latter adjusted with UN national accounts estimates of property income.

(26) Niger, population (1960): Morrisson, pp. 194, 204 (allocation between 0–60% and 60–80% estimated on basis of classification 1A by income concentration on p. 194; 0–40% estimated by curve fitting).

(27) Nigeria, population (1959): Jean Marchal and Bernard Ducros, *The Distribution of National Income* (New York, 1968), p. 405 (shares of 0–40%, 40–60%, and 60–80% estimated by curve fitting).

(28) Pakistan, households (1963–64): Asbjorn Bergan, "Personal Income Distribution and Personal Savings in Pakistan, 1963–64," *Pakistan Development Review*, 7, no. 2 (Summer, 1967), pp. 160–212.

(29) Panama, households (1969): UN, ECLA, *Economic Survey of Latin America, 1969*, Fig. 37, p. 366 (share of 40–60% interpolated by curve fitting).

(30) Peru, population (1961): "Income Distribution, 1961," Instituto Nacional de Planificacion, private communication (shares of 60–80% and 95–100% interpolated by curve fitting).

(31) Philippines, population (1961): Eustaquio O. Ordono, "The Pattern of Post-War Income Distribution in the Philippines," *Economic Research Journal*, 11, no. 3 (1964): 144 (share of 60–80% interpolated by curve fitting).

(32) Rhodesia, population (1946): Morrisson, pp. 194 and 205 (allocation between 0–60% and 60–80% estimated on basis of classification by income concentration 6B on p. 194; share of 0–40% estimated by curve fitting).

(33) Senegal, population (1960): Morrisson, pp. 194 and 205 (allocation between 0–60% and 60–80% estimated on basis of classification by income concentration on p. 194; share of 0–40% estimated by curve fitting).

(34) Sierra Leone, households (1968): "Sierra Leone Household Survey," *Africa Research Bulletin*, Feb. 14, 1968, p. 917 (shares of 40–60%, 60–80%, and 95–100% interpolated by curve fitting).

(35) South Africa, population (1965): Republic of South Africa, Bureau of Statistics, "Report No. 11–06–03, Survey of Family Expenditure, Ten Principal Urban Areas and the Urban Areas of the Vaal Triangle and the Orange Triangle and the Orange Free State Gold Fields, November, 1966, Family Income"; G. R. Feldmann-Laschin, F. E. Radel, and C. de Coning, "Income and Expenditure Patterns of Coloured Households, Cape Peninsula" (Pretoria: Bureau of Market Research, University of South Africa, 1965; adjusted with UN demographic data on population distribution, with all rural income assumed to be distributed as in the Cape Peninsula; property income adjusted with UN national accounts data).

(36) Sudan, households (1969): "Omdurman Household Budget Survey," Republic of the Sudan, Department of Statistics, p. 24.

(37) Surinam, population (1962): "Surinam in Figures, No. 44," Algemeen Bureau Voor de Statistiek, March 1967, p. 3 (share of 40–60% interpolated by curve fitting).

(38) Taiwan, households (1961): Kowie Chang, "Report on Pilot Study of Personal Income (and Consumption) in Taiwan" (prepared under the sponsorship of the working Group of National Income Statistics Directorate-General of the Budget, Account and Statistics, the Executive Yuan), Table C (share of 40–60% interpolated by curve fitting).

(39) Tanzania, population (1964): "Priyatosh Maitra," pp. 96–97; and Hadley E. Smith, ed., *Readings on Economic Development and Administration in Tanzania*, Dar Es Salaam, IPA, UDY, no. 4 (distribution of wage income adjusted with estimates of sectoral distribution of income and employment; shares of 0–40% and 40–60% estimated on basis of similar distributions in similar countries).

(40) Trinidad and Tobago, population (1965): Nugent Miller, "Some Observations on the Income Distribution of Trinidad and To-

bago," *Income, Earnings of Individuals by Sex, In 1–1* (Trinidad and Tobago, Continuous Sample Survey of Population, No. 6), pp. ix and 1 (adjusted with UN national accounts data on rural income and profit income and UN demographic data on rural population; shares of 40–60% and 60–80% interpolated by curve fitting).

(41) Tunisia, population (1971): Ghazi Duwaji, *Economic Development in Tunisia* (New York, 1967), p. 189 (figures are projected; shares of 40–60% and 60–80% interpolated by curve fitting).

(42) Venezuela, households (1962): Cline, p. A7 (share of 40–60% interpolated by curve fitting).

(43) Zambia, households (1959): Robert E. Baldwin, *Economic Development and Export Growth: A Study of Northern Rhodesia, 1920–1960* (Berkeley, Calif., 1966), p. 46 (The British protectorate of Northern Rhodesia became independent Zambia in 1964; share of 40–60% interpolated by curve fitting).

CHAPTER FIVE

1. Simon Kuznets, "Economic Growth and Income Inequality," *American Economic Review*, 45 (1955): 1–28.

2. Paul A. Baran, *The Political Economy of Growth* (New York, 1957), chap. 5.

3. Gustav Ranis and John C. H. Fei, "A Theory of Economic Development," *American Economic Review*, 51 (1961): 533–65.

4. See Irma Adelman and Cynthia Taft Morris, *Society, Politics, and Economic Development* (2d ed.; Baltimore, 1971), pp. 259ff.

5. *Ibid.*, pp. 261–63.

6. This finding is supported by those of W. W. Rostow in *Politics and the Stages of Growth* (Cambridge, Eng., 1971), chap. 7.

7. Irma Adelman, Marsha Geier, and Cynthia Taft Morris, "Instruments and Goals in Economic Development," American Economic Association, *Papers and Proceedings*, 59 (1969): 409–26.

8. Vita Tanzi, "Redistributing Income Through the Budget in Latin America," paper presented at a Conference on Equity and Income Distribution in Latin America, Georgetown University, November 17, 1972.

9. Hollis Chenery proposes this approach in a recent internal working paper for the World Bank.

Index

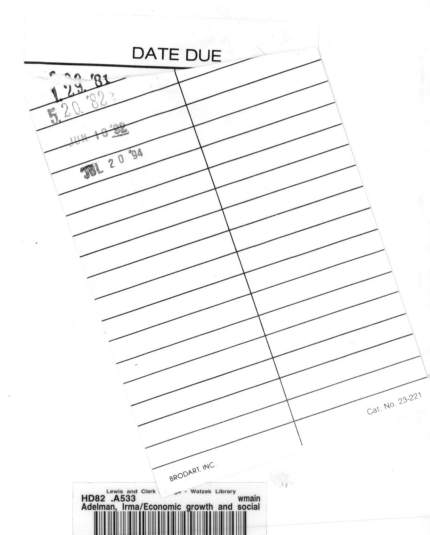

DATE DUE

1 23 '81	
5 20 '82	
JUN 10 '82	
JUL 20 '94	

Cat. No. 23-221

BRODART, INC.